Affinities

India and Korea

Past and Present

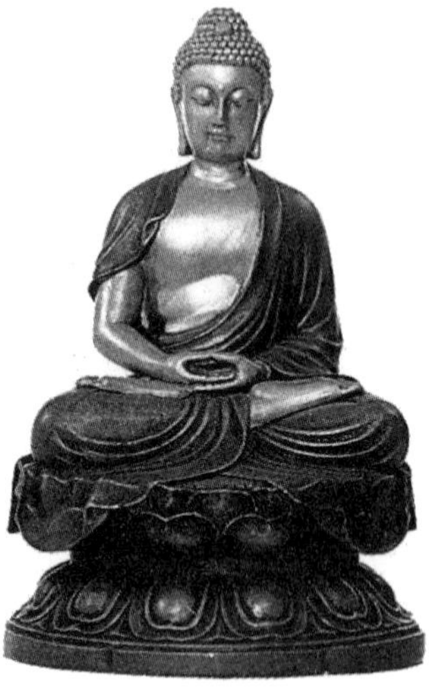

Affinities

India and Korea

Past and Present

Edited by

Pankaj Mittal

Daisy

Ravi Bhushan

Editorial Advisor

Kapil Kapoor

BPS Mahila Vishwavidyalaya

DK PRINTWORLD

Publishers of Indian Traditions

Cataloging in Publication Data — DK
[Courtesy: D.K. Agencies (P) Ltd. <docinfo@dkagencies.com>]

International Conference on "India-Korea Relations : Past and Present" (2012 : Bhagat Phool Singh Mahila Vishwavidyalaya)
Affinities : India and Korea : past and present / editors, Pankaj Mittal, Daisy, Ravi Bhushan ; editorial adviser, Kapil Kapoor.
p. cm.
Includes bibliographical references.
ISBN 9788124606933

1. India – Relations – Korea – Congresses. 2. Korea – Relations – India – Congresses. I. Pankaj Mittal. II. Daisy. III. Bhushan, Ravi, 1974- IV. Bhagat Phool Singh Mahila Vishwavidyalaya. V. Title.

DDC 327.540519 23

First published in India, 2014
ISBN 978-81-246-0693-3

Published by:
Bhagat Phool Singh Mahila Vishwavidyalaya
Khanpur Kalan, Dist. Sonepat (Haryana)

and

D.K. Printworld (P) Ltd.
Regd. Office: Vedaśrī, F-395, Sudarshan Park
(Metro Station: Ramesh Nagar)
New Delhi – 110 015
Phones: (011) 2545 3975; 2546 6019; *Fax*: (011) 2546 5926
E-mail: indology@dkprintworld.com
Website: www.dkprintworld.com

Printed by: D.K. Printworld (P) Ltd., New Delhi

Preface

THE "Look East Policy" of India has accelerated her relationship with all Asian countries. As part of this initiative, University Grants Commission (UGC) established the Centre for Indic–Asian Studies at Bhagat Phool Singh Mahila Vishwavidyalaya, Haryana, in 2011. Korea, which had a historic relationship with India, is continuing strong relationship with India in the arenas of culture, education, trade and commerce. These two strong democracies share a special bond.

Having sustained a strong association between both the countries from early first millennium, much through Buddhism, both the countries are vying to strengthen the mutual relationships in all walks of modern life — culture, defence, economics, education, social development and rural reconstruction. To cement the existing relationship between both India and Korea, the Centre for Indic–Asian Studies organized a bilateral International Conference at Bhagat Phool Singh Mahila Vishwavidyalaya (BPSWV), Khanpur Kalan, Haryana, on 18-19 July 2012.

This book is a collection of lectures delivered in the conference on "India–Korea Relations: Past and Present", where scholars from India and Korea have presented their views on the history of relationship and the multifaceted issues confronting both the countries. This International Conference, the first of its kind in the Area Studies Programme, examined historical, cultural, economic, commercial, educational, and social and rural reconstruction experiences in India and Korea.

We hope the academic community — national and international — will find this a useful contribution towards mutual understanding and co-operation in a world, which is increasingly becoming interdependent.

Contents

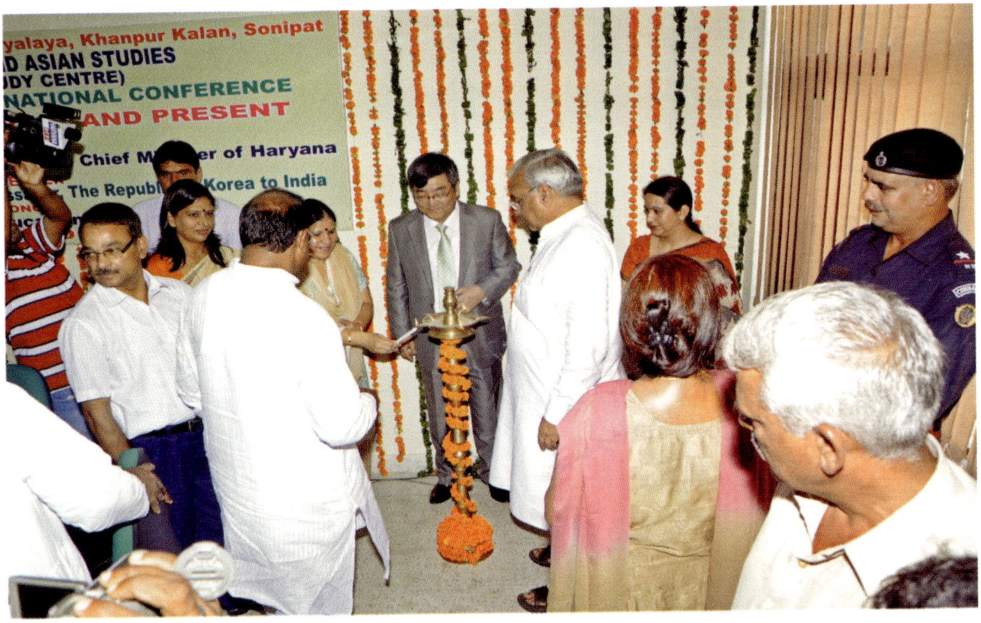

1. Let this light enlighten all! Dignitaries lightening the lamp

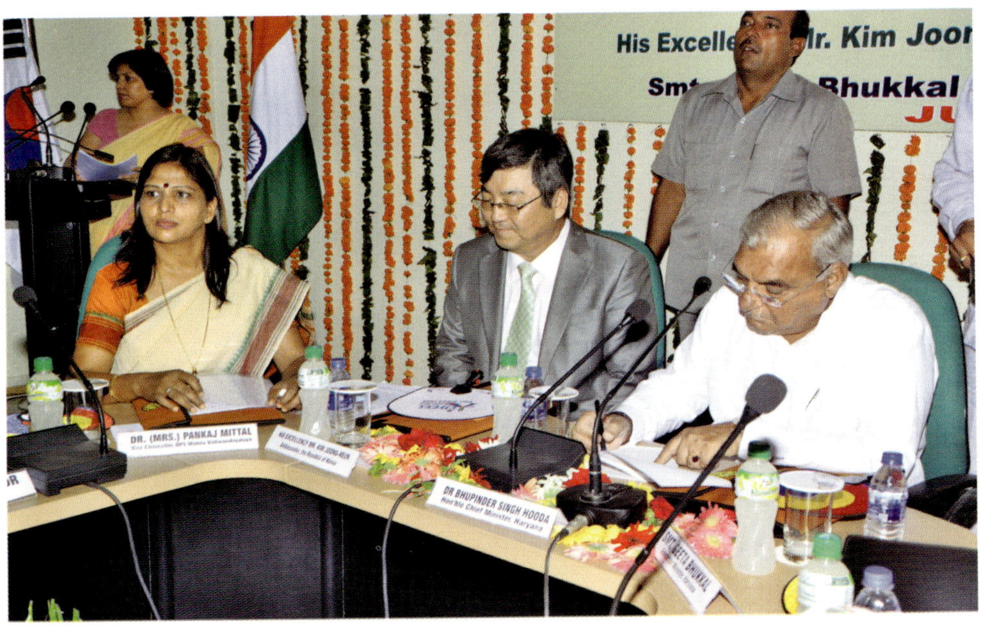

2. (L-R) Dr (Mrs) Pankaj Mittal, Vice-Chancellor, Bhagal Phool Singh Mahila Vishwavidyalaya, His Excellency Mr Kim Joong-Keun, Ambassor of Embassy of the Republic of Korea, Dr Bhupinder Singh Hooda, Chief Minister, Haryana

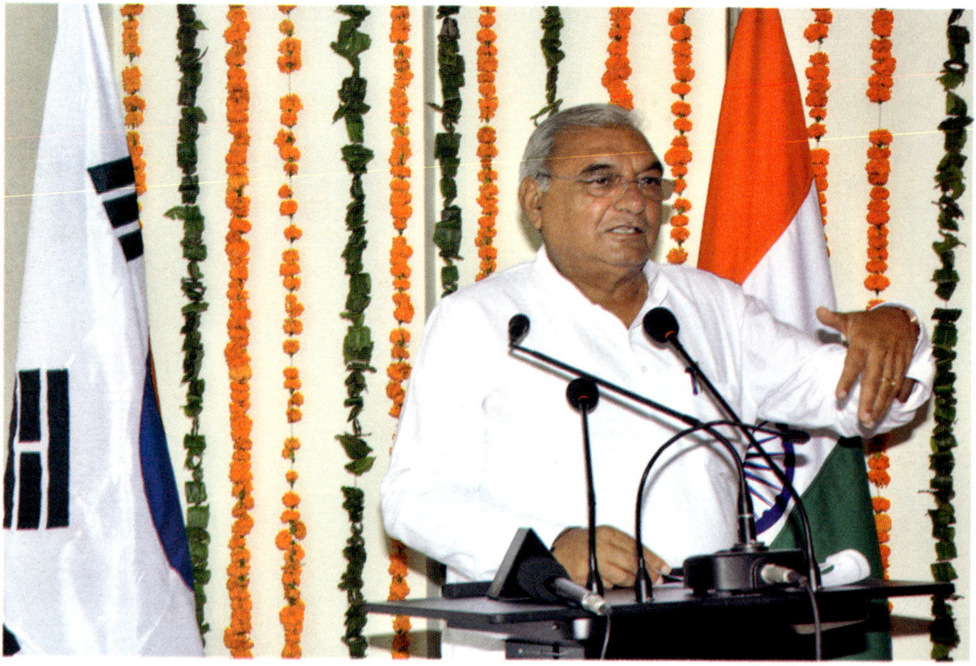

3. Making the ground clear: Dr Bhupinder Singh Hooda

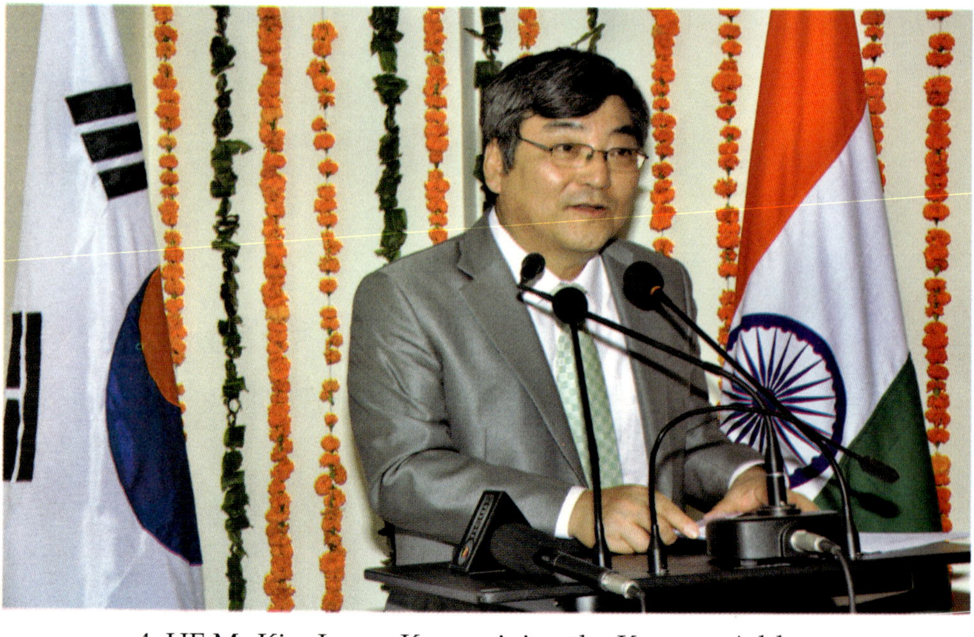

4. HE Mr Kim Joong-Keun, giving the Keynote Address

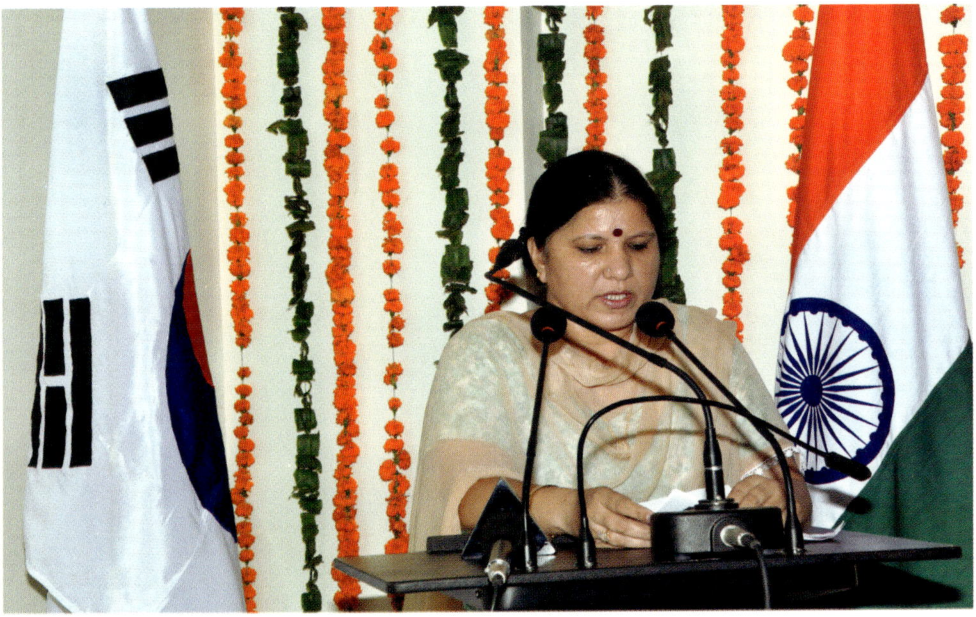

5. Offering more opportunities: Mrs Geeta Bhukkal, Minister of Education, Government of Haryana

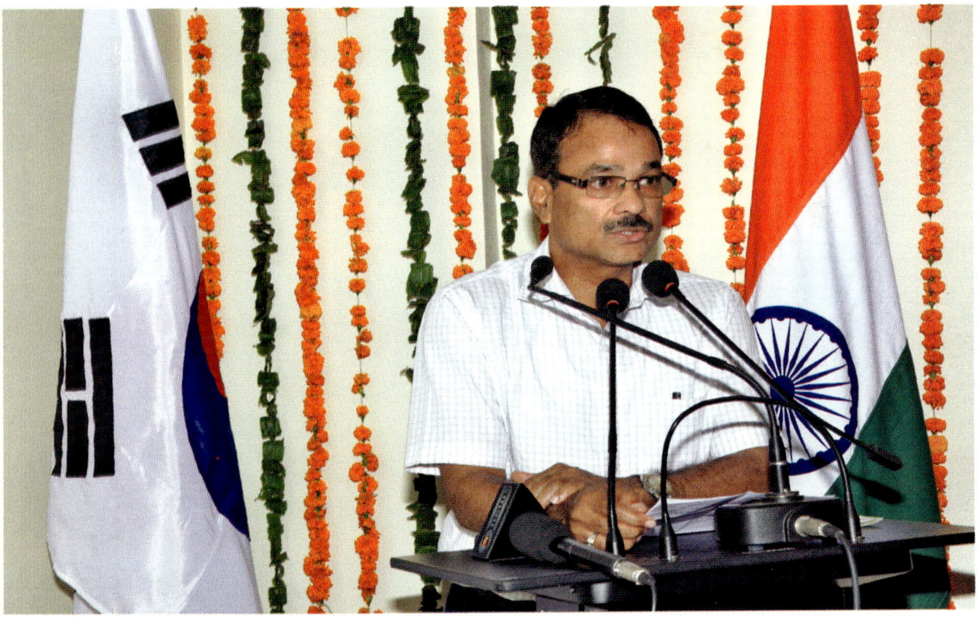

6. Lessons in Economy: Mr S.S. Prasad, Financial Commissioner & Principal Secretary, Govt. of Haryana

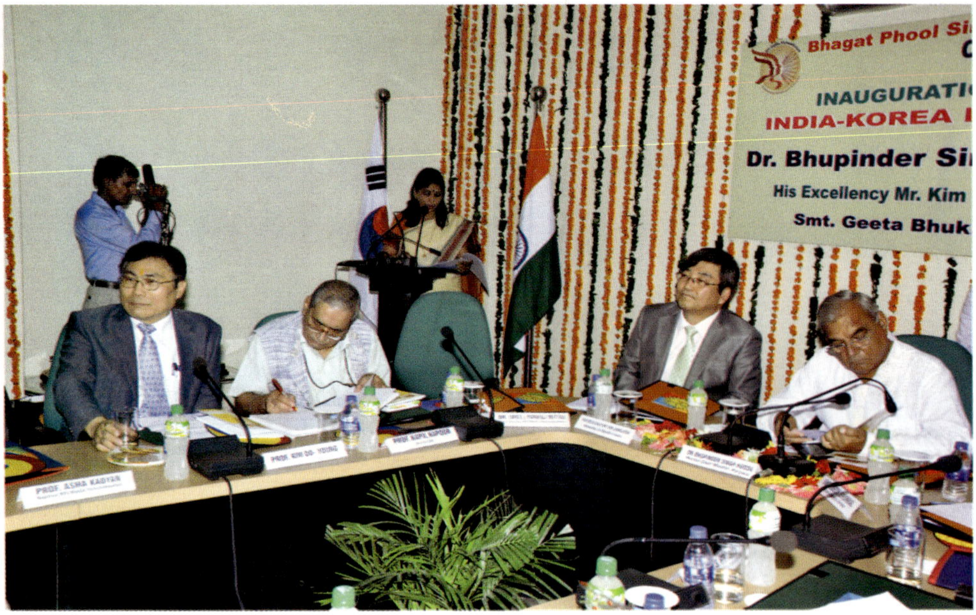

7. Dr (Mrs) Pankaj Mittal addresses the gathering.
Seen (L-R) are Prof. Kim Do-young, Prof. Kapil Kapoor,
HE Mr Kim Joong-Kuen and Dr Bhupinder Singh Hooda

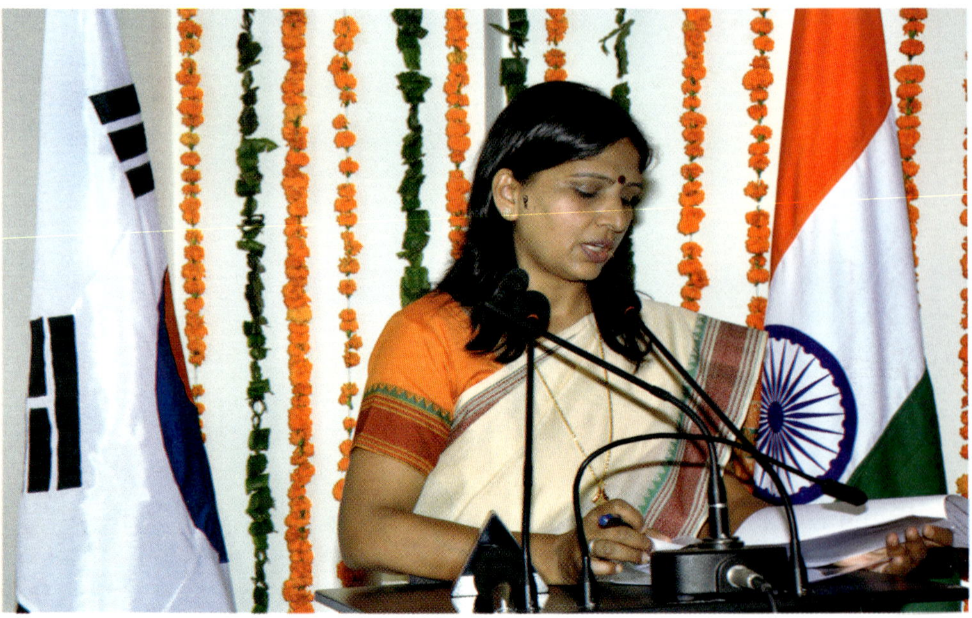

8. Dr (Mrs) Pankaj Mittal

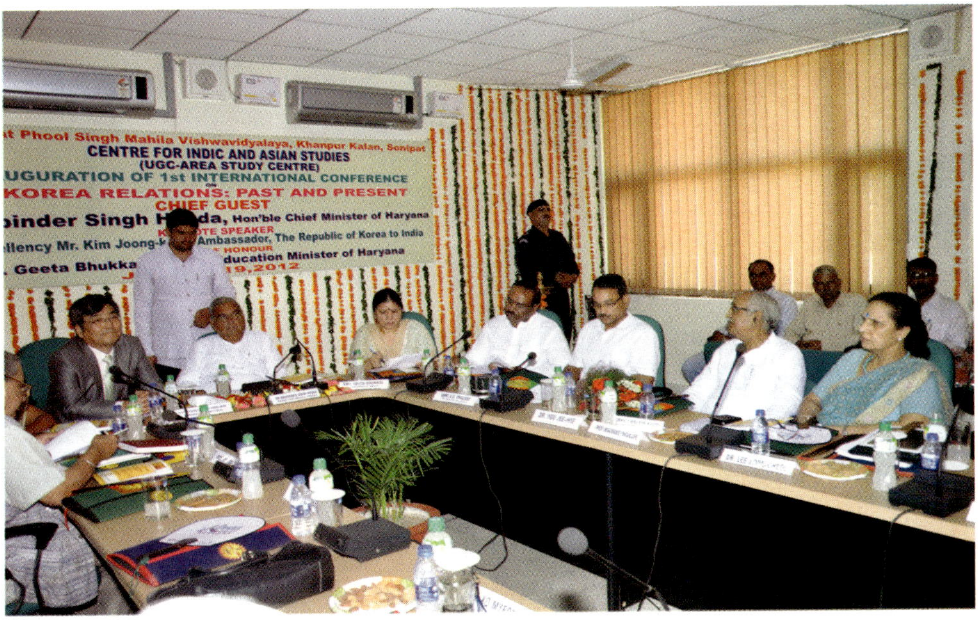

9. The felicitators (L-R) Prof. Kim Do-young, Prof. Kapil Kapoor, HE Mr Kim Joong-Kuen, Dr Bhupinder Singh Hooda, Mrs Geeta Bhukkal, Mr S.S. Prasad, Dr You Jee-hye, Prof. Makarand Pranajape and Mrs Balbir Kaur

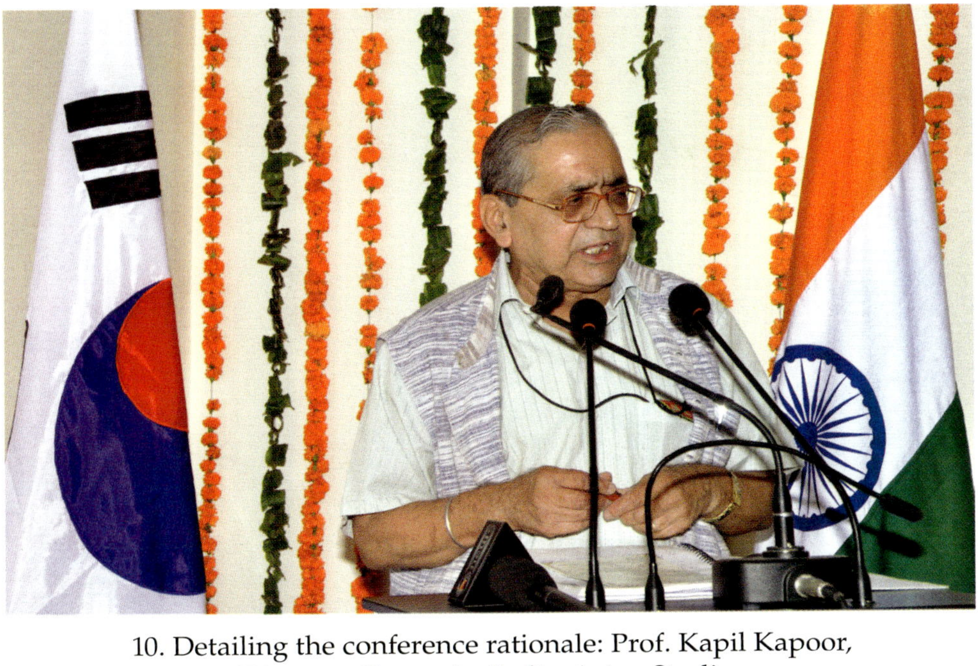

10. Detailing the conference rationale: Prof. Kapil Kapoor, Director, Centre for Indic–Asian Studies

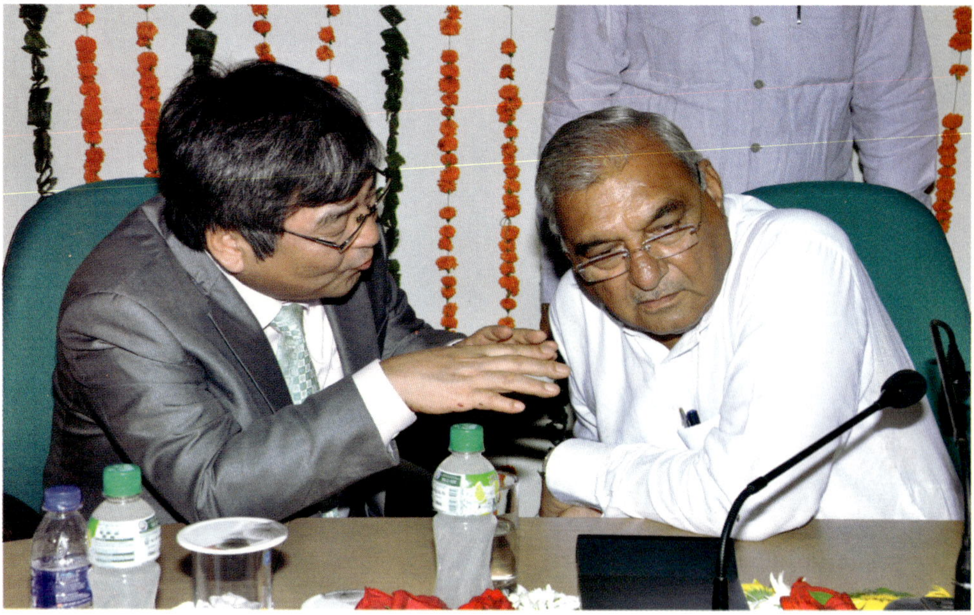

11. Let us scale up: HE Mr Kim Joong-Keun and Dr Bhupinder Singh Hooda

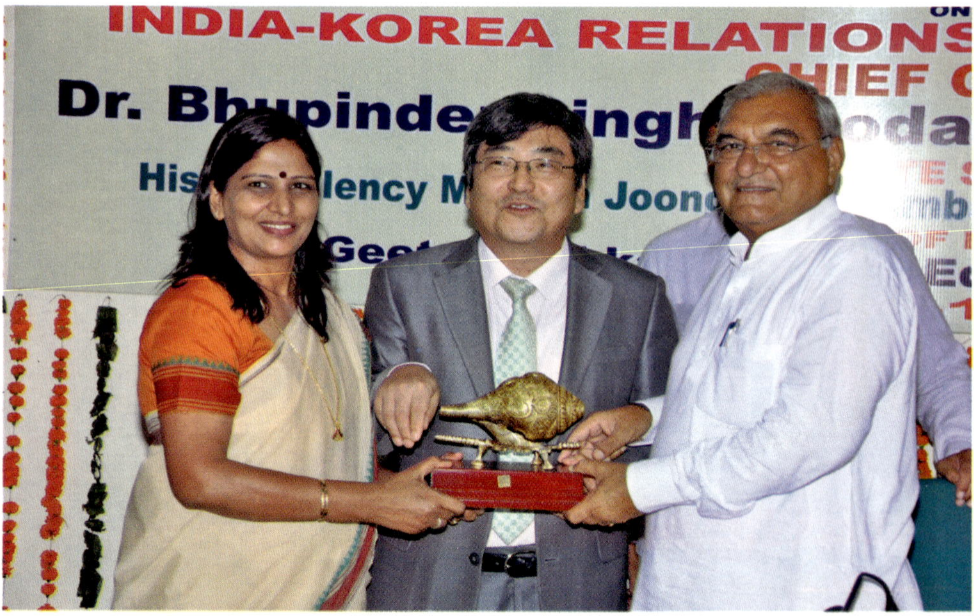

12. Dr (Mrs) Pankaj Mittal and Dr Bhupinder Singh Hooda presenting a momento to HE Mr Kim Joong-Keun

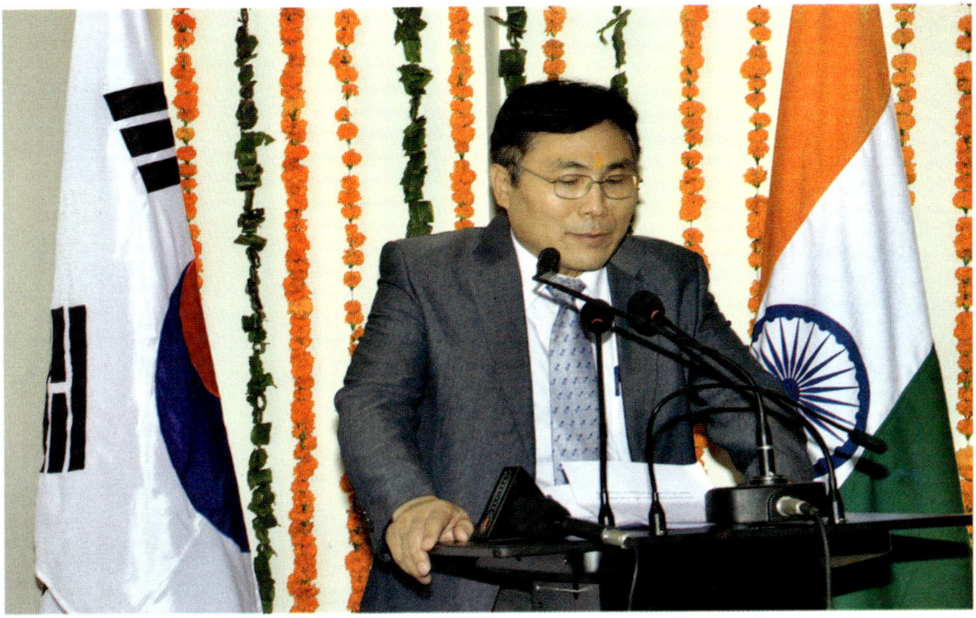

13. Connecting the past to the present: Prof. Kim Do-young, Visiting Professor Korea Foundation, Dept. of East Asian Studies, University of Delhi

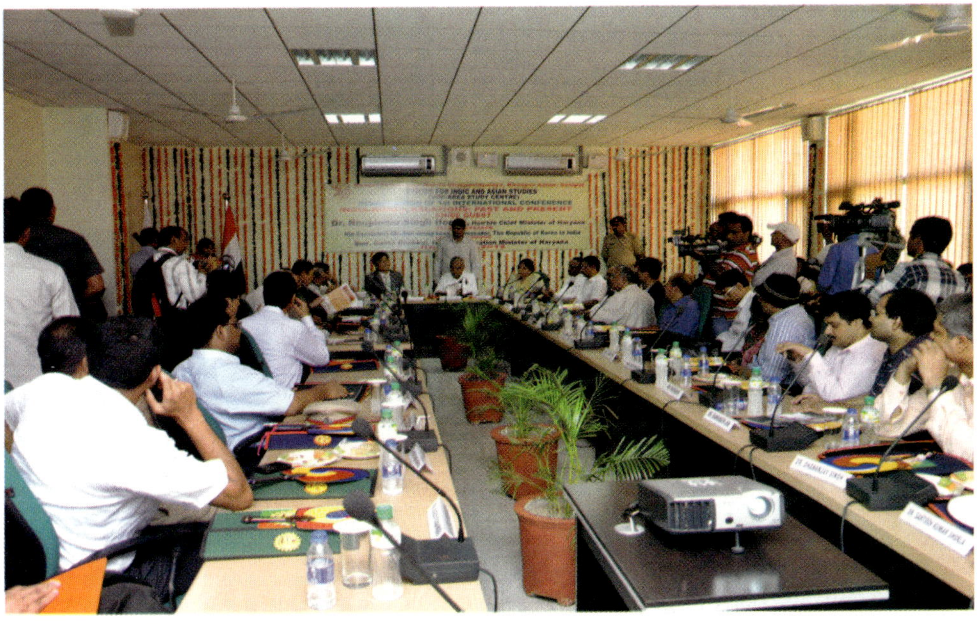

14. The Conference in progress

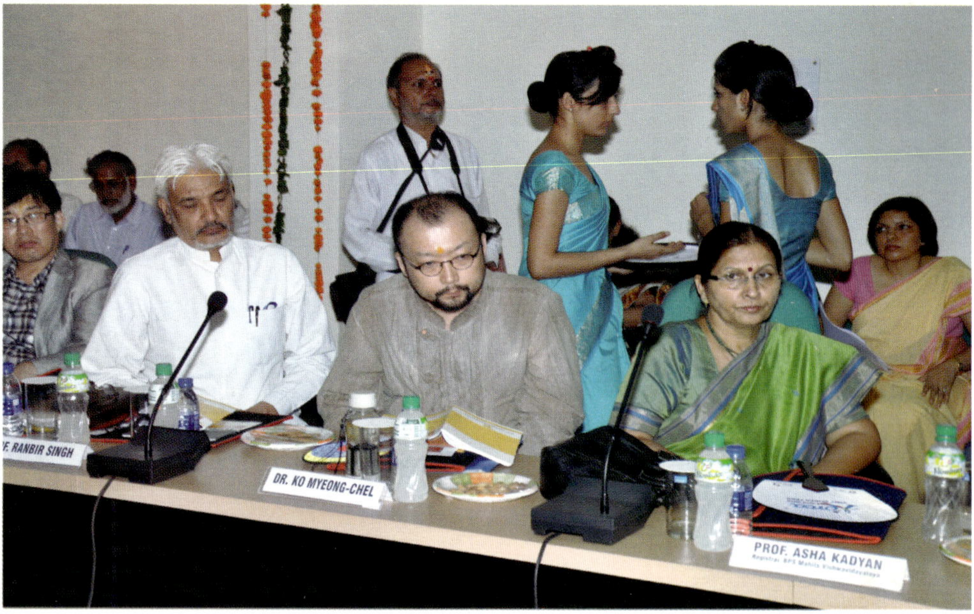

15. (L-R) Dr Lee Kwang-su, Prof. Ranbir Singh, Head, Dept. of Indology, Kurushetra University, Kurukshetra, Dr Ko Meong-chel and Prof. Asha Kadyan, Registrar, BPS Mahila Vishwavidyalaya

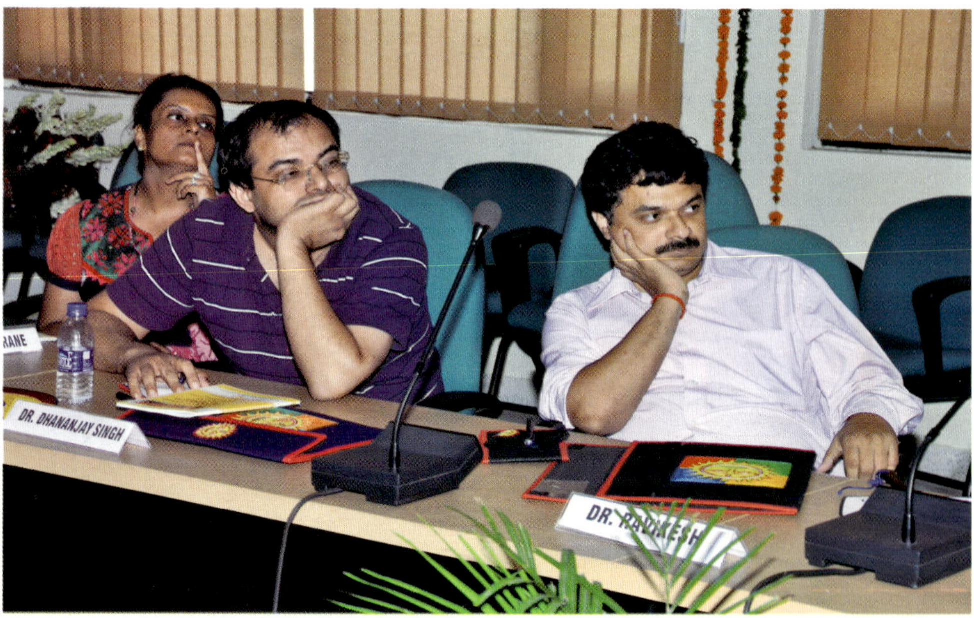

16. Dr Alokka Dutta, Dr Dhananjay Singh and Dr Ravikesh keenly listening to the talk

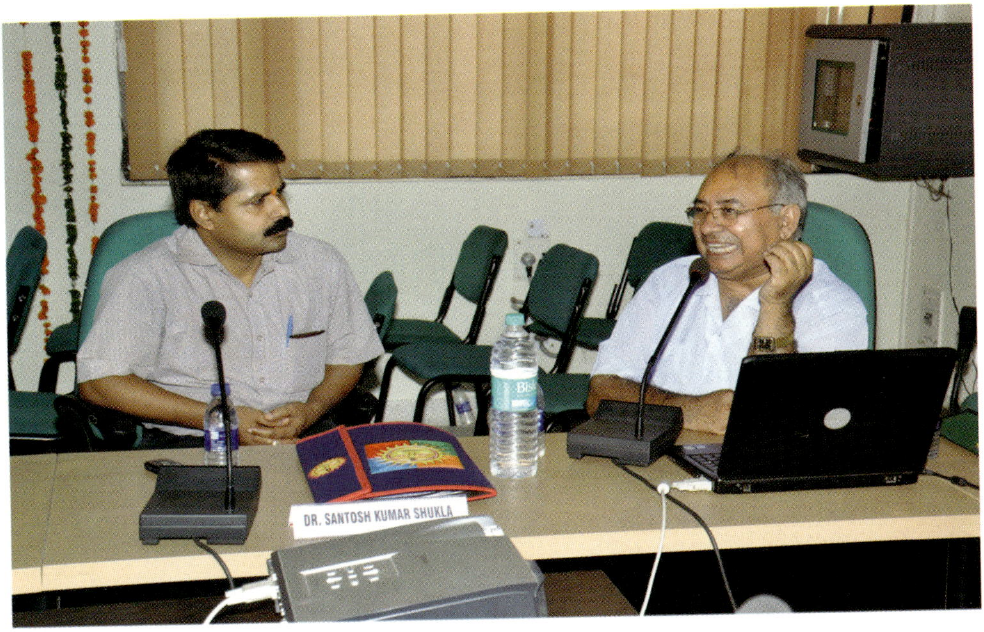

17. Dr Santosh Shukla and Prof. R.C. Sharma

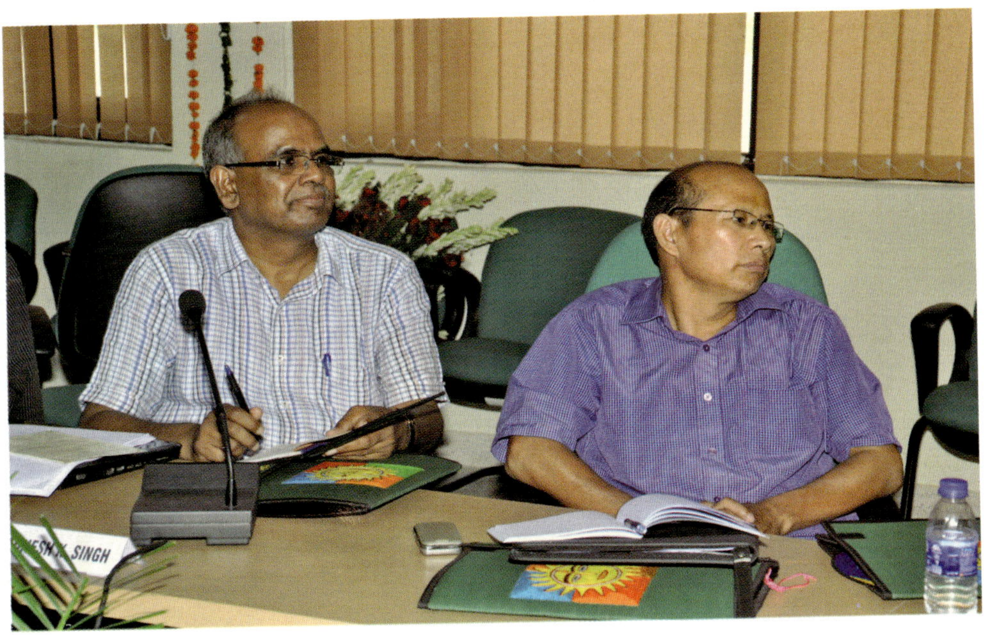

18. Keenly listening: Prof. Avadhesh Singh and Dr A.S. Yaruingam

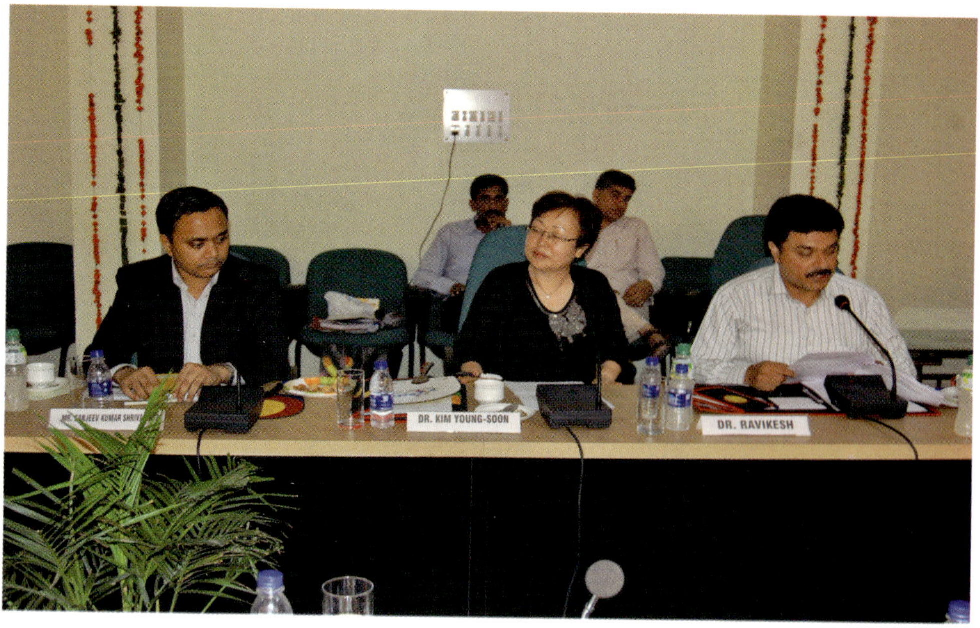

19. (L-R) Dr Sanjeev Shreevastav, Dr Kim Young-soon,
Dr Ravikesh at the Conference

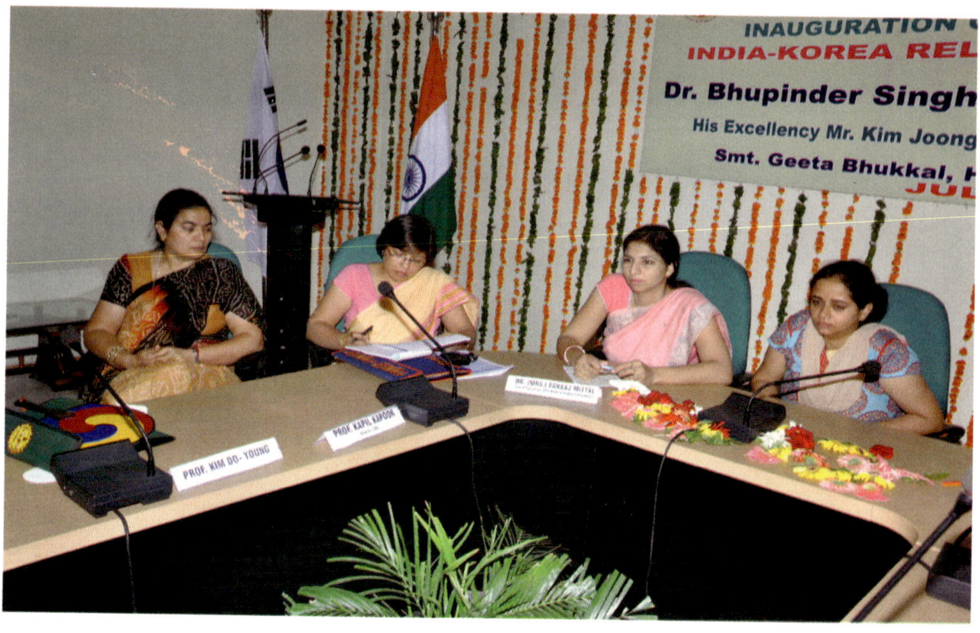

20. (L-R) Dr Sneh Sangwan, Dr Daisy, Dr Shefali Nagpal and Mrs. Priya

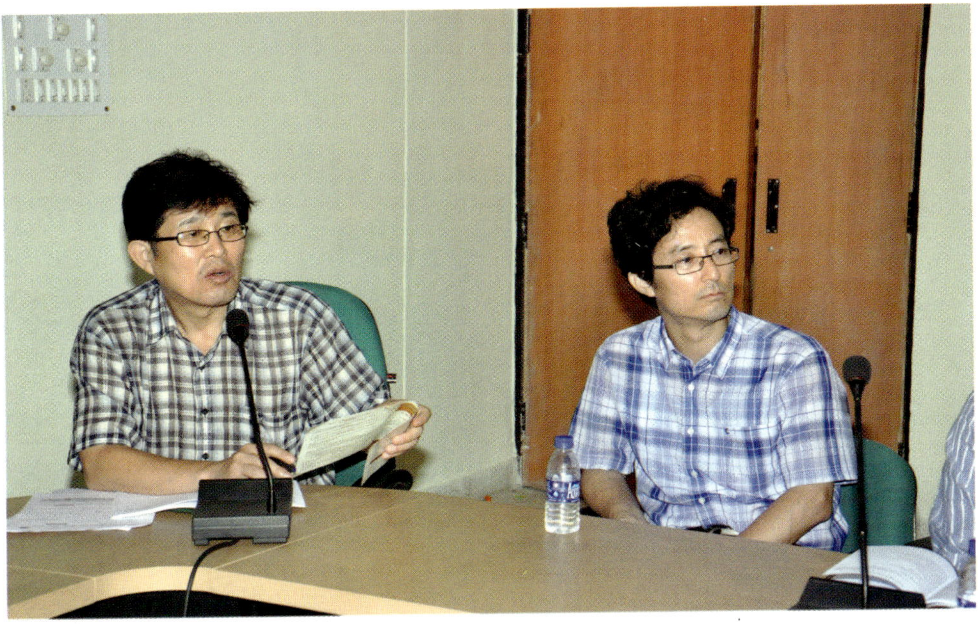

21. Prof. Lee Kwang-su and Mr Kyung-hee Lee

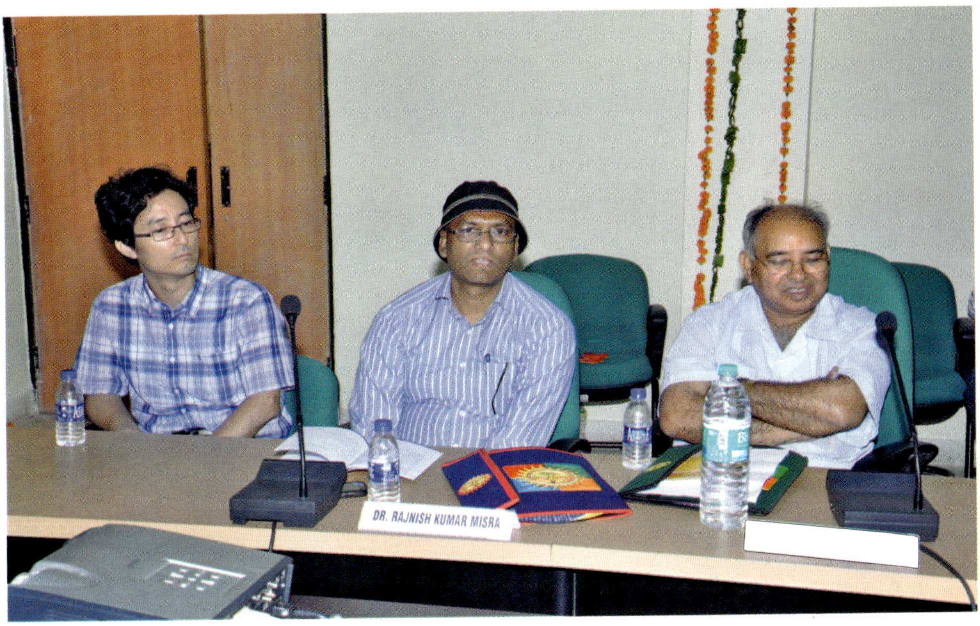

22. (L-R) Mr Kyung-hee Lee, Dr Rajnish Kumar Mishra and Prof. R.C. Sharma

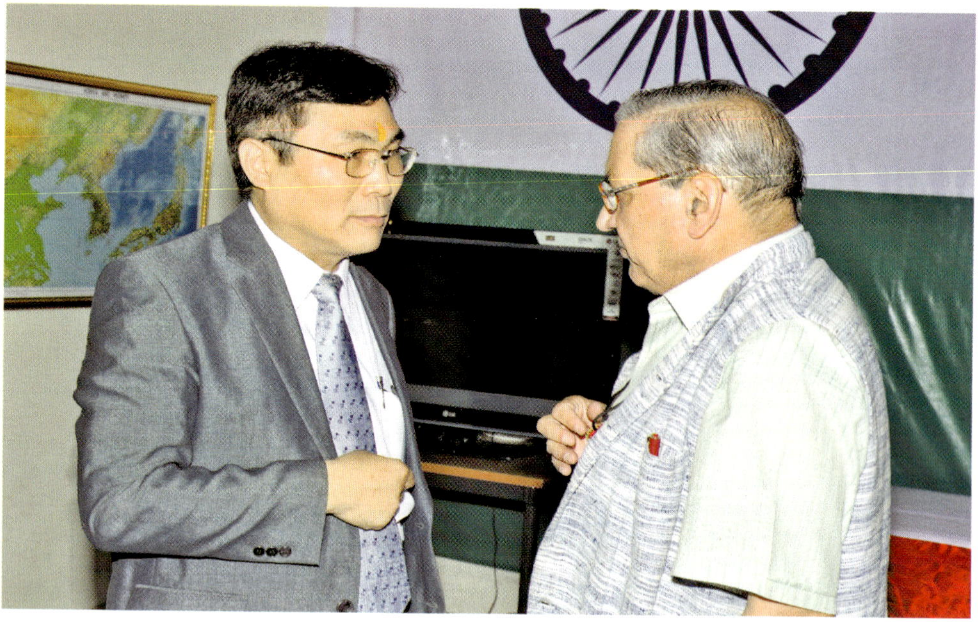

23. Prof. Kim Do-young and Prof. Kapil Kapoor

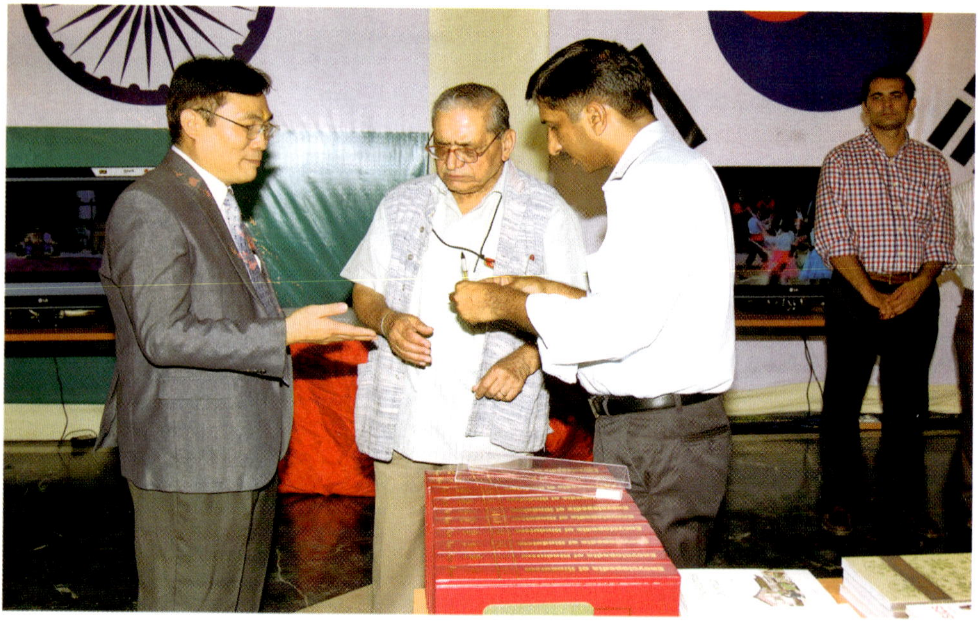

24. Conference co-ordinator Dr Ravi Bhushan with
Prof. Kim Do-young and Prof. Kapil Kapoor

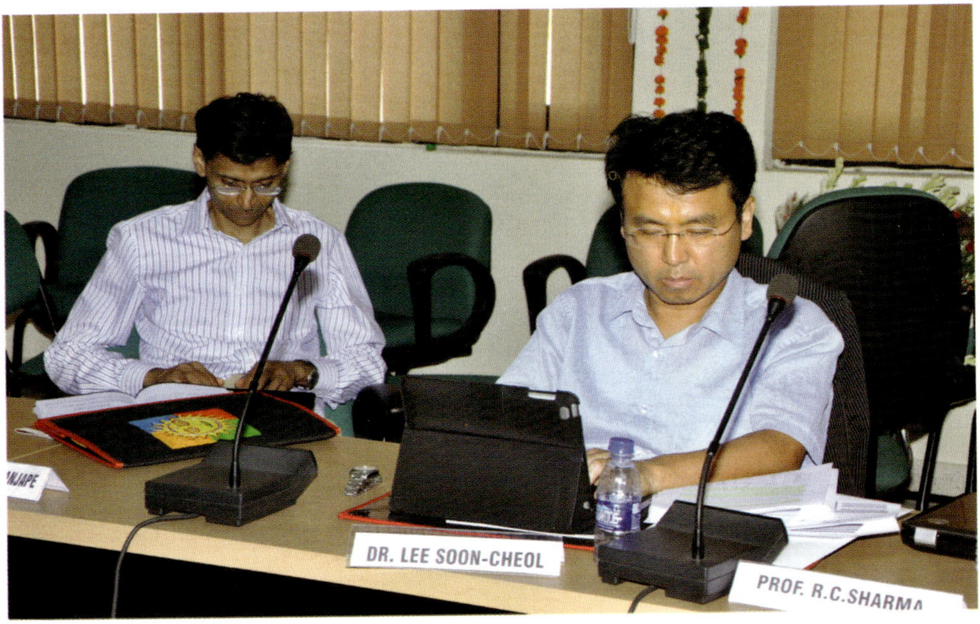

25. Prof. Makarand Paranjape (L) and Dr Lee Soon-Cheul

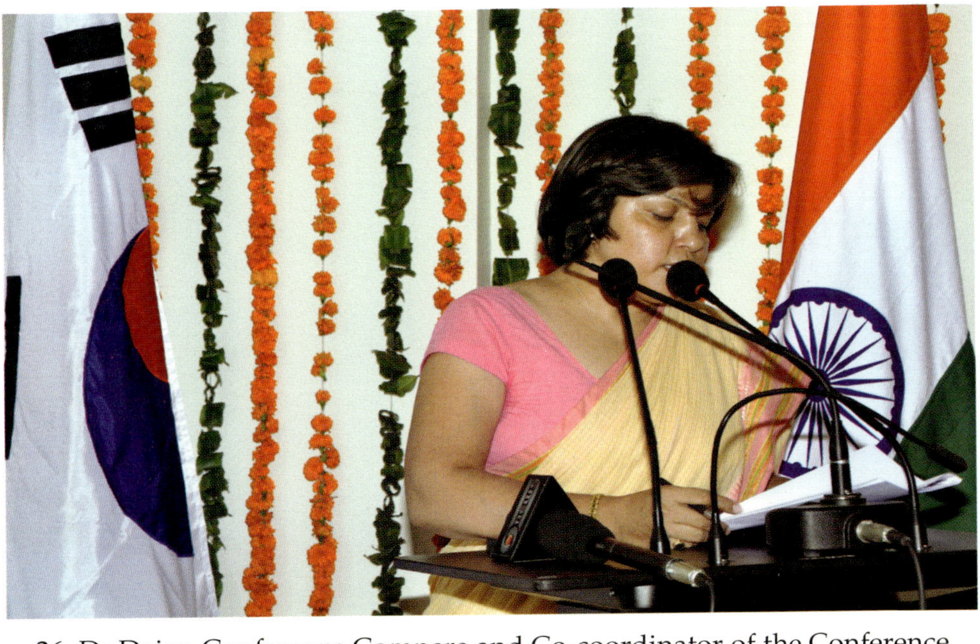
26. Dr Daisy, Conference Compere and Co-coordinator of the Conference

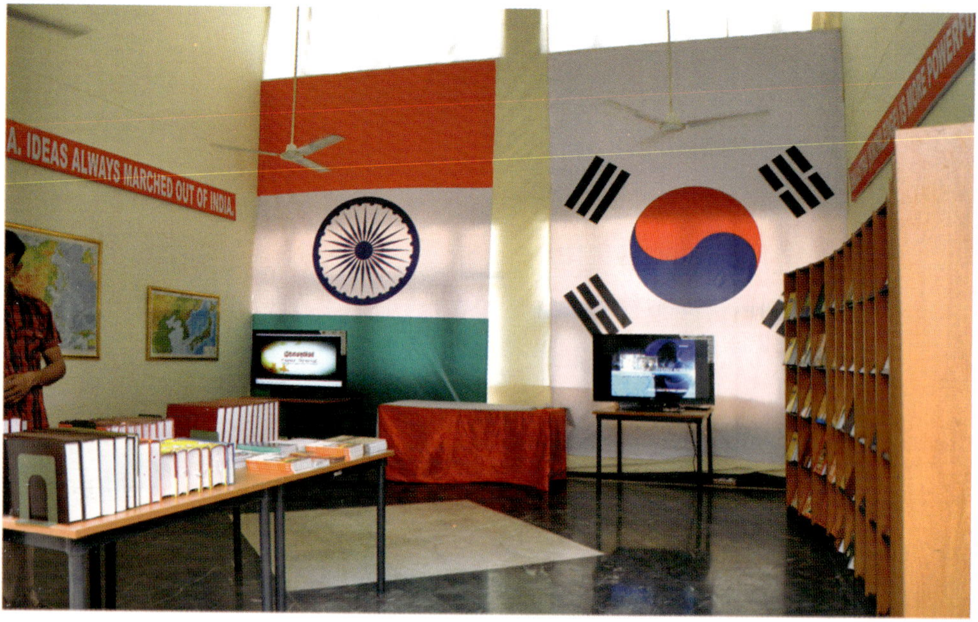

27. The Display Area

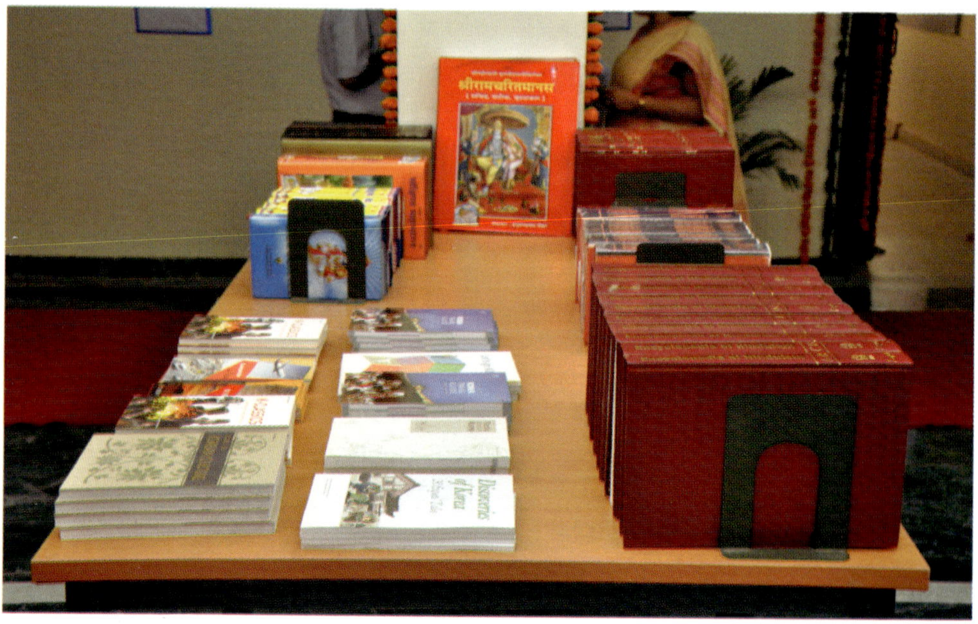

28. The Display Area

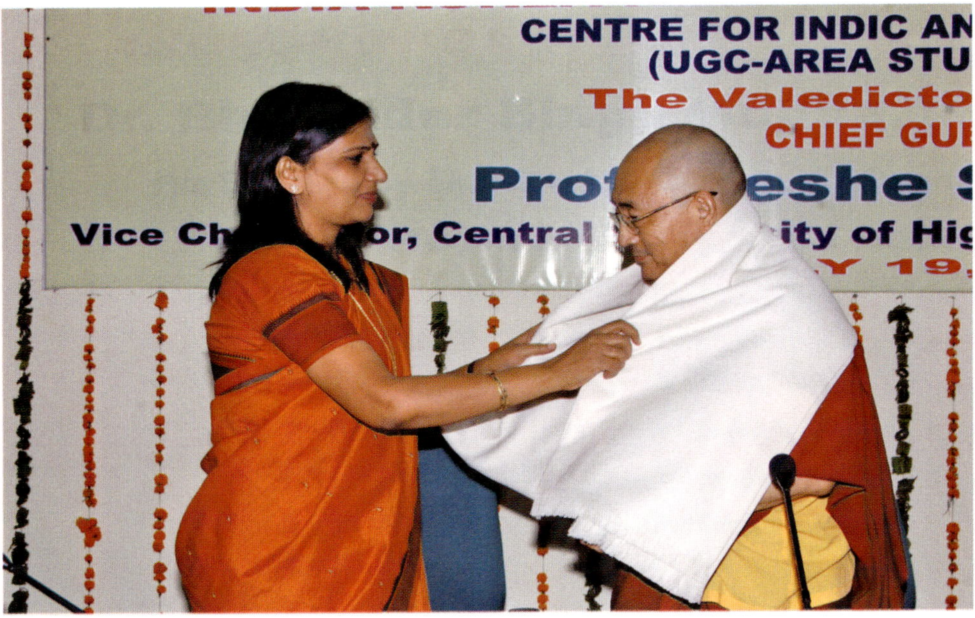

29. Dr Pankaj Mittal honouring Prof. Geshe Samten in traditional Indian style

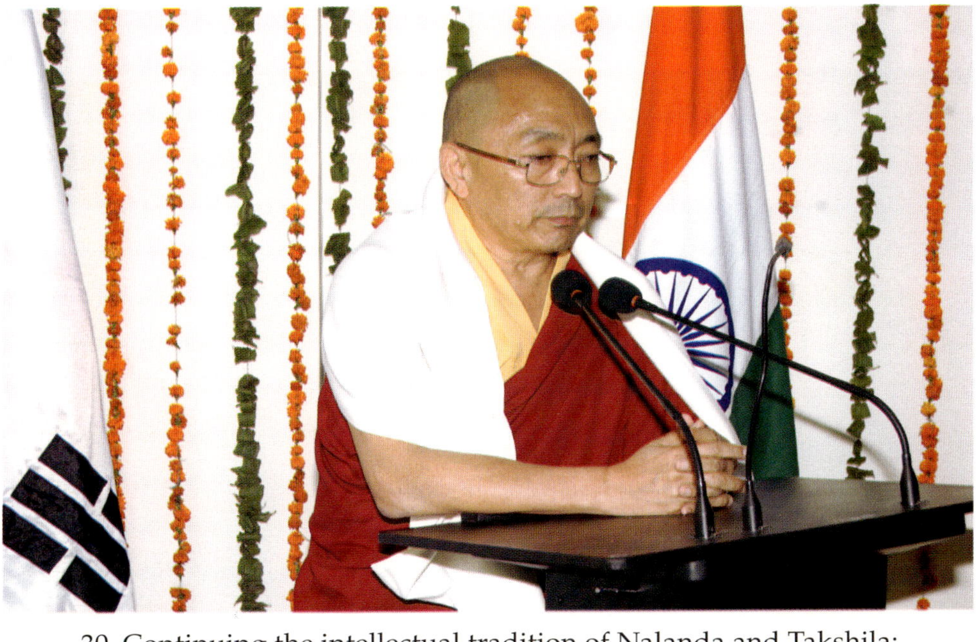

30. Continuing the intellectual tradition of Nalanda and Takshila:
Prof. Geshe Samten, Vice-Chancellor,
Central University of Higher Tibetan Studies, Sarnath

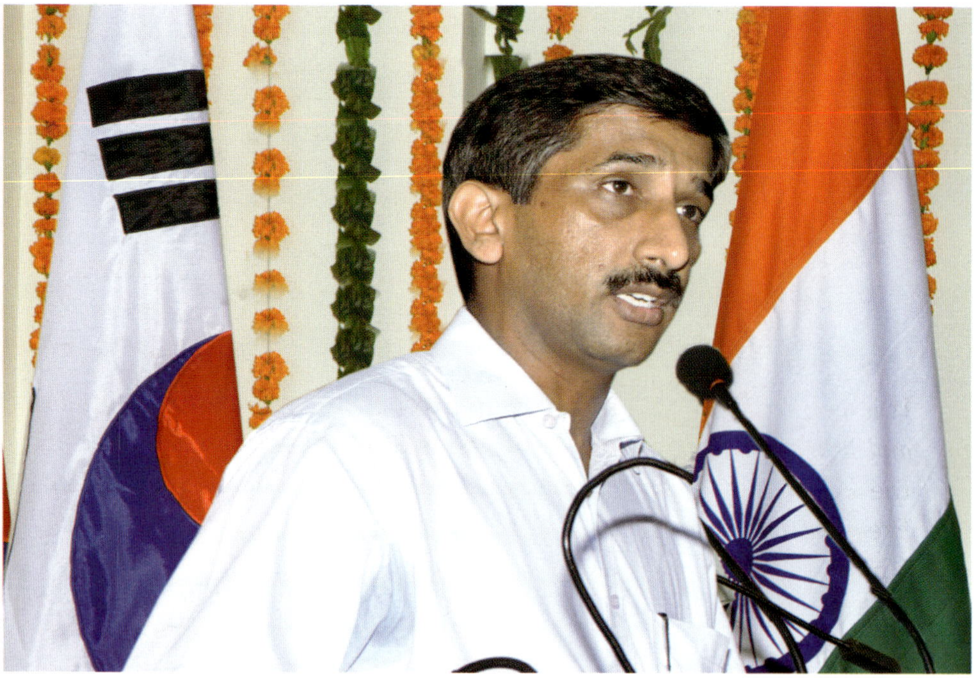

31. Presenting vote of thanks: Dr Ravi Bhushan, Conference Co-ordinator

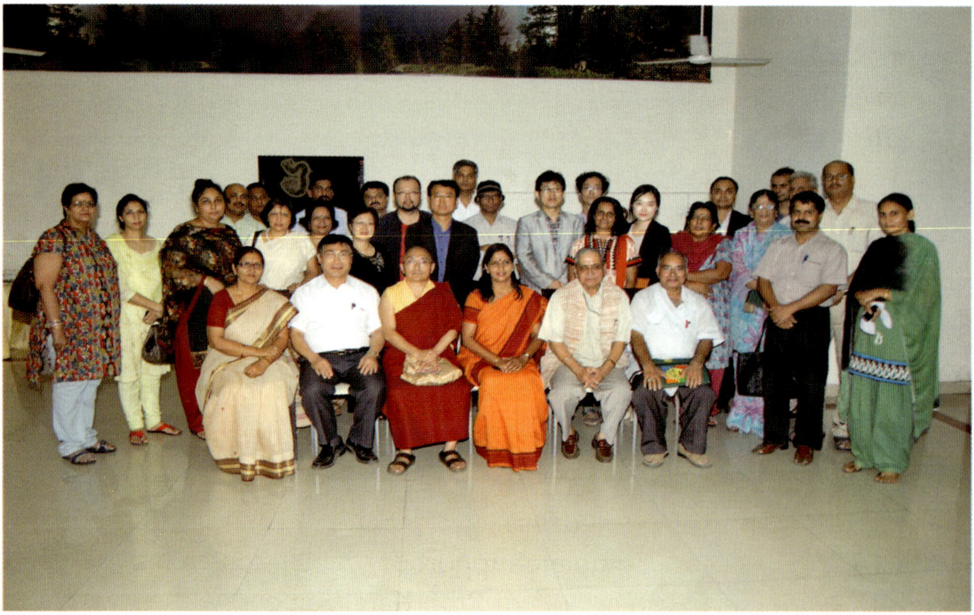

32. The participants, group photo after the valediction ceremony

Acknowledgement

It is our pleasure and privilege to present this book *Affinities: India and Korea — Past and Present* which is a set of lectures delivered in the International Conference on "India–Korea Relations: Past and Present" held on 18-19 July 2012 at BPS Mahila Vishwavidyalaya, Khanpur Kalan. In this first international conference organized by the Centre for Indic–Asian Studies (CIAS), many eminent professors/scholars from India and South Korea presented their research papers on a variety of affinities (cultural, historical, social, legal, economical, religious, etc.) between India and Korea. We express our gratitude to all our esteemed contributors who acceded to our requests and found time from their extremely busy schedules to come and grace the occasion by actively participating in the conference.

Prof. Kim Do-young deserves our special thanks for he has been an extraordinary help not only during the conference but before and after that too.

We are deeply grateful to the Doyen of Indic–Asian Studies, Dr. Lokesh Chandra, who has very graciously and kindly allowed us to include three of his articles on India–Korea relationship in art, architecture and philosophy.

We would also like to thank Ms Sonia Kathuria and Ms Farhana Sayeed, our research scholars, who helped us by providing us the written version of some of the speeches of our distinguished guests after listening to the recordings.

We are also grateful to Shri Joginder and Ms Mina Malik both of CIAS for extending complete support during the conference. Above all we are indebted to our *guru* Prof. Kapil Kapoor, without whose guidance, we would not have come out with this book.

Editors

1

The Conference Rationale

Kapil Kapoor

WHY this conference on India–Korea Relations: Past and Present? Because there is a need to renew intimate intellectual, emotional and moral relationships among Asian neighbours. India, over the last two millennia, has shared and disseminated across different countries of Asia its knowledge in various disciplines such as mathematics, language, philosophy, poetics and logic among others, besides Buddhism, India is held in some respect by the people of Asia and it is time for Indians to rediscover their relationships with Asia. India is not only the actual geographic base of Asia but is also the core of the Asian mind.

Korea is a very important partner in India's current economic and commercial growth. For that reason, since 1974 there has been an increasing focus on the study of Korean language and literature. I was myself associated with this process in Jawaharlal Nehru University (JNU) where I was instrumental in initiating the Korean PG programme. But this new focus on Korea cannot be limited to Hyundai, LG and Samsung. It must encompass the whole gamut of relationship, including culture and value system. Both the countries have deep affinity so much so that when our students study Korean literature they feel some kind of oneness with it. Today this relationship — intellectual and commercial — is strengthening through our students and teachers.

We have taken this initiative in this perspective. This is the first conference of this kind in India. We have never had so far a conference in India on India–Korea relationship. I may also draw attention to the historical connection between the two countries. In CE 42 the princess of Ayodhyā landed in Kumahya and married the King of Korea and the king in gratitude to the ocean, to the sea through which the princess had travelled, set up a Temple of Water of Grace. Beginning with that came up some of the earliest Buddhist monasteries in Korea. That historic connection is still alive in our shared value system and habits. It was very pleasant to discover that in Korea you had a choice between a Korean five-star hotel where you could sleep on the floor and and a five-star hotel in the Western mode. It was a pleasure because it is close to what we Indians were also used to — sleeping on the floor. And they also sit on the ground and eat, like we do and they greet people the same humility and politeness. We have changed a good deal unfortunately. India has exported many of its virtues and imported many vices and much is lost. But when we go there, we discover how close we are.

Apart from this I have had the pleasure of having been associated with some Korean pioneering scholars like Prof. Kim who set up the Korean Centre at Jawaharlal Nehru University and then in the University of Delhi. Through him I have been in contact with Korean poets and others. It is high time we start a Korean programme here in our university because our students after learning Korean will have better employment opportunities as most of the companies nowadays look for trilingual young people who can work in Hindi, English and Korean. Therefore the girls of this university, a rural women university and first of its type in north India, should be exposed to new trends, new minds and they should begin to have a new vision of not only India but also of the world and what role they can play in it.

2

India–Korea Cultural Relations
Past to Present

Kim Do-young

His Excellency Mr Kim Joong-Keun, Ambassador of Embassy of the Republic of Korea, Honourable Mr Hooda, Chief Minister of Haryana State, Dr Pankaj Mittal, Vice-Chancellor of Bhagat Phool Singh Mahila Vishwavidyalaya, and all the eminent scholars and professors!

I am very delighted to present the theme speech in the International Conference on "India–Korea Relations: Past and Present" organized by the Centre for Indic–Asian Studies, Bhagat Phool Singh Mahila Vishwavidyalaya.

Indo–Korea relationship has been developing steadily for the last thirty-nine years after establishing the diplomatic relationship in 1973. Both the countries are entering the forty years of diplomatic relationship anniversary, next year. From 1991 onwards, the relationship of both the countries has been evolving drastically in the view of economic ties. Last year, the total volume of Indo–Korea trade was above US $4.7 billion. It is more than 250 per cent increase within four years. Along with this kind of development of economic ties, cultural and educational development of counterpart was also becoming visualized and deep. In Korea, three universities teach Indian languages to more than 300 students and develop their study on Indian language and literature. In the past, Indian language meant only Hindi. But now, a few universities carry on their research on Indian culture, Indian economy, Indian law, international relationship, etc.

Korean language was introduced in India in 1973 as a "one year-certificate course" at Jawaharlal Nehru University (JNU). It has developed to MA programme now. The University of Delhi also has a two-year postgraduate course which will be connected to MA in Korea in 2013.

Of the Indo–Korean cultural relationship, Indo–Korean relationship has a long history. One of the major Korean history books *Samguk Yusa* reveals that one princess of Ayodhyā of India came to Korea and married the king of Gaya, King Kim Su-ro. It is supposed to be in CE 42. The king's lineage is originated from Kimhae Kim family, which I belong to. In 2007, the then Indian Ambassador to Korea, N. Parthasarthi wrote his novel *The Silk Princess*. This was written based on the same mythology of establishing a kingdom "Gaya" which welcomed the princess of Ayodhyā. Some centuries later, during the eighth century CE, one Korean Buddhist monk came to India and visited five kingdoms of north India. He had studied at Nālandā. While going back, on his way to China, he had written down what he had experienced and seen in India. It became a well-known essay titled "Wang-o-cheonchuk-guk-jeon" (A Story of Visiting Five Indian Kingdoms).

In contemporary ages, India has been keeping deep relation with Korea since the Korean War. India had sent her medical troops during the Korean War. Just after finishing the Korean War, prisoners of war of North Korea, captured by South Korea were supposed to be classified as real North Korean soldiers or forced soldiers. The former were supposed to be sent back to the North and the latter were given their own choices; the South or any third country. Finally, eighty-eight people chose to go to the third country neither North Korea nor South Korea. Six of them decided to live in India and finally arrived at Madras. Five of them have passed away and only one is alive. Hinted by their lives, a renowned Korean novelist came to India and had an interview with one of the two survivors. Based on this he has written a novel *Guwangjang* meaning "Open Square" describing the story of a North Korean officer who had chosen to come to the Third World and finally settled in India. This novel portrays the agony of the then Korean intellectuals very well; they couldn't choose to go back to the North or to stay back in the South. So in various ways, India has been related with Korea.

This conference focuses on the past and the present of India–Korean relationship which will be enlightened by eminent Indian and Korean scholars. The most distinctive character of this conference is to see the root of past and present the fruits of deepening mutual relationship. Indian scholars who want to research on Korea can share their aspects enough, and Korean scholars who want to expose the relations in the view of language, literature, culture, history, economy on India can do the same. In this sense, this conference will be a sketch of India–Korean relationship. I hope this conference may give a clear picture of the past and the present, and set a way for future relationship.

Thank you.

3

Korea and India
Lessons in Economy

S.S. Prasad

THIS is the first project of its kind in Haryana and also for organizing this international conference on relationship between "India and South Korea: Past and Present". In the address given by His Excellency, he has covered every aspect of India–Korea relationship. Before coming to this conference, I tried to link the historical relationship between the two countries. South Korea has made amazing progress. South Korea got independence on 15 August 1945, two years ahead of India. They also fought a bloody war, which cost four million lives and thousands were wounded. India has fought five wars with its neighbours and lost so many lives. But losing four million people for a small country like Korea is a colossal loss and having started building on the rubbles of the war and coming to this stage in just six decades is by any standard a spectacular achievement.

Anybody, who has been overseas, knows that apart from the West and Japan; Korea, with a small population of five crore, has got at least six international brands. China, a major economic power in the world, to my knowledge, doesn't have a single international brand. We have our share of success. India is now one of the fastest developing economies in the world. We have, what is being termed, the demographic dividend. We have got the largest pool of young manpower and that is our dividend for future growth. Our people are very intelligent and bright. The Indians are one of the finest brains in the world; there is no doubt about that. Every Indian is an entrepreneur. Now that India has tasted progress and growth, there is no looking back. The tempo of growth that we have made during the last decade will continue in future also. But there are many challenges and problems both for Korea and India. The nature of problem may be different but the problems are there and we have to find out solutions. And we have to learn a lot from the teachers' experiences and, there, this study centre at BPS Mahila Vishwavidyalaya is an important one and the initiative Dr Pankaj Mittal has taken for conducting this conference is timely and I am very sure it will go a long way.

Two things need to be specified here. One, the relationship between these two countries has been centred on industry and commerce, and now this needs to be broadened. Education is one such sector which needs the attention and particularly higher education should form an important aspect of the study and the process that has started today in the conference should be taken to its logical conclusion. His Excellency will vouch for what I am saying that the development of human resources is the key for the economic development. One of the reasons why South Korea has succeeded so well is its human resource. But this is true not only in the context of South Korea, this is equally true for India, or for that matter any country. South Korea has invested heavily in education; we are doing the same in the last couple of years. Our capacity expansion at all levels, whether family education, middle education, or higher education, has been spectacular. Two, there are other challenges: the challenge of quality, the challenge of employability, the challenge of offering courses which are required by the society and the industry and we have to do a lot of work and, therefore, our co-operation and learning from each other's experiences are extremely vital. With these remarks, I would like to conclude and thank Mrs Mittal. And the very fact that the honourable chief minister is here is a testimony to the fact that Haryana government gives so much of importance to the relations between these two countries and whatever is required from the state goverenment's side, I can take the liberty of promising on behalf of the honourable chief minister that it will be forthcoming.

Thank you.

4

Korea and India
Interchange of Technology

Geeta Bhukkal

HONOURABLE Dr Bhupinder Singh Hooda, Chief Minister, Haryana; His Excellency Mr Kim Joong-Keun, Ambassador, the Republic of Korea; Shri S.S. Prasad; Dr Pankaj Mittal, Vice-Chancellor, BPS Mahila Vishwavidyalaya; Vice-Chancellors of all other universities of this State, Prof. Kapil Kapoor, Director of Centre for Indic–Asian Studies (CIAS); and learned scholars, both from India and South Korea, I am very happy to be a part of this international conference. Indeed, it is a privilege to be invited for such an academic event of international repute. At the very outset, I congratulate CIAS and in particular Dr (Mrs) Pankaj Mittal for organizing this international conference on "India–Korea Relations: Past and Present". Having known that BPS Mahila Vishwavidyalaya is a favourite project of our beloved Chief Minister Dr Bhupinder Singh Hooda-Ji, the university has truly become a centre of excellence for girls' education. Being a witness to the multiple happenings at BPS Mahila Vishwavidyalaya, I have always enjoyed coming to this university.

As is often said, BPS Mahila Vishwavidyalaya is "a university with a difference", its commitment to the empowerment of women through qualitative education and unique faculties like Centre for Society–University Interface and Research, and Centre for Indic–Asian Studies, makes it truly different from others. I wish the university continues to grow and proves to be the best place for girls' education. The theme of this conference "India–Korea Relations: Past and

Present" fascinated me. Even if the relationship between India and Korea is not very old, the two nations have always been a guiding force for each other. In this age of technology, especially research and development in electronics, it is of immense help to India. Besides technological exchanges both the countries share socio-cultural and political ethos. Both being republics, sustaining democratic values is a challenging task. Education determines the growth of a society. I, being the education minister of this state, offer mutual exchange of educational opportunities between South Korea and Haryana. The possibilities of higher education in Haryana are immense and we have state-of-the-art infrastructure in place. Our state provides wonderful opportunities for international students. I look forward to have considerable academic exchange programmes between India and South Korea, especially in Haryana.

I am sure, a variety of themes and topics proposed to be presented by the scholars will definitely discuss the relation between India and South Korea. Certainly the deliberations of this conference will be seminal in deciding the future course of action for Indo–Korea relations.

I must congratulate Centre for Indic–Asian Studies for beginning their series of conferences with South Korea and other Asian countries like Indonesia, Nepal and Thailand. These countries are equally important in terms of socio-cultural relations with India.

The Republic of Korea has shown its social commitment by initiating "model village project" in Haryana with Garghi Sapla. This conference will reinforce and extend a chain of activities for giving a fillip to the overall growth of the region.

I sincerely congratulate the BPS Mahila Vishwavidyalaya for being awarded with the Centre for Indic–Asian Studies and hosting this international conference. I thank Dr Pankaj Mittal for giving me this rare opportunity of participating and interacting with scholars of India and South Korea. I extend my best wishes and all support to the organizing team of this conference.

Thank you.

5

An Indian State and Korea
The Road of Co-operation

Bhupinder Singh Hooda

HIS Excellency Mr Kim Joong-Keun, Ambassador, the Republic of Korea; my colleague Mrs Geeta Bhukkal; Vice-Chancellor of this University Dr (Mrs) Pankaj Mittal; vice-chancellors of other universities of this state; Director, Centre for Indic–Asian Studies; ladies and gentlemen, and dear students, I am extremely happy to be here. Indeed it is a pleasure to be invited to this international conference on relations between India and the Republic of Korea.

For me, coming to Bhagat Phool Singh Mahila Vishwavidyalaya is always a home coming. Since its inception in August 2006, this university has always been my cherished dream. Seeing girls being empowered through qualitative education at BPS Mahila Vishwavidyalaya gives me great joy. In fact, the university was established with an aim to provide the best and affordable education to the rural female students. I am elated to know that BPS Mahila Vishwavidyalaya is doing its best to realize the dream of Bhagat Phool Singh-ji, who was a noble soul. I am told that the university has made its presence felt on international arena through academic and cultural exchange programmes. Holding this conference is a testimony to that. I congratulate the staff, students and especially Dr Pankaj Mittal for their hard work and commitment to the cause of women empowerment. I appreciate the idea of organizing an international conference on the relations between India and the Republic of Korea in the past and present. In fact, this very theme made me to be a part of this academic exercise. Relations between India and Korea have always been very good and strong. Both the nations being republics share many common values, including democracy. In fact, both are the representatives of Asian cultural, economic and political life.

I am told the Centre for Indic–Asian Studies will be holding a series of international conferences on Asian countries such as Nepal, Philippines, Sri Lanka and Vietnam. Holding the first such conference on the Republic of Korea is laudable.

The presence of his His Excellency Mr Kim Joong-Keun, Ambassador, the Republic of Korea, gives me an opportunity to explore the possibilities of Korean investment in our state of Haryana. The possible areas for investment could be agricultural technology, education, agro-economics, culture, etc. The scholarly discourse by both Korean and Indian scholars present here would certainly suggest some more potential areas of mutual exchange between India and Korea.

Having said that we live in the age of technology and the globalized world, there is an urgent need for strengthening the relations between India and Korea. Besides academic enrichment I am sure this conference would define paradigms of socio-cultural, economic and technological growth of both the countries. In spite of the fact that the world is fast progressing technologically and becoming modern day-by-day, the importance of our traditional knowledge cannot be overlooked. India has a lot to offer in this regard. I am sure the Centre for Indic–Asian Studies will make all efforts to preserve and propagate the treasure of knowledge available in Indo–Asian region. The galaxy of scholars participating in this conference would certainly suggest viable ways to achieve this mammoth task which will be a great service to humanity and wonderful gift to our posterior generations.

I am thankful to His Excellency Mr Kim Joong-Keun, Ambassador, the Republic of Korea, for agreeing to be a part of this international conference and taking keen interest in patronizing such an academic endeavour of international importance. I once again congratulate Dr Pankaj Mittal for holding this conference and offer my best wishes to the participating scholars.

Jai Hind!

6

The Ambassador's Keynote

"Korea and India: Past, Present and Future"

Kim Joong-Keun

Introduction

It is with a sense of great joy that I am with you today at Bhagat Phool Singh Women University and have the opportunity to deliver the keynote address on "India–Korea Relations". I take this opportunity to express my sincere gratitude to Dr Pankaj Mittal, distinguished Vice-Chancellor of the university, for her kind invitation.

I am delighted to learn that the university enjoys the distinction of being the first State women university in north India. This casts a heavy responsibility on you as the students of this university to be the standard bearer of Indian women, their values and heritage. I think that women in India have been subject to multiple discriminations. Spread of female literacy and education as well as growing social awareness can act as bulwark against discrimination against women. Against this backdrop, the motto of your university to empower women through education is, indeed, quite befitting.

Times have changed. Today, women are trying to take charge of their own lives and to break free from the stereotypes imposed upon them. More and more women are entering the fields which were previously considered as exclusive male domain. Nowhere, the progressive rise of women is so glaring, as in India.

It is a matter of great pride to the Indian womanhood that the country has a woman President and a woman Speaker of Lok Sabha. The president of the ruling party and the chairperson of ruling coalition is a woman. The leader of Opposition in the Lok Sabha is also a woman. There are several women ministers in the Union Council of Ministers and three of Indian states have women as chief ministers. Many Indian women also occupy top positions in the corporate world, and in the field of science and technology and sports. I am sure when you graduate from this great university, you will also make India proud as successful scientists, businesswomen, entrepreneurs and leaders.

As Ambassador of the Republic of Korea to India for almost two years, I have always felt that despite very strong relations between our two countries, there is general lack of awareness about Korea in India. I have, therefore, been interacting with the academic community, in the colleges and universities so as to enhance the understanding about Korea in India. I must admit that always I have emerged confident about our enduring bilateral relations from my interactions with students. With this abiding optimism, I am going to share with you about Korea's past, present and future.

Korea Past

The Republic of Korea occupies the southern portion of the Korean peninsula. Therefore, it is popularly known as South Korea. In terms of geographical area, the Korean peninsula, North and South Korea combined, is almost of the same size as that of the United Kingdom.

The history of undivided Korea dates back to over 5,000 years. Go-Chosun was Korea's first kingdom which was founded when a tribal chieftain Dangun united warring tribes into a nation state in 2333 BCE. In the first century BCE Go-Chosun kingdom declined and gave way to the emergence of three kingdoms of Goguryeo, Baekje and Silla which ruled the Korean peninsula and a part of Manchuria. In the seventh century, Shilla defeated the other two and unified the peninsula. The "Unified Silla Period" (CE 668–936) was the golden age for Korean culture.

In the early tenth century Goryeo dynasty succeeded Shilla. The name "Korea" is actually derived from "Goryeo". In 1392, the Joseon dynasty took over the area and remained in control until 1910. The

Choseon dynasty was the peninsula's last dynasty. During this period, the Korean alphabet "Hanguel" was invented and Hanyang, now known as Seoul, was established as the capital city. In 1910, Choseon dynasty fell under Japanese colonial rule largely due to its "closed door policy" and failure to adapt to the changing geopolitical landscape. For the proud people with 5,000 years of history and culture, 1910 marked the beginning of one of the darkest periods.

Japanese colonial rule ended with its defeat in the Second World War and surrender to allied powers on 15 August 1945. However, the end of colonial rule did not lead to the emergence of an independent nation. The country faced the tragic division of North and South along the 38th parallel line with the United States occupying the South while erstwhile Soviet Union, the North.

Three years later in 1948, elections were held in the South under UN supervision and the Government of the Republic of Korea was inaugurated. However, the joy of a new beginning was short-lived. On 25 June 1950, North Korea launched an unprovoked invasion of South Korea leading to a full-scale war that lasted for three years. The devastating war left four million people killed or wounded and the Korean economy completely destroyed.

Under the flag of the United Nations, sixteen nations sent their combat forces and six nations, including India, sent their medical contingents to help Korea meet this challenge. A cease-fire was signed in July 1953 to end the conflict. But, no peace treaty as yet, so we are still at war technically.

Korea Today

South Korea's meteoric rise from a poor and destitute country to an economic power is a truly incredible "rags to riches" story. Korea, devastated by the Korean War, was one of the poorest countries in the world just six decades ago. Today, Korea is an economic powerhouse with GDP over US $ 1 trillion and per capita income over US $ 22,000. As one of the most dynamic trading countries, it is the world's ninth biggest trading nation with annual trade volume of US $ 1 trillion.

Today, Korea is world's largest producer of memory chips and the second largest producer of semi-conductors and cellular phones. It ranks second in shipbuilding, fifth in automobiles manufacturing, sixth in steel production. It also has the distinction of being one of highest internet-connected countries in the world. Korean enterprises have unprecedented global presence. Major Korean companies like Samsung, Hyundai and LG are household names across the globe and have won recognition and respect for Korea.

Such remarkable economic achievements just within a span of six decades are nothing sort of a miracle and that is why Korea has come to be described as "Miracle on the Han River". These achievements become even more incredible if one considers the fact that these economic achievements have taken place despite the nation's poor endowment of natural resources, small size of domestic market and its preoccupation with constant national security threats from North Korea.

Korea was also once described as a barren land for democracy but today it is a vibrant democracy. It is the only country in the world to have achieved economic development and democracy almost at the same time. The deepening of democracy in Korea is reflected in the spread of democratic idea, the rule of law, the freedom of press and independent judiciary.

In tandem with its economic and democratic achievements, Korea's international standing and prestige have also risen. The country is no longer a hermit kingdom, dislocated from the global community. Today it occupies a centrestage in international politics and economics. As you may recall, in November 2010, Korea hosted G20 Summit to pool together the collective efforts of the world community to overcome the global economic crisis. In March 2012 it hosted the Second Nuclear Security Summit to contribute to the international efforts for making the world safe from nuclear and radiological terrorism.

Korea's leadership role in the field of culture and sports has also grown at a spectacular pace. Korean Wave of pop culture or Hallyu as it is known in Korean language which includes popular music as well as television dramas, movies is enchanting millions of hearts across the world and this has even touched the Indian shore.

Korea has also hosted major sporting events like the Summer Olympics in 1988, FIFA World Cup in 2002, World Athletics Championship in 2011 and will be hosting the Winter Olympics in 2018.

Inter-Korean Relations

The most important strategic challenge before South Korea is the maintenance of peace and stability in the Korean peninsula.

Korean peninsula is the only remnant of the Cold War. As I already said, the two Koreas are still technically at war because of no peace treaty between them till date. North Korea continues to indulge in armed provocations, challenging peace and security on the Korean peninsula.

Establishment of peace on the Korean peninsula is the most important priority of the foreign policy of South Korean government. South Korean government has consistently pursued reconciliation with North Korea. But the Communist regime has taken South's efforts for reconciliation as sign of weakness and has reciprocated the latter's sincerity with belligerence and armed provocations. North Korea torpedoed and sank a South Korean warship "Cheonan" in March 2010, killing 46 South Korean soldiers. Without taking any responsibility for sinking Cheonan, North Korea repeated its act of aggression by shelling "Yeonpyeong Island" in November 2010 which claimed the lives of four South Koreans, including two civilians. These unilateral, unprovoked and premeditated attacks by North Korea have made inter-Korean relations highly tense. In April 2012, despite strong opposition from the international community, a defiant North Korea went ahead with the launch of a long-range missile dressed up as a rocket, which failed. The launch was a clear violation of the United Nations Security Council Resolution 1874, which prohibits any launch using ballistic missile technology, and a provocative act that threatened the peace and security on the Korean peninsula and in North-east Asia.

The failed effort to launch a rocket goes out to explain that despite the change of leadership after the death of Kim Jong-Il, there has been no change in the regime's tendency to indulge in reckless and destabilizing acts. At a time, when the North Korean leader is trying to consolidate his grip over power, there are genuine concerns that a failed rocket launch could spur North Korea to go for more reckless behaviour, endangering peace and stability on the Korean peninsula and whole of Asia. Today, it is North Korea's pursuit of nuclear weapons and proliferation of nuclear know-how and ballistic missile that threatens not just the peace and stability on the Korean peninsula, but Asia and the world as well.

My government's proposal is that if North Korea sincerely wants peace and stability in the Korean peninsula, it must make a clear and unambiguous commitment that it will desist from provocative acts in future. If Pyongyang abandons its nuclear ambitions, we are ready to work with international community to provide security assurance and implement our economic assistance package and lead the effort for international assistance and support to North Korea.

Korea Tomorrow

President Lee Myung-bak announced a vision of "Global Korea" in 2008, a fully-advanced Korea which stands tall in the global arena and which looks beyond the security of the Korean peninsula to contemplate the world's problems and plays a leadership role in finding a solution to these problems — be it war in Afghanistan, economic and financial stability or nuclear terrorism.

Korea understands that Global Korea can't be truly possible without taking global responsibilities. So, Korea hosted G20 Summit in 2010, High-Level Aid Effectiveness Forum in November 2011, Nuclear Security Summit in March 2012 and APEC Education Summit in May 2012 in its efforts to be at the forefront of tackling global issues. For this, Korea has decided to raise its Official Development Assistance (ODA) which was US $ 300 million in 2005 and currently US $ 900 million to over US $ 3 billion by 2015 — a tenfold increase in its foreign assistance in a decade. Korea will also expand its peacekeeping forces which are currently operating in fourteen countries as a part of UN and multinational peacekeeping forces so that they contribute more to maintaining peace and stability in the world.

In order to achieve the goal of Global Korea, it wants to become a hub of international trade and it sees Free Trade Agreements (FTAs) as powerful means to achieve this goal. Seoul has signed FTAs with forty-five countries including India. It is the only country in the world to have signed FTAs with both the US and the European Union (EU).

Korean government, its diplomats and Korean people are working together relentlessly so that they could realize the vision of Global Korea.

Evolution of Korea–India Relations

Korea and India established their diplomatic ties in 1973 but until the early 1990s, bilateral relations between the two countries remained relatively low, despite enormous potential for growth.

There were two main reasons. First, India's policy of Non-Alignment during the Cold War period was in sharp contrast to Korea's alliance with the US which hindered the two countries from drawing close to each other. Second, in the economic sphere, India adopted inward-looking import substitution model of development, whereas Korea consistently pursued an outward-looking export-oriented development path and opened its market to the world. This difference in economic policy orientation prevented the growth of economic ties between the two countries.

However, things began to change in the early 1990s. The end of the Cold War and India's adoption of market-oriented economic reforms removed the impediments to the growth of bilateral ties. In other words, these two developments provided the right environment for growth and marked the beginning of a new era in our relations, which I often refer to as a phase of "economic and commercial co-operation". Korean companies were among the first to repose faith and confidence in India after it opened its economy. They entered

India in a big way and as a result bilateral trade and investment surged and became the defining feature of Korea–India bilateral relations.

However, real turning point in Korea–India relations came in 2010. Two important developments took place in the year, which truly transformed the bilateral relations. First, our two countries implemented Comprehensive Economic Partnership Agreement (CEPA) to realize the full potential of trade and investment. Second, President Lee Myung-bak paid a historic state visit to India as the Chief Guest on India's Republic Day celebration and together with Prime Minister, Manmohan Singh, decided to upgrade the bilateral relations to a "Strategic Partnership". The official visit of Prime Minister, Manmohan Singh, to Korea in March 2012 has further deepened our Strategic Partnership.

India's "Look East Policy" and Korea

India announced its Look East Policy in the early 1990s keeping in view its economic interests and strategic imperatives. The policy came to symbolize as one of the most important policy initiatives of India in recent past. Ironically, neither India nor did countries of South-East Asia or North-East Asia attach much importance to the policy in the first decade. For the whole period of the 1990s, India though looked East but actually went West. The response of East Asian countries to India's much avowed policy decision was at best lukewarm. Given the fact that India was embroiled in too many domestic problems, its economy was in shambles and the countries of the region did not expect economic rise of India any day soon, hence, quite evidently, attached much less importance to it in the regional affairs.

Initiatives taken in the 1990s towards comprehensive reforms of Indian economy began to show results in the early 2000s, signifying country's fundamental economic regeneration. Indian economy began to register impressive growth and with rising economic stature, India's strategic importance also got significantly enhanced.

The countries of South-East and North-East Asia began to factor India in their foreign policy making and look at India as partner in stable balance of power in Asia. The growing importance of India for the countries of the region came to be reflected in a flurry of high-level mutual exchange of visits between India and countries of the region, and number of strategic and free trade agreements that India signed with them as well as India's entry into East Asia Summit (EAS).

An economically strong India with its renewed strategic importance commanded the respect of the region as also the world at large. Korea did not miss to recognize the new profile of India and evinced much interest in building strong bilateral ties on a range of issues. India, too, realized the importance of Korea as a partner in the emerging geo-political scenario.

Korea complimented India's Look East Policy with its New Asia Initiative which President Lee Myung-bak announced in 2008. India's Look East Policy and Korea's New Asia Diplomatic Initiative have much the same common focus and direction.

So, when India invited President Lee Myung-bak as the chief guest on its Republic Day in January 2010, the message was clear: New Delhi perceives its engagement with Seoul as one of its foreign policy priorities and desires a very special relationship with Korea. President Lee Myung-bak reciprocated New Delhi's desire for special partnership and paid a historic state visit to India. During their summit meeting, President Lee and Prime Minister Manmohan Singh decided to give strategic dimension to what till then largely was mercantile relations.

Since the establishment of strategic partnership, there has been an increased co-operation between the two countries in security and defence matters, so much so that some of the future investments from Korea in India are planned from strategic point of view.

Current State of Bilateral Relations

The present phase of "Strategic Partnership" has witnessed substantive engagement between the two countries not only in economic field but also in the field of security and defence.

In the economic field, CEPA has worked as catalyst and surged bilateral trade and investment. In two years, since the effectuation of

CEPA on 1 January 2010, the two-way trade has increased almost by 70 per cent. In 2011, bilateral trade crossed US $ 20.6 billion. The two countries have now set an ambitious trade target of US $ 40 billion by 2015. I am sure we will be able to achieve the new trade target before its scheduled time.

Today, Korean investment in India stands at around US $ 3 billion. Indian companies have also invested around US $ 1 billion in Korea. As Korean companies are keen to bring more investment to India, they have identified civil nuclear power, ship-building and defence industry as new sectors for future investment. These are the areas in which Korea excels and I am sure Korean investment will flow into these sectors in future which will take our investment relations to a new high.

The single most important new development in Korea–India relations in the post-2010 period has been the steady strengthening of strategic aspect of our relations. This has been necessitated by the changing geo-strategic realities of the world and the desire of the two countries to protect and promote their mutual interests.

As students of politics and economics, you must be aware that the world politics is currently undergoing a major transformation. The relative decline of established powers and the emergence of new powers have put the balance of power that prevailed in Asian region in a flux, putting regional peace and stability under strain. And, it is in this backdrop, Korea and India are working closely together bilaterally as well as in the regional and international fora to ensure a peaceful and stable regional order.

And, one of the ideas we are working on is the trilateral co-operation between Japan, India and Korea, second, third and fourth largest economy in Asia, respectively. Korea, India and Japan are three most important countries in the Asian region with significant economic and strategic weight in the world. We enjoy excellent relations with one another; our mutual relations are distinguished by convergence of our world-views; our three countries share common values; we have a broad range of common interests in diverse areas impacting regional peace and security; all three of us — Korea, India and Japan — are the US close allies. Significant complementarities in three countries make an important case for a trilateral co-operation which could be a factor of peace and security in the Asia-Pacific region.

As a first step in this direction, we launched this dialogue at Track II level between the think-tanks of three countries in June 2012. We do expect that this dialogue at non-governmental level will gradually evolve into a dialogue at the governmental level.

Both Korea and India are committed to develop comprehensive bilateral relations. We are hopeful that with growing engagement across the spectrum, we will be able to break new ground and achieve many more milestones in the coming years.

Thank you.

7

Korean Language Education and Korean Studies in India

Kim Do-young

Introduction

KOREAN studies in India have been a backbone of maintaining and developing Korea–India cultural relationship, although it didn't have a great number of specialists nor various channels to approach to it. Desire for further development between two countries has been growing bigger, and it came visualized gradually after being inseminated with consulate relation between the two countries. In fact, beginning and progress of Korean studies in India are to be mentioned earliest after late 1960s when a few Indian students came to Korea for learning languages and studies.

The period of early 1970s to early 1980s was the time for sporadic insemination of Korean studies and languages producing researchers or a few batches of language courses in 1970s. Early 1980s to late 1980s was the time of status quo in view of external development, however, concept of area studies and languages was assorted in the 1990s, more precisely, from 1995 it has been progressive conspicuously in quantity as well as in quality along with clearer concept of both.

Institutionally it may be proper to speak about establishment of Korean language programme and area studies at Jawaharlal Nehru University (JNU) and University of Delhi, respectively, since Korean studies have been developed based on the root in the two. These two prime universities out of 263 universities in India have been playing the pivotal role in Korean studies since no other university has set up any programme related with Korea. Though a few private institutes bearing the title "Korea" are discovered being influenced by successful achievement of Korean corporates in India, they are insignificant in view of cultural influence as well as augmentation in number. Therefore, focus of Korean studies should be on tracing development from JNU to University of Delhi as a mainstream. Along with this development and transition, it is anticipated that more universities in India may set up Korean language and study programmes in near future and Indian understanding on Korea may be expanded and deepened.

Jawaharlal Nehru University

DEVELOPMENT

In 1971, the first Vice-Chancellor G. Parthasarthy initiated Korean language programme with appointment of R.R. Krishan as an assistant professor. R.R. Krishnan and Vipan Chandra, who had studied Chinese studies at University of Delhi, had been selected and supported by the Korean government scholarship for three years in 1968. Though it is not exactly the step of JNU, Alka Gupta who had been selected as a scholarship student in 1972 by the help of JNU may be mentioned here as a partial development.

Korean language programme began one-year Pre-Degree Diploma course as a part of African–Asian Language at JNU, which had instituted School of Foreign Languages. The course was opened to the students who had a bachelor degree. Its first batch students were Alok Roy, Pankaj and Vyjanti Raghavan. With internal problems of the varsity in early 1980s, problems of pre-degree courses were specified and reduced to certificate courses. Accordingly, Korean language programme was downgraded to one of the certificate courses. With lapse from 1986 to 1988, Korean language programme couldn't recruit students and from 1989 it renewed its admission to a certificate course, which was developed to advanced certificate course later. In 1995, significant development was made by the help of Korea Foundation, which had donated US $ 45,000 to the university for employing faculty members. It had set a spur for degree programme at the university. Thereby Korean language programme was upgraded to BA degree programme and admitted twenty-five students in July 1995. Its first batch of twenty-two was produced in May 1998. As a part of integral MA, the programme was stretched to MA in Korean language successively. In July the same year and after two years it produced the first batch of nine graduates in the history of Korean studies in India. Their career was diversified according to conditions and choice. Along with the development of Korean language programme at the School of Languages, Literature and Cultural Studies, area study related to Korea has shown gradual expansion at the School of International Studies. It had produced twelve graduates of MPhil in Korean studies till July 2003, after its beginning in 1983. In fact, many of them were graduates of MA in Korean language programme at the School of Language, Literature and Cultural Studies.

KOREAN LANGUAGE PROGRAMME: SCHOOL OF LANGUAGE, LITERATURE AND CULTURAL STUDIES

Name of the Department: Centre for Japanese and North-East Asian Studies

This department has been branched out of Centre for East Asian Languages. Because Japanese language was one of the most dominant among Asian languages, it came up with the title Japanese, and Chinese has the same way, i.e. Centre for Chinese and South-East Asian Studies. The former includes three languages with different disciplines — BA, MA, pre-PhD in Japanese language, BA and MA in Korean languages and one-year certificate course in Mongolian. It may be a right direction for having an independent centre for Korean languages in the future.

BA and MA Course in Korean Language

This is a five-year, ten-semester BA and MA integrated course. At the end of the course, the student is expected to be able to converse fluently and flawlessly in Korean language using a fairly wide range of vocabulary, be familiar with 1,200 Hanja or Sino–Korean characters, translate materials from Korean into English and vice versa based on the vocabulary learnt in various courses and with the help of dictionaries. The student is also expected to acquire a sound knowledge and understanding of Korean history, culture and contemporary society.

SCHOOL OF INTERNATIONAL STUDIES

In 1972, School of International Studies, JNU, began Korean area studies offering a few courses to MA students. R.R. Krishnan started to give his lectures at Centre for East Asian Studies of the school, JNU.

Master of Philosophy (MPhil) Courses

In India, specialization in Korean studies of various fields is available only in this programme.

Steady and consistent research works are developed, although it has only one faculty member.

Doctor of Philosophy

A countable number of students who had finished MPhil are carrying on PhD course, although there is no one who has completed PhD at JNU. A few completed their PhD at Seoul National University in Korea.

University of Delhi

DEVELOPMENT

Department of Chinese and Japanese Studies, whose head was Sreemati Chakrabarti, initiated developing the programme to include Korean language and area studies in 2001. It was visualized in 2003 when it inducted a Korean visiting professor Do Young Kim into Korean language programme, and renamed it Department of East Asian Studies and offering certificate course (1st year part-time), diploma (2nd year part-time) and advanced diploma (3rd year part-time). The details of courses are as below.

KOREAN LANGUAGE COURSES

University of Delhi has a layer of Korean language courses. First of all, Department of East Asian Studies, Faculty of Social Sciences, holds two postgraduate diploma courses; one year postgraduate intensive diploma and one year intensive advanced diploma courses. Second is a part-time course: part-time Korean certificate course, Korean diploma course, and Korean advanced diploma course. Daulat Ram College has three courses in all, Delhi College of Arts and Commerce and Khalsa College have certificate course only.

The aim of the Korean language courses is to impart them in an integrated manner, the four skills of speaking, reading, listening and writing the language fluently. To achieve this, the students would be trained right from the beginning, in conversation as well as reading and writing. The oral comprehension of the students would be enhanced by using audio-visual aids in the language laboratory. By the time the students finish the three years of study, it is expected that they would be in a position to read Korean language newspapers and journals. At the end of the diploma course, the students would be able to translate and interpret, and at the end of the advanced diploma, they would be in a position to handle primary source materials. Thus the courses shall train the students not only to take up jobs requiring Korean language skills, but also equip them with the necessary academic background to enable them to take up Korea as a subject of study.

In the certificate course, the students would be introduced to Hanguel (the Korean script) and also 100 Hanja (Chinese characters). At the end of the certificate course, the students are expected to be proficient in day-to-day conversation and writing short paragraphs in Korean on simple topics.

In the diploma course, the students would be introduced to another 300 Hanja and also business terminology. The students would be trained in translation skill too. At the end of the diploma course, the students would be able to translate and interpret from Korean to English and vice versa and thus be in a position to take up jobs that require knowledge of Korean.

In the advanced diploma course, the students shall be taught another 400 Hanja. They would be introduced to aspects of Korean society and culture. Technical terms in the fields of history, politics, economics, etc. would be introduced and the students shall be encouraged to read Korean books and journals. Emphasis would be placed on improving reading comprehension skills. At the end of the advanced diploma course, since the students would be able to read and write 800 Hanja, they are expected to be able to handle primary source materials.

KOREAN STUDIES

It is proposed to introduce a two year full-time Masters Programme in East Asian Studies with the objective of promoting comparative as well as area-specific core studies of themes and issues which fall within the purview of the various branches of social sciences. The East Asian region is defined as comprising of the Peoples Republic of China, Japan and the two Koreas. The basic thrust of the programme will be to equip students with the fundamentals of East Asian civilization and its dynamics as it unfolded in the ancient, medieval, pre-modern, modern and contemporary periods, in order to enable them to pursue and undertake meaningful research on the countries that constitute this region. Courses related with Korea apart from Japanese and Chinese studies are as below:

1. Pre-modern Korea
2. Korea under Japanese Colonial Rule (1910-45)
3. Political Developments in South Korea (1953 to the present)
4. Political Developments in North Korea (1953 to the present)
5. Foreign Policy of South Korea (1953 to the present)
6. Foreign Policy of North Korea (1953 to the present)
7. International Economic Relations of the two Koreas (1953 to the present)
8. Development Experience of South Korea (1953 to the present)
9. Development Experience of North Korea (1953 to the present).

KOREAN RELATED ACHIEVEMENTS

2003 22-24 March: International Conference on East Asia "India and East Asia: Learn Each Other"

2004 26-27 March: International Conference on Korea "Korea into the 21st Century"

2004 21-24 November: Korea Week

2004 23 November: International Seminar on Korea: "Nativization of Korean Language"

2005 17-18 February: International Seminar on Korea: Modernizing Experiences of Korean and India

2005 21-25 November: Korea Week

2006 10-11 February: International Conference on Korea: "Korea in Search of a New Global Role: Current Concerns and Past Moorings"

Scholarship

University of Delhi has the scholarships of Shinhan Bank, LG and Korean Government Scholarship.

Magadha University

Language Centre of Magadha University began Korean language certificate course in 2007 and expanded it to as a diploma course.

English and Foreign Language University

It has two years postgraduate courses; one-year certificate and one-year diploma course.

Scholarship Students in Korean Studies

Students specializing in Korean studies or languages have been encouraged enormously by the scholarship offered by the Government of the Republic of Korea in two ways: Scholarship by Korea International Education Centre under the Ministry of Education and Human Resources, and Korea Foundation under the Ministry of Foreign Affairs. Private or Korean universities' scholarships are also noticeably on the rise, although their contribution is not discovered significantly.

KOREA FOUNDATION

Korea Foundation maintains two ways of offering scholarship: Research Fellowship for scholars and Language Training Scholarship for students.

Conclusion

Korean studies have been developed in India and spread for the last three decades. Along with this gradual and positive development, a few directions may be discovered. First quality matter should be focused. Compared to Chinese and Japanese studies in India, it is still on the establishing stage. Therefore, more universities should be encouraged to open Korean programme, and on the other hand, PhD programme should be inducted. Second, faculty members should be engaged in more research works for self-academic discipline. There is a great demand for Korean studies but the contents do not satisfy it. It can be solved by enhancing the level of their research and teaching contents. Teachers should be encouraged to complete their PhD, to hold seminars or conferences every year and to publish their research papers and textbooks. Third, scholarship students should be encouraged to come back to India after completing their study. Of course, present faculty members should make an effort to take them in to the academic fields. Conclusively speaking, academic level should be enhanced and it should be focused on, rather than expansion in number because such increase is a phenomenon which is naturally based on social demand.

References

PAPERS

Giri, Deshingkar, "Chinese Studies in India: An Appraisal", 1994.

Huang I-shu, "Pioneers and Cultural Bridges", 1994.

Kesavan, K.V., "A Note on the State of Japanese Studies in India", 1999.

Narsimhan, Sushila, "Area Studies in India: Case Study of Delhi University", Korea Research Foundation, 2003.

Vishwanathan, Savitri, "Othernesses of Japan, Indian Approaches to Japanese Studies", Korea International Education Center.

REPORTS

Embassy of the Republic of Korea, *Cultural Agreement*, 1974.

Electronics and Computer Software Export Promotion Council.

Language Related Market Access Facilitation Initiative in the Japanese IT Market, 2002.

Japanese Language Teachers Association of India, *Annual Report*, 2002.

Korea Economic Daily, 1 August 2003.

Korea Foundation, Haewoi Hongukhak Boekseo, Seoul: Eurya publication, 2005

1. *Korean Language Training Fellowship*
2. *Research Fellowship*
3. *Report of Madras University*
4. *Report of Calcutta University*

The committee for commemoration of the 30th Anniversary of Korea–India Diplomatics Relations, *30 years of Korea–India Relations*, Seoul: shingu publishing co., 2003.

8

Korea's Indian Connection and the Tradition of Language Learning and Translation

Ramesh Chand Sharma

LANGUAGE sets the human beings apart from rest of the animals in as much as language happens to be far more important to the crucial nexus of human brain as the material basis for language and cognition on the one hand and the social dimensions of language on the other. As a biologically evolved functional tool, language happens to be the most suited fundamental basis of human communication and knowledge acquisition, and thus happens to be crucial to psychological and sociological dimensions of human existence. The question overemphasized at the outset can, in a way, be examined in relation to the emergence of Korean language as a national identity and some of the processes that have shaped the national identity. Korea has had an old Indian connection, and the tradition of language learning and translation. Korean tradition of Indian studies and languages of India is closely linked to their history and the emergence of their national identity.

Korea has historically remained largely an isolated country for a variety of reasons, but mostly due to the self-assumed vassal status *vis-à-vis* China on the one hand and historically being overshadowed by two dominant civilizations of China and Japan in the neighbourhood. The fact that evolution and growth of Korean society and civilization spans over long history is attested by not only archaeological evidences and historical resources, but also the factors which have defined and shaped its growth and evolution. A vexing question, however, remains to be addressed: Why did Korean language wait so long as a language to emerge as a vital means of standardization, modernization, and socialization; and also as an eventual manifestation of "Koreanness"? Why did Koreans wait so long to have Hangul as a recognized and accepted writing system for Korean language? It is a question of paramount significance and needs to be addressed particularly as it also relates to the wider and more acceptable manifestation of Korean identity. The focal issue at the bottom of this question, at best, can be seen in relation to not only "the being of Korean", but also the fact that Korean has been lodged between the two important and culturally rich Chinese and Japanese societies has meant that Korea is often overlooked. "It has been difficult for Koreans to emerge from the shadow of their East Asian neighbours and to make their presence and their cultural knowledge to the rest of the world" (Seth 2006).

The long-term homogeneity of Korean society and language has grown from a historical synthesis of varied peoples, as pointed out by Seth, through gradually forging a society characterized by cultural homogeneity and political unity, and certainly one of the oldest continuously unified states in the pre-partitioned Korea, thus gradually merging into a single ethnicity, sharing one language. "Thus, Korea became one of the few lands where ethnicity, membership of a language community and a state were continuous. The unity and homogeneity that emerged over the centuries have become an important part of the Korean identity" (Seth 2006: 1-20) and has also contributed the remarkable continuity as a distinctive feature of Korean history.

Historians as well as linguists would initially be surprised with a peculiar coexistence that Korean has had with Chinese, adopted as an elite language for such a long time. The situation was neither a diglossic nor similar to the status of Persian during medieval history of India which was at least one of the major factors to contribute to the emrgence of Hindi initially as a *lingua franca* and later as a modern Indian language. For, the historical coexistence of Korean and Chinese did not give rise to any striking metamorphosis which could have created a new language. It can be reasonably argued as to why such a historical eventuality in terms of linguistic history could not take place in the context of Korea. One, Korean community has always been a highly homogeneous ethnic and linguistic community and thus a strong nationalistic attitude to their language must have prevailed upon the minds of the people to maintain their language. Two, unlike Persian, Chinese had no genetic affinity with Korean. Three, Chinese existed in a specific space of "order" rather than usage. It created a kind of undefined "tolerance" of Chinese by the language of the native people of Korea without warranting the rise of a diglossic situation where in either two dialects or usually closely related languages are used by a single language community and hence giving rise to the status of one as a language variety of every-day routine communication ("L" or "low" variety), a second language the status of a highly codified variety ("H" or "high") meant to be used in certain situations such as literature and formal discourse. Chinese (as it is, with no genetic affinity with Korean at all), supposedly the high variety in this case, was neither an older stage of the same language, nor a distinct yet closely related present-day dialect thus one being the colloquial dialect and the other potentially being the official, literary standard. Even the scholars of literary history of Korea are aware of this historical fact of the existence of Chinese and Korean for such a long time in Korean history. Kichung Kim explains this in his book (1996):

> . . . *Hanmun* — literally "letters of Han", that is Chinese characters — was the written language of practically all literate Koreans from about the beginning of Korea's recorded history to the end of the nineteenth century.

No doubt Koreans have a well-established national tradition and they have always maintained and have been proud of their national identity even during the times of their country's occupation. The predominant Chinese influence on Korean thinking and culture, maintaining the long historically viable national identity as they did, can be seen since the extermination of the first recorded Korean state by the Chinese establishment of an imperial outpost in 108 BCE and the subsequent Chinese impact on the three kingdoms that emerged later in Korea as well as on the unified Koryo and Joseon period of Korean history. Chinese influence can also be gauged from Chinese impact on Korean adoption of Buddhism which has flourished as an important religious philosophy and even to date it happens to be one of the major religious inclinations of the Korean people. Chinese influence prevailed and remained dominant all through the history of Korea through the three kingdoms period to the unified Korea ruled by the three successive royal dynasties — three kingdoms unified by Silla which giving way to Koryo in CE 936 and Koryo to Choson in 1392 and the Choson ruling until Korea's occupation followed by annexation by Japan in 1910 to its independence. Macdonald (1996: 11) writes:

> Buddhism flourished in the Silla and Koryo dynasties; Confucianism became the state philosophy of Choson, which evolved a political and social structure transcending in some respects its Chinese model. Each dynasty brought forth cultural and aesthetic accomplishments: Silla, for example, had its pottery, gold and silver ornamentation, and architecture; Koryo the beautiful celdon ware that has never been fully reproduced; Choson, a scientifically correct phonetic alphabet to replace the ill-fitting Chinese ideographs.

Scholars in Korea have historically shown a strong attitude as well as a keen desire for learning foreign languages and knowledge systems though its isolation over long time of history owing to a variety of reasons was highly unfavourable to their quest for knowledge and languages. First of all, ever since the establishment of the Korean people in ancient times, the three ancient kingdoms to the Joseon dynasty, Korean powers always assumed a vassal status in relation to their more towering neighbour China. It is true that China provided not only Confucianism and Buddhism to Korea, but also "the model for literature, art, music, architecture, dress, and etiquette" (Seth 2006: 2). This, though, does not mean that Koreans could not develop their love for nature and natural world into their beliefs and artistic expressions.

In spite of the fact that a scientific writing system for Korean language had already evolved due to the initiative of King Sejong (1418-50), Chinese language has had the pre-eminent position in the pre-modern Korea. Apart from being language of the elite, and a medium of intellectual and religious discourse, Chinese language also dominated to negatively impact the growth and development of Korean language. Such domination of Chinese detrimental to the emergence of Korean as a language of intellectual and artistic expressions can be seen to be reflected all through the stages of Classical Korean literature — through Hyangch'al, Idu and Shizo (Kim 1996). One may ask why until the Silhak movement, Hangul was not popular for writing in Korea?

It is true that Korea's Chinese connection as well as its geographical proximity to China were extremely significant in the import and spread of Buddhism in Korea. But, at the same time, one cannot ignore the crucial role of the Indian connection right from the beginning of Buddhism in Korea. Ilyeon's *Overlooked Historical Records of the Three Korean Kingdoms* and *Lives of the Eminent Korean Monks* as well as the *Samguk Yusa* mention about the role of Indian monks who visited Korea and contributed to the rise of Buddhism there. Sundo came to Konguryo in CE 372 during the rule of King Sosurim and brought Buddhism there. Ado, an Indian monk followed after some years, probably around four years. Even though Ilyeon mentions that Sundo came from China to Korea, he is categorical in mentioning that Sundo's origin is unknown. Keeping in view the fact that there is an analogical similarity with other such names of Indian monks who visited Korea those days and also the fact that even today in Korea, an Indian name like Pankaj is transformed into "Pangoji", it is very likely that Sundo was also an Indian monk who visited Konguryo after spending some time in China. Nanto (Malananda), an Indian monk, brings Buddhism to Paekje in CE 384 and with the issuance of the royal decree by King Asian of Paekje in CE 392 began the spread of Buddhism there. Another Indian monk Ado came to Silla and is largely credited with laying the foundations of Buddhism in Silla. Discrepancy concerning the dates of Ado's life and arrival in Silla is noted by Ilyeon in the "Haedong

Kosung Chon" (*Lives of Eminent Korean Monks*) though after death of Nulji until the time of Popkong (514-40), the 23rd king of Silla. Buddhism did not make much progress in Silla. In 534 a monastery was built and Buddhism began to flourish in Silla. The early Mahāyāna school had already identified Sanskrit as language of their identity (as opposed to Pāli of Theravādins), so most of the translations those days took place from Sanskrit to Chinese and the same were used by the later Korean monks. But, what is noteworthy is the fact that several Sanskrit terms are found replete in Ilyeon's literature which not only points out that early Buddhist scholars of Korea were all well versed with the Buddhist literature in Chinese but were also used to refer to several Sanskrit terms. The fact that the ease with which Ilyeon refers to the original sources in Sanskrit and their translations (in Chinese) also supports that scholars like Ilyeon not only knew Sanskrit and Chinese languages, but were well aware of the several translations that had been done those days by various scholars.

Many Korean monks and scholars in ancient Korea travelled to India at different times visiting places of pilgrimage and learning. Ilyeon's *Overlooked Historical Records* and *Lives of the Eminent Korean Monks*, many monks from Korea, particularly from Silla, had travelled to India in ancient times. Several of them knew Sanskrit or learnt it in India and used their knowledge of Sanskrit for further learning, for translating books of Buddhist philosophy and discourse, and for further improving the already existing translations. These include majority of monks from Silla though monks from other Korean ancient Korean kingdoms also travelled to India. A monk named Hyeop during the era of Chen Kwan travelled to India traversing the vast desert of moving sands and climbed the steep ridges of the Himalayas. He visited the Mahābodhi and Nālandā monasteries. He read the *Vimalakīrti-Nirdeśa*, compared it with the T'ang translation and expounded it thoroughly and systematically. While doing copying of the works in Sanskrit, he died in the Nālandā monastery. Sok Hyenyun, a native of Silla (with an assumed Sanskrit name of Prajñāvarman) travelled to India with another senior monk Hyonjo and on their pilgrimage they stayed at the Ciñcavihāra monastery of Amarāvatī for about ten years. Later he moved further east and lived in the prosperous Gandharchanda monastery frequented by with foreign monks. Hyenyun knew Sanskrit well and studied thoroughly the *Abhidharma Kośa*. Monk Hyonjo was also accompanied by Sok Hyon'gak, another monk from Silla. They reached the Mahābodhi monastery in India and found many other Korean monks there.

Travelled to India with another senior monk Hyonjo, and on their pilgrimage they stayed at the Ciñcavihāra monastery in the country of Amarāvatī and reached the Mahābodhi monastery in India where already some Korean monks were staying. Sok Hyonyu, a native of Konguryo, visited many places in India and finally returned to the eastern India, where he constantly learnt from eminent monks and lived near them. Ilyeon records in *Lives of Eminent Korean Monks*:

> Early in life he showed a marked propensity for *prajñā* and *dhyāna*. He probed the depths and fulfilled the measure of the doctrine. He went forth empty-handed and returned heavily laden.

Another monk Hyont'ae (with an assumed Sanskrit name Sarvajñānadeva) also travelled to India and stayed in the Mahābodhi monastery, studied carefully the scriptures and treatises, and observed the local customs before he returned. Emulating the courage of these early monk-scholars who travelled to India those days, Kakhun says:

> They traced the steps of Fa-hsien and Hsuan-tsang. They went back and forth in the deserted regions, regarding them as lanes and streets. They can be compared with the envoys Chang Ch'ien and Su Wu.

Reference is also made of the stay of Indian monk-scholars Kumārajīva and Bhikṣu Asaṅga in China. Asaṅga had received a copy of *Bodhisattvabhūmi* from Maitreya which was translated from Sanskrit by Tan-Mo-Ch'an (Dharmakṣema 385–433) at Kutsang. The *Mo-ho-yen lun* was written by Bodhisattva Nāgārjuna and translated by Kumārajīva (344–413) upon his arrival in Changain. Knowledge of

Sanskrit and Chinese was not confined only to Indian and Chinese scholars which encouraged a faster exchange of ideas but also to some of the contemporary Korean Buddhist scholar-monks. Initially they must have learnt Sanskrit in China or from the direct contacts with some Indian monks who happened to come on visits to Korea. This also reflects that Indian monks too were not only well versed in Chinese but also in Korean which enabled them to communicate with the common people, a factor so essential to the meteoric growth of Buddhism in ancient Korea. A strong desire to communicate in the language of the masses could not have made much progress owing to the dominance of Chinese as a language of the court and elite in Korea on the one hand and as a language of the intellectual discourse, on the other. Another factor that seems to have delayed the emergence of Korean language as a symbol of Korean identity is the large isolation of Korea as a "hermit kingdom" and the overall absence of any determined bid to identify Korean language as a tool of literacy, standardization and as a language of artistic expressions. Only with the development of the Silhak and Donghak movements and other factors such as the spread of Christianity, growth of modernization and reassertion of Korean identity as a response to Japanese colonization and hegemony over Korea, came Korean language as a symbol of Korean identity; thus it was a larger response of the reassertion of Korean nationalism. Silhak brought "practical relevance" and the "Korean identity and nationalism" into focus.

Significant changes took place in the mid-seventeenth century reflecting in agriculture as well as knowledge and understanding which shifted the focus to matters of practical relevance. This resulted in the theoretical groups committed to four sectors of Korean life and society: (i) comprehensive administrative and educational reforms; (ii) commerce and technology; (iii) a critical appraisal of the Confucian classics which had hitherto dominated and defined the polity, society and administration; and (iv) the study of history, geography and language of Korea. This soon resulted in the emerging Korean literature art and all kinds of creative expressions which by now turned to be

"Korea- and Korean-centric". The Independence Club movement of Philip Jaisohn, adoption of Hangul for all creative expressions and knowledge acquisition, the Tonghak Rebellion of 1894-95 and the demise of Qing Dynasty in China consolidating Korean nationalism and identity could carve a perspective and milieu for the emergence of Korean language as a symbol of Korean identity.

In the beginning of the twentieth century, the Buddhist scholars also realized the importance of original sources of the Buddhist literature in Sanskrit and thus began to study and translate them into Korean language. Emergence of modern economy in South Korea has also created the needs for Koreans sending their children abroad, including India, for higher education and thus enthusing the Korean economy as well as education system with new ideas on the one hand and on the other enabling the emerging Korean economy reap fruits of advantageous trade and business contacts by learning foreign languages including modern Indian languages. Hindi is taught not only in Hankuk University of Foreign Studies and Pusan University of Foreign Studies, but also in some other major and minor universities along with other courses such as Indian economy and business, law and culture. Development of Indian economy has also created further needs for learning Hindi and these courses. The present year is remarkable as a professor at Hankuk University of Foreign Studies (HUFS), Seoul, Lee Jeong Ho has been honoured with the coveted George Grierson Award by the President of India and HUFS is completing forty years of teaching Hindi in Korea. India and Korea have also signed a new agreement. Moreover, since 2004, when Korea and India agreed to establish a Joint Study Group to study the feasibility and necessity of the Korea–India FTA, called Comprehensive Economic Partnership Agreement (CEPA) at the summit meeting between Korea and India, relations between the two countries have gained strength and in line with the growth of relations both the countries have hammered the CEPA signed between South Korea and India as an ambitious free trade agreement on Friday, 7 August 2009 that slashes tariffs, encourages investment and promotes exchange of skills in a bid to double fast-growing commerce over the next decade between two of Asia's biggest economies. It seems to herald a fresh outlook of the tradition that obliquely began as a connection of translating the religious literature and making pilgrimage in ancient times. Academic interest in South Asia in general and India in particular will definitely be driven by this agreement as it has already created a broader interest in learning of Hindi (Koreans have already started a broader plan of encouraging learning of English for a global upfront in business and commerce which is also turning to be an added advantage for their growing interface with India) and the courses in economy, politics, society and culture of India.

References

Ilyeon, *Overlooked Historical Records of the Three Korean Kingdoms* (Eng. tr. Dal-Yong Kim), Jimoondong, Seoul, 2006.

———, *Samguk Yusa* (Eng. tr. Tae-Hung Ha and ed. Graffton K. Mintz), Yonsei University Press 1972.

Kakhun, *Lives of Eminent Korean Monks* (The Haedong Kosung Chon, tr. Peter H. Lee), Cambridge, Mass., Harvard University Press 1969.

Kim, Kichung, *An Introduction to Classical Korean Literature: From Hyangga to Pansore*, M.E. Sharp, New York: 1996.

Lee, Peter H. (ed.), *A History of Korean Literature*, Cambridge, Mass, 2004.

Seth, Michael J., *A Concise History of Korea (from the Neolithic Period Through the Nineteenth Century)*, Oxford: Rownaa & Littlefield Publishers, 2006.

9

Indic–Asian Studies Towards an Alternative Cosmopolitanism

— A Brief Note —

Makarand R. Paranjape

THIS is not a learned paper but a brief note or presentation in a response to the call from the UGC Centre for Indic–Asian Studies (CIAS) at Bhagat Phool Singh Mahila Vishwavidyalaya, Khanpur Kalan, Haryana, which is the host of this conference. Inspired by Kapil Kapoor, CIAS has proposed an "alternative paradigm of area studies from the perspective of post-colonial societies" that "shall promote a holistic understanding" of Asia as an area "with its cultural, social, economic and strategic specifications in an interdisciplinary programme encompassing various disciplines of social sciences, language and culture, and science and technology". Furthermore, CIAS wishes to bring an "Indian perspective" to this programme, especially in its bold call to examine and uncover "the undoubted strong undercurrent of *puruṣārtha*-relatedness of Asia". In sympathy with some of these objectives, this presentation aims at suggesting some ways in which such a task may be begun, if not done.

It would be useful to start with the note circulated by the late swarajist scholar-researcher, Dharampal-ji, several years back, but revised in September 2003. Dharampal-ji argued that India's relations with its large neighbourhood both to its West and East constitutes what might be termed as an enduring Indian Ocean oecumene. British imperialism did, no doubt, alter the social, cultural, political and economic structure of this region. But, in the longer run, it might be considered more as an interruption in a longer and more enduring geo-cultural sphere. It could not, we might argue, effect an irrevocable alteration in the character and disposition of those who live in the region. Therefore, after colonialism, it behoves us to recover and restore our relationships with our older neighbours. According to Dharampal-ji:

> Such a recovery of knowledge and self-awareness requires a major scholarly effort to work on the past in all its manifestations and detail, say from CE 1500 backwards to 600 BCE. Regaining of such knowledge would require search of original sources not only in India, but initially perhaps much more in China, Korea, Japan, SE Asia, etc. where such sources seem to be more known and perused by scholars in recent times.

This is indeed an ambitious, even daunting project, but a beginning must be made somewhere, even in a conference such as the present one.

The newly-established UGC Area Study Centre for Indic–Asian Studies is, therefore, in some sense, a partial fulfilment of this urgent need as enunciated by Dharampal-ji. Even before Dharampal-ji's call, scholars like Janet Abu-Lughod, in her pioneering book, *Before European Hegemony: The World System CE 1250-1350* (New York: Oxford University Press, 1991) not only gave a detailed description of our larger geo-political neighbourhood before European hegemony, but also called India the "crossroads" of the entire region, literally on the "road to everywhere". For every important intellectual, political, and cultural current from East to the West and from West to the East, India became the point of transition, mediation, or even fruition. To name two major such currents consider the West to East movement of Buddhism and, later, of Islam, or the East to West movement of science, from China all the way to Europe. If we try to make Dharampal-ji speak to Abu-Lughod, then we would start thinking and planning for a world after Western hegemony too; in such a world, India's relations with its Eastern neighbours would assume paramount importance.

An Indic contribution to Asian studies, in other words, would entail a shift from a Western style, politically motivated study of Asia to a culturally and spiritually directed endeavour to recover older traditions of mutuality, peace and prosperity. If domination, control, surveillance and economic exploitation are the aims of Western-style Asian studies, surely we need to find other ways to interact with one another in Asia. Rabindranath Tagore, who is such an influential figure in Korea, thanks to his consistent and courageous stand against Japanese militarism and imperialism, may be the most suitable figure to whom to turn to for such an alternative.

The moment we agree that we have to find a different, non-Eurocentric way of conducting Asian Studies, we shall find other resources both in our past and in our present. Let me give few examples. Nearer home, we might turn to the Asian Relations Conference, March–April 1947, held in New Delhi, on the eve of India's Independence. In his address to the conference, the prime minister of India in waiting, Jawaharlal Nehru, said:

> . . . Asia is again finding herself . . . one of the notable consequences of the European domination of Asia has been the isolation of the countries of Asia from one another. . . . Today this isolation is breaking down because of many reasons, political and otherwise. . . . This conference is significant as an expression of that deeper urge of the mind and spirit of Asia which has persisted. . . . In this conference and in this work there are no leaders and no followers. All countries of Asia have to meet together in a common task. . . .

It would be possible to trace a direct line from this conference to the Afro–Asian Conference, Bandung, 1955. These were some political initiatives for an alternate Asia.

Intellectually, closer to our times and also expanding from our own location outwards, I would look at exciting recent initiatives like *Another Asia: Rabindranath Tagore and Okakura Tenshin* by Rustom Bharucha (New Delhi: Oxford University Press, 2009) and *Asia as Method: Toward Deimperialization* by Kuan-Hsing Chen

(Durham, NH: Duke University Press, 2010). Both are outstanding accounts, the former more specific and practical, the latter more theoretical and speculative, of an alternate way of doing Asian studies. Both books alleviate anxiety over theory. What Chen calls "Duplication of the Imperialist Eye"— applies to both, Taiwan, where he stays, and India or Korea, which are the subjects of this seminar. There is a sort of "sub-imperialism" to all these societies, the shadow of the US and now China over Taiwan, of the US over Korea, and of the West over India for the last 200 years. That is why Chen says:

> The ex-colonized now, in terms of both the psychology and the practice, becomes talented in co-operating with the ones stronger and more dominant than itself in the game of global capitalism. In the meantime, it learns to exploit those who are weaker and more vulnerable than itself in the same game.

The new way of doing Asian studies would certainly resist this paradigm of a hierarchical chain of exploitation and domination to try to replace it with the discourse of co-operation and *sarvodaya*. Here, India does have options and alternatives, both in terms of ideas and practices.

A new way of doing Asian studies must address concomitant issues like the crisis in area studies, regional perspectives, translating back diversities to the dominant conditions for the production and dissemination of knowledge, self vs. the other, Asian comparative studies, decolonization, many Asias, and so on. Many of these issues are highlighted in Prasenjit Duara's much discussed essay, "Asia Redux: Conceptualizing a Region for Our Times". (*Journal of Asian Studies*, 69.4, November 2010.)

From such readings it is clear that we need to develop comparative methodologies, inter-Asian dialogues and intellectual exchange and multiple points and frames of reference. In the process, we may produce a new "theory" of Asian studies. Not theory in the sense of (mostly continental) "high" theory, as exemplified by, say, Jacques Derrida, a very cerebral, slightly obtuse "post-structuralist" type of discourse or theory as opposed to methodology, an abstract conceptualizing not fully integrated with actual research or pedagogical practices, or even theory, mostly Western, as opposed to data, mostly Asian. Instead, what we need is theory as "situated knowledge", theory as a way of making sense of vast and diverse bodies of knowledge or thought worlds, theory as a way of understanding and formulating perspectives, ways of seeing and organizing knowledge, and, ultimately about making intelligent and enabling generalizations; to that extent, it is essentially an inductive, even pragmatic enterprise, even if it is actually epistemological. In our case, it would be theory as a sort of reflexive way of doing Asian studies, the idea being to destabilize received notions and contribute something meaningful.

What was actually interesting about our seminar was that though there was an assumption that we all understood each other or shared an understanding of the keywords or concepts that we discussed, actually, there was little shared understanding, let alone consensus. Each session became, as it were, a field of difference, with some possible strategic groupings, rather than an area of convergence, let alone consensus. For me, this was a reality check, but a very good revelation of the challenges that needed to be overcome before we could form a cohesive working group based at the UGC Centre for Indic–Asian Studies at Bhagat Phool Singh Mahila Vishwavidyalaya. Indeed I was a trifle disappointed, not to speak surprised, to find that the very name of the centre was different on the banner than what the initial letter of invitation indicated; instead of "Indic–Asian" the banner said "Indian and Asian". Anyhow, what we may still need to learn from our Asian friends is the possibility of collaboration, working together and forming research collectives. To me this possibility is actually exciting because Indian academics, to risk generalization, are very individualistic, rarely successful in working together. Here, the far Eastern culture might serve as supplying more helpful, co-operative models.

10

Constructing a Trajectory of Cultural Transactions Through Translation Between India and Korea

Avadhesh Kumar Singh

LET me begin with a few statements in the form of a few caveats. In India it is stated that all of us are a part of the Infinite *Brahman* that is *pūrṇa* (complete). Despite it, the fact is that no individual is complete. I am neither complete nor do I know how much incomplete I am. I do not know myself and know so less about my own country. More I know about my own country, more I realize that I know so less about it. In such a situation, how can I claim that I know about Korea? Despite it, the fact is that by knowing about Korea I become less incomplete. Moreover, for us South Korea is the Korea for different reasons at the moment because we have even less knowledge about North Korea, as North Korea has not opened itself to the world outside. In this context I remember meeting two Korean students in my block seminar in Heinerich Heine University, Dusseldorf in Germany in the last week of June 2012. They were friendly and looked almost like brothers. During interaction with them I came to know that one of them was from North Korea and another from South Korea. The elder one from South Korea used to take good care of his counterpart. On being asked he told me that his younger colleague needs attention and affection, as he is like a brother from a divided family. Sooner or later they would become one. So why should they waste their time in a state of adversarial relationship that pervades between the two nations for political reasons. Unification is the destiny of both the

Koreas. It has a message for us as well. Sooner or later the two will become one.

Let me hasten to add that I have been extremely sceptical to the category called "area studies", as it is primarily a Pentagon category that came into existence in the post-Second World War period. Toby Valkman who was a Ford Foundation Programme Officer has brought it out in her pamphlet published in 1999. Area studies were considered indispensible for American interests. The US wanted to control the world after the Second World War, by dividing it into knowable categories because knowing is controlling and possessing too in the end. The office of secretary of state had departments after these areas, and accordingly the funding for research projects in areas studies in universities was provided. However, it was later realized that areas like the South-East Asia, West Asia, Middle East among others were not self-contained, as was assumed. Hence they were followed by intercultural studies, and multiculturalism. It is necessary to know the inherent politics and economics of areas so that the area studies in India can move in a meaningful direction of dialogue among cultures. Only then, we, who subscribe to the notion of the entire world as a family (*Vasudhaivakuṭumbakam*) would contribute to the area of intercultural studies, and give a positive dimension to area studies.

The present paper is an exercise more in trying to understand Korea and less in research, more in speculation or in agenda-preparation and less in critiquing the obtaining cultural transactions, for that is rather limited and rather a recent phenomenon.

India is among the forty-nine major civilizations of the world. Human mind excelled in different domains of knowledge and aspects of life. Max Müller rightly mentioned regarding it:

> If I were asked under what sky the human mind has most fully developed some of its choicest gifts, has most deeply pondered on the greatest problems of life, and has found solutions, I should point to India. — Max Müller 2007: 5

It is one among the principle reasons which has contributed to the continuity of Indian civilization against the ravages of time. Indian civilization was a knowledge civilization, a fact attested by still extant knowledge texts and manuscripts. To avoid the risk of being a dated Charlton jingoist, it would be appropriate to cite not so distant views of Peter Schraf, an American scholar, who comments on comparative state of manuscripts in Sanskrit on the one hand, and Greek and Latin on the other, "the manuscripts in Sanskrit number one hundred times those in Greek and Latin combined" (Schraf 2003: 23). Not just the quantity of knowledge manuscripts, the attitude towards the *hetu* (means) and *prayojana* (objectives) was different in it, as the main objective of knowledge was not dominance over others, but emancipation from the cause(s) of suffering or *puruṣārtha catuṣṭya* (realization of the fourfold ends of life), i.e. *dharma* (righteous conduct), *artha* (attaining material prosperity under the conditions of *dharma*), *kāma* (gratification of human desires under the conditions of *dharma* and *artha*) and *mokṣa* (liberation from the cause of suffering). The acquisition, preservation, creation, dissemination and application of knowledge were institutionalized in the form of its *viśvavidyālaya*s (universities) like Takṣilā and Nālandā at least 1,500 years before Europe could have its first universities. No wonder that India attracted people from various parts of the world in different ages. It led to the creation of many sites of cultural transactions, and have been acknowledged and studied accordingly.

Travel, trade and translation routes are interrelated. In the history of human civilization, large-scale movement of human beings for whatever reasons — natural disasters, religious persecution, social, economic, political considerations, or natural human curiosity — has led to exploration to new terrains and establishment of routes — silk and rugged — opening up possibilities of appropriation of economic resources through legal means, i.e. trade, and through illegal means, i.e. theft. The encounter between trading parties was not limited to trade/theft, as it was not possible without interaction through translation. It impacted "base" and "structure", i.e. fine arts and useful arts, if some of us cannot understand a phenomenon without them for too long.

Writing on "Early Art and Architecture", P.S. Rawson observes that very few people yet realize

> how great a debt the art of the world — especially that of the eastern world — already owe to India. It is true to say that without the example of Indian forms and ideas the arts of the whole of South-East Asia, of China, Korea, Mongolia, Tibet, and Japan would all have been radically different, and would have lost by that difference. — 1975: 197

He adds that modern Western art too, especially architecture and painting would have also suffered. As regards the South and East Asia, the stream of cultural influence and reception was even more focused and diffused as well because apart from regional contiguity that put the whole of the region in the category of the Orient, the Indian philosophical traditions like the Sanātana Dharma in the initial period and Buddhism in particular later on, as journeyed with travellers, scholars and traders. Translation was a means of constructing the bridge between the knowledge systems and cultural traditions of the region.

According to Rawson, Buddhism was a "merchant's religion *par excellence*, and vehicle for this artistic excellence" (ibid.). It was "the chief vehicle for this artistic influence, though Hinduism did penetrate South-East Asia and the islands; and Buddhist art, at home in India, owes a good deal to the Hindu art that flourished alongside it" (ibid.). He adds:

> Monks from Gandhāra and Khotan travelled east; converts from inner China travelled back towards India. Texts were transmitted from India and translated into Far Eastern Languages. The art styles which became canonical, first in China, then in Korea and Japan, were closely based, for doctrinal reasons, upon types established first in Khotan and Gandhāra, and transmitted, probably, by pattern works. Even today Buddhist artists in Japan create images which contain echoes of Gandhāra. — Ibid.: 201

The great importance of this cultural transaction was that the Buddhist art of the region impacted East Asia in general and China, Korea and Japan, in particular. It was "an effect only modified, not replaced, by later waves of influence". Buddhism being "a merchants" religion, wherever India's merchants went during these centuries Buddhism and its art followed in the region of Gandhāra, the eastward land routes over the Pāmīr, through the kingdom of Khoṭan, and around the northern and southern fringes of the desert Tarim basin.

The transmission of knowledge was possible through translation which needed fixed written source texts. Indian, particularly Sanātana (called Hindu subsequently), tradition was oral, so translation was difficult. Buddhism made it possible because Buddha asked his disciple to preach his teachings to others. Moreover, as Robert Thurman mentions Buddhists began writing down their teachings in the vernacular at a time when Hindus thought their sacred texts ought only to be transmitted orally by brāhmaṇas in Sanskrit. It was Buddhist rejection of the caste system, adds Thurman, that led so many of the merchant castes to join Buddhism. These merchants used writing more than anyone else because of their commercial requirements. Once people got used to reading texts, Sanātanīs also began to write theirs down into Sanskrit. Also Buddhists had to write down their texts so that they may participate in serious debates in universities like Nālandā and respond precisely to arguments attacking their tenants. Interest in Buddhism persuaded various scholars from East Asia particularly from Tibet and China, to visit India because, as Marie-Louise Friquegnon notes in her book on Śāntarakṣita, India was the purest source of Buddhist teaching because it was after all the native land of Buddha, and had "a network of monasteries and universities which were repositiories of over a thousand years of Buddhist studies" (2001: 34). Indian Buddhist scholars travelled to Tibet and China in the first century CE and laid the foundation of the process of the earliest translations of Buddhist texts into Chinese.[1] Indian scholars like Śāntarakṣita, the author of *Tattvasaṁgraha* and *Madhyamakālaṁkāra*, visited Tibet as a consequence of this quest and others did go to China.

Buddhism acted as a bridge between India and Korea via Tibet, China and Japan. Various scholars visited India and Indian scholars

---

1 For discussion, see Ramesh Krishnamurthy in Baker et al. 1998, p.452.

were invited. The visitors returned to their lands with scores of translations and texts to be translated later. Buddhism considered Buddha's message as the central and did not attach sacredness to language. Buddha used Pāli for communication with people and did not mind using Sanskrit for the construction and preservation of the message. Buddhism promoted translation for its own sake. Christianity refused to translate its sacred texts.

Islam believed that their sacred texts be read only in their original languages. Else they lose original meanings. Contrary to it, Buddha believed that meaning and reasoning can be preserved even in translation. He encouraged rendering of his words for the people of different languages. To quote from *Vinayamātṛkā*:

> Two monks came to Buddha and asked, "Among your followers, there is someone from a certain family in a certain country. His language is different from yours and thus is incorrect: it thus destroys the correct meaning of your speech. Enlightened One, please allow us to compile the *sūtra*s based on the *chanda*s (verse) and discussion, and thus the original sound and meanings can be recognized." The Buddha told these monks, "In my teaching there is no concern for fine language. As long as the meaning and reasoning are not lost, that is all I wish. You must teach according to the sounds that people prefer, and thus they can understand." For this reason there is a saying, "to compose in accordance to the country".
>
> — *Taisho Shinshu Daizokyo*, vol. 24, p. 822

It becomes evident from the study of above practice that apart from commerce Buddhism was a major catalyst for preparing the source texts for translation. As far as translations in Korean are concerned, they were often not attempted directly from Indian languages but they were indirect translations from Chinese and Japanese, as Korea for geographical and historical reasons was influenced by both the countries. India's translational interaction with Korea was routed indirectly through China. China was the centre of the world for Korea for long because of territorial proximity, and model of development. China had a long tradition of translation, as early as the Zhou dynasty in the ninth century BCE, there were special government officials known as *sheren* (tongues-man) in-charge of translation and interpreting who were always present at meetings with foreign emissaries. The current Chinese word *yi* (translation) was the official title adopted since the Han dynasty. During the Han dynasty *yizang* (translators/interpreters) were employed routinely by merchants on their long trips to South Asia and China (Baker 1998: 370). The spread of Buddhism gave impetus to the translation activities in China. The most unique attribute of this transaction was that Indian ideas travelled far and wide in most of the case, and its army. Hu Shih, former Ambassador of China to USA, rightly stated it, "India conquered and dominated China culturally for twenty centuries without ever having to send a single soldier across her border".

China has had a great influence on Japanese intellectual, religious and socio-cultural life. The first record of official contacts between Japan and China dates back to CE 57. Incidentally, Korean scribes are credited with introducing the Chinese script to Japan in the third and fourth centuries that did not have script of their own. According to Twine the two indigenous Japanese phonetic scripts were developed by the eighth century that enabled Japanese to be written without taking recourse to Chinese characters, the latter has been in use because of their consciousness, formality and prestige (1991: 35). In 1639 the Tokugawa shogunate had issued a series of seclusion orders closing the country off from destabilizing external influences. Traders and missionaries were banned, particularly Christians. Since Portugese did not attempt proselytizing so they were allowed to stay in the town of Hirado in Kyushu. The Chinese were restricted to Nagasaki and the Koreans were permitted to trade only in Tushima. It had adversely affected translational activities (1991: 469).

India did not send armies, but sent its ideas and knowledge traditions till the end of the first millennium to its East and West. By the West, I mean the real West to India, i.e. the Arab and Persian world. Indian traders took Indian ideas and knowledge with them. From the second half of the eighteenth century onwards, a major part of India came to be occupied by the East India Company from 1757 to

1857 and colonized from 1858 till India's ndependence in 1947. Though this was the period of India's political subjugation, Indian influence on the Western thought became the harbinger of the second European renaissance. Ironically, Europe which may be termed as India's second West became the first, and obliterated the immediate West which came to be called as the Middle East, for the American called it so according to its area studies under the Pentagon strategies.

The West captured Indian psyche to such an extent that India forgot its East, the West compartmentalized it in the East. There was a brief period of exception when Subhas Chandra Bose diverted his attention to the East when he opened the Eastern front against the British with the help of Japan. Thereafter, Indian disillusionment with the slogans like "Panchsheel" and "Hindi Chini Bhai Bhai" in the form of the debacle of the 1962 war led to diversion of its focus.

Between them, India and Korea offer a rich site for comparative cultural and literary studies, for they share terrains at different levels. The earliest references of cultural transactions between India and Korea include the legend of the Princess Heo or Suro's dream and travel to North Korea with gold, silver, tea plant and "a stone with two fish kissing each other", a symbol of Gaya kingdom (Royal family in Ayodhyā) in CE 48.[2] The next reference is made to Hyecho, a Korean Buddhist monk from Silla, who came to India in 723, on the advice of his Indian teacher in China and is accredited with writing *An Account of Travel to the Five Indian Kingdoms*.

By the mid-second century CE translation of Buddhist *sūtras* from Sanskrit into Chinese gave birth to a massive translation movement that went on for the next nine centuries.

FIRST PHASE

The translators were primarily monks. There were translation forums

[2] For detailed discussion of the legend, see Lee Kwang-su, "Legend of a Princess from Ayodhyā and Myth Making in Buddhist Temples in Korea", *Buddhism in East Asia: Aspects of History's First Universal Religion Presented in the Modern Context*, ed. Anita Sharma, Delhi: Vidyanidhi Prakashan, 2012, pp. 185-97.

(*yichang*) with a respected monk as the chief translator (*yizhu*). Partha Masiris from Parthia was the first translator of Buddhist *sūtra*s into Chinese and good example of this practice.

SECOND PHASE

In the second phase translation activities flourished under prominent foreign monks particularly Indians. Kumārajīva (344–413) with the help of 800 monks translated more than 300 volumes of Buddhist *sūtra*s.

Kumārajīva is the culmination of the Chinese institutional translation. Teamwork in the Chinese institutional translation played a crucial role in the transmission of Buddhism and in form(ulat)ing trade and diplomatic ties. It was instrumental in ensuring the spread of Buddhism in China and other parts of East Asia like Korea and Japan. The initial endeavours to translate Buddhist scriptures (around the second century BCE) later evolved into large-scale projects carried out by teams.

The process of translation of *sūtra*s had many stages. It began in the translation hall in which a West-oriented *maṇḍala* was built, probably because of the land Lord Buddha came from, i.e. "India", in the West. The translation would begin with *pūjā* (prayer). Paṇḍit, a scholar of Sanskrit, would recite a Sanskrit *sūtra*. He would check the *sūtra* as well heard, before the translators get on to the work to avoid mistakes. The *sabda* of the *sūtra*s would be jotted down thereafter, i.e. from *sūtra* to *su da lan* in Chinese. The jotted Chinese *śabda*s would be translated into Chinese meanings, i.e. from *su da lan* to *jing*. Since Sanskrit *vākya* (sentence structure) is different from the Chinese, they would be made into a regular Chinese structure, i.e. from *buddhyāya smārta* to *smārta buddhyāya*. This would be followed by different stages of proofreading, revision, modification and necessary embellishment. (These stages are based on the notes taken from the lecture by Yin Xi'nan, Sichuan University, Chengdu, China in School of Translation Studies & Training, Indira Gandhi National Open University, New Delhi on 3 February 2012.)

The process was systematized in the third and fourth century CE, with explicit procedures for collaboration in distinct roles:

(i) *yizhu* (chief translator), a highly revered master, presided over the translation by orally explicating the Buddhist concepts;

(ii) *chuanyu* (interpreter) interpreted chief translator's explication into Chinese;

(iii) *bishou* (recorder) compiled the text in Chinese. The final stage of translation included checking the recorder's notes and cross-checking them against those taken by the monks and scholars in the audience for verification. The chief translator was often a foreign monk unable to speak Chinese.

However, even after the linguistic need for adopting this format disappeared with the emergence of Chinese monk-translators, teamwork in *sūtra* translation continued. The Chinese tradition of institutionalized team-work translation which is known now also as collaborative translation or team translation constitutes an important part of in the history of collaborative translation which invites comparison with other traditions in the world, particularly translations of the sacred texts like the Bible, as the principles were enunciated in the Preface to the translation of the Bible by Wycliffe.

THIRD PHASE

In this phase the process of theological explication was separated from the translation and the number of translation forums was considerably reduced. In this prolific period Xuan Zang (602-64) rendered over 1,300 volumes of *sūtra*s into Chinese. Xuan Zang vowed to travel to the land of Buddha in 621 to learn the truth because the *sūtra*s were open to the extremely diverse interpretations. During his visit he visited temples, learned Sanskrit and studied *sūtra*s. He returned in 645 and devoted remaining years of his life to the translation of Buddhist *sūtra*s. The decline of Buddhism in India and change in the government policies led to the erosion of translation forums from eleventh century onwards. Henceforth translation of Buddhist text became an individual rather than a collective activity. In this phase, the process of theological explication was separated from the translation and the number of translation forums was considerably reduced. These translations from Sanskrit to Chinese, later on, were translated into Korean. Indian medical texts were translated into Korean, along with Khotanese, Tibetan, Mangolian, Chinese and Arabic (R. Krishnamurthy in Baker et al. 1998: 453). Among others, Yi Jing (? - CE 695) translated 200 volumes. of *sūtra*s.

Institutions like Nālandā University played their role in training translators from fourth century onwards. Kumārajīva went to China in 401 and translated the *Life of Nagarjuna* into Chinese and Fa-hsien came to India to collect more texts. Paramārtha went to China in the fifth century and translated *Life of Vasubandhu*. Hsuan Tsang and I-Tsing came to India in the seventh century and studied at Nālandā. The former is accredited with the translation of more than thirty volumes of Buddhist texts. Dharmadeva (960–1000) translated 118 Buddhist texts into Chinese. About 8,000 Indian texts dealing with mathematics, astronomy, medicine, Hinduism and Buddhism were translated into Chinese are preserved in the Sung-pao collection. They are printed from wooden blocks which as a technique came to China from Tibet. The other Nālandā scholars like Āryadeva, Śīlabhadra and Dharmapāla went to Tibet and their works were translated into Tibet. Śāntarakṣita and Padmasambhava transmitted Buddhism in scholars. *Mahāvyutpatti* is an instance of Indian, Chinese and Japanese co-operation. Śāntarakṣita (eighth century CE) was invited by Thri srong Deutsen, the thirty-eight king of Tibet in search of "the perfect Buddhist master". He told the king about his doctrine, "to believe what is in accordance with reason, what is not in accordance with reason".

Xuan Zang (600-44) lived in Nālandā University in the modern-day state of Bihar from CE 629-45. He is also known as Mokṣadeva and Mahāyānadeva, and referred to as "collecting Buddhist Sūtras from heavenly India". He is credited with translating 300 volumes of *sūtra*s. He proposed his *anuvāda siddhānta* (five non-translational principles):

1. *Amitābha*: The sacred word might be translated in its sound.

2. *Bhagvān, bhikṣu*: The ambiguous word could be translated in terms of its pronunciation.
3. *Buddha, Jambu*: If target language has no such word, so it can be translated as its pronunciation.
4. *Anubuddha* (Confucius): Some words should be translated in a traditional way since the older version of translation has been popular.
5. *Prajñā, bodhisattva*: Some words would be understood in an honourable manner if translated according to their pronunciation.

Transplantation changes the co-habitation of region in which new plant is planted, but the plant does not remain the same, and gets transformed in the new soil. This is true about idea and ideational texts. Buddhism did not remain the same in the new habitat in China and Korea, as it was mediated through translation in the context of native socio-political situation and institutions. Naturally, it got transformed in the process of its plantation in the new environs. The question for which I have not been able to find any answer is: What happened to the Chinese tradition of collaborative translation in Korea when Buddhist *sūtra* texts in particular were translated in Korea?

The Korean Situation:
"Speaking Korean, Writing Chinese"

The trajectory of cultural transaction between India and Korea through translational activities, indirect as it was, was mediated by China and Japan. It reached there initially via Tibet. The translations of Buddhist *sūtras* in Korea were mediated by China. Buddhism is a common heritage between India and Korea. However, it did not reach Korea directly. As a case of indirect influence, Buddhism reached Korea via China. Therefore it would be interesting to discuss Korean linguistic situation and cultural transaction between Korea and China.

The Korean linguistics situation may be understood taking recourse to the narrative of the creation about the *Mahābhārata*. Veda Vyāsa has composed the *Mahābhārata* but wanted to an amanuensis to write it. Gaṇeśa, on the request of gods agreed to do so with conditions, of course.[3] Vyāsa and Gaṇeśa represent the speech and writing traditions that went into making of the *Mahābhārata*. Korean was Gaṇeśa and Chinese Ved Vyāsa. Korean was a native language, in which the Koreans expressed themselves. However, it had no script. Koreans borrowed not only vocabulary but sooner accepted the system of Hanja, a Chinese script. Used for spoken Korean as late as 1894 when Hanguel (literally meaning "great script"), the Korean script, developed in 1443 by King Sejong of the Joseon dynasty (1392–1910) replaced Hanja. In a way, the modified representation of the spoken Korean in Hanja was an activity of translation. On the other hand, it was like the split between speech and writing in the Western tradition.

Various efforts to bridge the gap between Chinese pictographs and Korean phonetics resulted in translational endeavours in Korea. Consequently Koreans found out two principles: (i) ignore pictographic meaning, and adopt a phonetic function of Chinese characters; and (ii) ignore phonetic pronunciation and adopt the pictographic meaning of Chinese characters only for purely Korean words.[4]

During the period of the Goryeo dynasty, Buddhism flourished along with the codification of laws and introduction of civil service system. Buddhist *sūtra*s were made available in the period in Hanja. Sayeokwon at beginning of the Joseon dynasty supported Chinese studies, but set up Yeokhak (translation studies). It included Chinese and Japanese studies.

Yeokgwans were government officials responsible for translation and interpreting. These officials were known as "Yeok-in", "Seol-in" and "Sang-seo". Yeokgwans were usually from the lower classes, but

---

3 For detailed discussion of the narrative, see Avadhesh Kumar Singh, "Theory of Creative Process in Narratives About the Rāmāyaṇa and the Mahābhārata: Mythic Narrative as Mode of Constitution of Knowledge", *Revisiting Literature, Criticism and Aesthetics in India*, New Delhi: D.K. Printworld, 2012, pp. 43-56.

4 See Ji-won Ki, "The Korean Tradition of Translation: From the Primeval Period to the Modern Era", *Journal of Language & Translation*, March 2008: 41-60.

later with the acceptance of translation learned persons from upper classes joined the profession.

Printing record from 1318 to 1968 of *Tripiṭika Koreana* (Goryeodaejanggyeong) from Goryeo dynasty, collection of text and wooden printing blocks (81,340) are available in Gasan Yi Ji-Gwan (1992: 229-31), and they become a site of good case study of translational enterprise (see Table 1).

Korean tradition of translation has not earned as much attention as it deserved. *Routeledge Encyclopaedia of Translation Studies* edited by Mona Baker and Gabriela Saldhanna discusses thirty-two translation traditions in the world including South-East Asia but it spares no space to Korean tradition. Korea is mentioned more than a dozen times in it but in case of organized collective translations attempted in house for business and official purposes. According to a study, 72.6 per cent of 223 South Korean public institutions including local government translations is taken care of by in-house personnel, mostly in teams (Lee et al. 2000: 57-107).

However, there are a few endeavours to disapprove the false impressions and establish the Korean tradition of translation, as does Ji-won Ki in "The Korean Tradition of Translation: From the Primeval Period to the Modern Era" (2008).

The similarities between them are curious and dissimilarities interesting. The similarities between Indian and Korean cultural experience in the last two centuries in particular compel us to consider them comparatively as the literary and cultural phenomena.

Buddhism was a common heritage between India and Korea, though indirectly mediated by China and Japan. Buddhism declined considerably in the land of its origin, though human psyche has been fascinated to Buddhist way of thinking and living that does not lay demand on one's being proselytized to Buddhist. Korea has moved ahead and established itself as one of economic powers of the world. Therefore, what may be of some emotional interest to us in India may not necessarily mean much to the modern Koreans. However, apart from Buddhism, there are a few common patterns of cultural

Table1 : Publication of Translations of *Tripiṭika Koreana* from Gasan Yi Ji-Gwan, Having Record of the Printing from 1318–1968 (Gasan Y: Ji-Gwan; 229-31)

Printing Year	*No. of Copies*	*Organizer*	*Purpose*
1318	Unknown	King Chungsuk	Filling the mission copies
1328-96	Unknown	Naong	Unknown
1378	Unknown	Unknown (monk)	Unknown
1381	Parts	Yi Saek (Confucian scholar)	Heavenly bless of his father
1393	Unknown	King Taejo	Blessing of the country
1399	Unknown	King Taejo	Heavenly bless of his sons and vassals
1413	Unknown	King Taejong	Blessing of the country
1439	Unknown	King Sejong	Unknown
1458	50	King Sejo	Blessing of the country
1500	20	Queen Sin	Blessing of longevity for the king and prince
1520	1	King Jungjong	Blessing of the country
1865	2	Yeonggi and Nammyeong (monks)	Unknown
1899	4	King Gojong	Blessing of the country
1906	parts	Lady Im (court lady)	Filling the mission copies
1915	3	Terauch Yamaguchi (Japanese Resident-General of Korea)	Preserving
1937	2	Puyi (the Emperor of Manchuria)	Gift to the emperor of Japan
1963-68	13	Kim Duho (private person)	To send to the famous libraries of the world

and historical realities and experiences that bring India and Korea together, and inveigle upon us to consider for study.

Both India and Korea suffered colonization, the former by the British and the latter by Japan. Both of them resisted colonization in their different ways, and are now busy charting out their courses as post-colonial societies[5]. In case of India, it is to be stated that during the nineteenth-century India with the translation of its knowledge texts from Sanskrit to European languages was a cause of the second renaissance in the West, as discussed by Raymond Schwab in his book *The Oriental Renaissance: Europe's Rediscovery of India and the East 1680-1880* (1984).

India and Korea suffered colonization and both of them chart out as post-colonial societies. India and Korea waged their struggle for freedom against their colonizers and attained their independence in twentieth century by employing different strategies. However, the similarity between the two is that their nineteenth century was a period of nationalism and renaissance which, some scholars in the case of Korea, term as the enlightenment.

Korea and India suffered the tragedy of their partition: one on ideological grounds as North Korea and South Korea, and the other on the religious grounds as India and Pakistan. Qurat-ul-Ain Haider's *Āga kā Daryā*, Bhishma Sahani's *Tamas*, Rahi Massom Reza's *Ādhā Gāoṅ*, Manzoor Ehtesham's *Sūkhā Bargad*, Khushwant Singh's *Train to Pakistan* (in English), Salman Rushdie's *Midnight's Children* are significant voices of this discourse. The Partition captures the imagination of different generations of Koreans, its legacy is not a matter of the past but a living present that haunts as a nightmare. As relations between the two Koreas rise and fall the history of the Partition remains a subject of negotiation between scholars and ideologues. As of today Kim Wonil's *Spirit of Darkness* (1973) that remembers the Partition as a part of nationalist memory or Pak Wanso's short story *In Remembrance of*

---

5 For the discussion of resistance in India in the colonial period, see Avadhesh Kumar Singh, "Theorising/Narrating Resistance and Colonisation in India", in *Discourse of Resistance in the Colonial Period*, New Delhi: Creative Books, 2005.

Things Unrecovered (2006) and *The Naked Tree* dealing with traumatic experience of the Partition are not available to us. The translations are attempted by scholars, as did Seunghei Clara Hong for her research. The memory of the past haunts the psyche of both countries, as the creative writers try to exorcise the ghost by articulating them.

The post-colonial discourses in India and Korea demand being comparatively studied. India has five major discourses: Dalit discourse, feminist discourse, regional discourse, rural (village-centred discourse) and diaspora discourse. Korea would have its own. They are good cases for comparative studies.

Literary translations in twentieth century are marked mainly by the Bible's translations and Buddhist translations, e.g. Yongsung's translation of Buddhist text into Hanguel until 1962 and Dongguk University project 2007. Also there is emphasis on the study of translation of English literary texts in Korean as may be discerned in the case of translations of Byron in Korea in the form of Ch'oe Namson's Cantos the First *Childe Harold's Pilgrimage*, Canto the Fourth translated by Orang.

The translational scenario may not be highly encouraging in both the countries. An article like "The State of Translation in Korea", *Pinyin News*, 21 January 2006 speaks about it. Park Sang-ik, Professor of Western History in Woosuk University, discussed how few translations of Western classics have been produced in comparison to their translation in Japanese. Park speaks about his disillusionment and shock at the quality of translation. He took the case of translation of *Divine Comedy* by an Italian language professor which is full of mistranslations and grammatically wrong expressions. Park is frank enough to accept that it is customary for professors to just let or make graduate students do translations with their own credits which have spawned bad cross-cultural texts. Indian situation is no better in terms of quality and quantity of translation. However, Indians cannot even complain to their Korean translator brethren, as Indian classical texts have not been translated to a good measure; Indians too do not have much to show in terms of translation of Korean texts in Indian languages. Kim Bumik's *Samguk Sagi* of the twelfth century, Il Yeon's

Samguka-Yusa in the thirteenth century, Lee Kyu-bo's *Dongguk Isang Gukjip* and Lee Seung-Hui's *Jewang Ungi* are not even heard by many of us, leave aside their translation. They are in Hanja, not in Korean. Hence, without wailing about lost opportunities, our endeavour can make up for it.

The world has come closer in an unprecedented manner, and hitherto inaccessible parts of the world are just a click of Google earth away. Information and Communication Technologies (ICT) and fast means of transport have accelerated the process. Nicolas Boureaud has rightly pronounced that in the twenty-first century the discourse of postmodernism has come to an end, and it has been replaced by altermodernism. Consequently, translation, sub-titling and dubbing have come to the centre.

Human sciences with joint projects between India and Korea can play their role in it. In an age of science and technology, to speak of culture and humanities might appear like fighting for the numerically weaker side. However, in the Indian epical wars, i.e. the Lanka War and the Mahābhārata War, the numerically weaker side ultimately won the war. Moreover, what Plekhonov said about humanities is relevant even today about culture. "So long as there is humanity, there shall be stupidity. And as long as there is stupidity, there shall be need for humanities." The world is neither flat nor near its end so soon. It has come close in an unprecedented manner. Newer cultures and worlds are being exposed to us every- day. In such a situation, there is no other way but to know each other and cultures, facilitated by translation. The United Nations, despite being vulnerable to the pressures of the superpowers, serves the function of providing forum for dialogue between warring factions. And that has become a reality, translation has to play its definite role in it.

Korea and India have realized the significance of translation and also of the fact that for the survival of humanity, along with the United Nations, the "United Nations of Cultures" is indispensable which can come into existence only through translation. The important thing is that the similarities between Indian and Korean cultural experiences in the last two centuries in particular compel us to consider them comparatively as the literary and cultural phenomena. The similarities between them are curious and dissimilarities interesting. Indians wish to see Korea beyond and behind Hyundai. A rich array of worlds beckons all of us. Let us not use cultural flyovers or over bridges. Rather we should make new and direct bridges. Just imagine that if the best of Korean literature is translated into Hindi, it would reach 600,000,000 people. Moreover, imagine the day when the knowledge texts from Sanskrit are translated into Korean, the Korean would have access to knowledge texts and manuscripts in one language that has them 100 times more than their number in Greek and Latin put together. It would lead to "placing" of two literary discourses and consequently to "mutual illumination".

In case of placing, it is to be admitted that more often than not Indian English Writing (IEW) is often considered as the representative of India. It leads to distortion and misrepresentation of Indian reality. Hence, for cultural transaction through translation literatures in Indian languages need to be the focal areas without oversighting IEW.

Let Heos dream again; on both sides and reach out for each other and contribute to a new cultural order.

References

Baker, Mona et al., eds., *Routeledge Encyclopedia of Translation Studies*, London & New York: Routeledge, 1998.

Friquegnon, Marie-Louise, *On Shantarakshita*, New Delhi: Cenegage Learning, 2001.

George, P.A., ed., *East Asian Literatures: An Interface with India*, Delhi: Northern Book Centre, 2006.

Hyun, Theresa, "Byron Lands in Korea: Translation and Literary/ Culture Changes in Early Twentieth Century Korea", http://id.erudit.org/iderudit/037288ar.

Ji-Gwan, Gasan, *Gayasan Haeinsa ji*, Seoul: Gasan Bylygo Munhwa Yeongueon, 1992.

Ki, Ji-won, "The Korean Tradition of Translation: From the Primeval Period to the Modern Era", *Journal of Language & Translation*, March 2008: 41-60.

Kim, Jong Min and Ravikesh Mishra, *Korean Proverbs with Hindi and Equivalents*, New Delhi: Manak Publishing, 2011.

Kim, Won-H, "Eodumui Hon", The Spirit of Darkness (1973), *Modern Korean fiction*, Bilingual Edition: Asia Publishers, 2012.

Kwang-su, Lee, "Legend of a Princess from Ayodhyā and Myth Making in Buddhist Temples in Korea", *Buddhism in East Asia: Aspects of History's First Universal Religion Presented in the Modern Context*, ed. Anita Sharma, Delhi: Vidyanidhi Prakashan, 2012.

Lee, Seung-Jae et al., "The Present Situation of Translation in Korean Public Organisations", *Penyekhak Yenkwu/The Journal of Transalation Studies*, **2**(2): 2000, pp. 57-107.

Max Müller, F., *India: What It Can Teach Us*? New York: Cosmico Classics, 2007, 1st edn. 1883.

Pak, Won-so, "Pokwon foeji motan Kottul ul Wihayo, (in Remembrance of things Unrecovered) Na in Kajang Najong Jinni-in Kot (My Very Last Possessions), Seoul: Nunhek Jongue, 2006, 184-85.

Rawson, P.L., "Early Art and Architecture", in A.L. Basham, ed., *A Cultural History of India*, Delhi: Oxford University Press, 1975.

Schraf, Peter, "Introduction", *The Ramayana in the Mahābhārata*, London & New York: Routeledge, 2003.

Schwab, Raymond, *The Oriental Renaissance: Europe's Rediscovery of India and the East 1680–1880*, trs. Gene Patterson-Black and Victor Reinking, New York: Columbia University Press, 1984.

Sharma, Anita, ed., *Buddhism in East Asia: Aspects of History's First Universal Religion Presented in the Modern Context*, Delhi: Vidyanidhi Prakashan, 2012.

Singh, Avadhesh Kumar. "Theorising/Narrating Resistance and Colonisation in India", in *Discourse of Resistance in the Colonial Period*, New Delhi: Creative Books, 2005.

———, "Theory of Creative Process in Narratives About the Rāmāyaṇa and the Mahābhārata: Mythic Narrative as Mode of Constitution of Knowledge", *Revisiting Literature, Criticism and Aesthetics in India*, New Delhi: D.K. Printworld, 2012.

Twine, N., *Language and the Modern State: The Reform of Written Japanese*, London & New York: Routeledge, 1991.

Valkman, Toby Alice, *Crossing Borders: Revitalising Area Studies*, New York: Ford Foundation, 1999.

———, "The State of Translation in Korea", *Pinyin News*, 21 January 2006.

Pak, Won-so, "Pokwon foeji motan Kottul ul Wihayo, (In Remambrance of Things Unrecovered) Na in Kajang Najong Jinni-in Kot (My Very Last Possessions), Seoul: Nunhek Jongue, 2006,184-5.

11

Buddhism: The India and Korea Connector

Kwangsu Lee

KOREA'S contacts with India commenced in the fourth century. Relying on the chronicles only, we have the following three names of Indian monks who came to Korea in ancient period. Yet, we have to notice the fact that they were the first missionaries to each of the three kingdoms and these three names represent an exhaustive list of Indian monks in ancient Korea.

The first Indian monk came to Korea from former Ts'in of China in CE 374. It is beyond our reach to ascertain the Sanskrit name of the Indian monk. It is maintained that Sun-do, the first monk who brought Buddhism with Buddha's images and *sūtra*s by order of King Fu-kien of former Ts'in in China must be Indian or Central Asian. He is popularly known as A-do which should not be a proper person's name but perhaps a pseudo name denoting "bald hair". His name is Marananta which must be transliteration of Sanskrit Malananda. He came to the other Korean kingdom of Paikche whose king greeted him with full respect in his court. As for his origin, we have no source at all. And by what route he came from India to China is completely unknown. But he was sent from the court of Eastern Ts'in in south China which had frequent contacts with south India and Sri Lanka through sea-route. There is a greater possibility of his coming from south India. Third Indian monk visited Silla Korea via Koguryo in CE 417 during the reign of King Nulchi. He was called A-do too with another name Muk-ho-ja meaning "dark complex foreigner". His identification is not possible due to the paucity of source material. Besides them there were some more monks from India. *Haedong-*

kosung-chon (*Biography of Eminent Monks of Korea*) in Taisho tells us the advent of three Indian monks during the reign of King Chik-pyong (579–631) — Bi-ma-ra-chik-che that may be Vimalacitta and Nong-gata, may be Luṅgadha from north India, and Bul-ta-sunga, i.e. Buddhasaṅgha from Mathurā.

Attempts to visit India were made by some Buddhist enthusiasts from the sixth century CE either with the purpose of learning Buddhism at first hand or to pay respect to the places hallowed by the memory of the Buddha. Moreover, the Buddhist intellectuals faced serious problems regarding the translation of Buddhist *sūtra*s and the proper disciplinary life in monasteries. Monk Kyom-ik was the first one who visited India with this purpose. In 526 he went up to India to study the sacred texts further, especially Vinaya texts. He visited a temple named Saṁghana in "central India" where he collected Sanskrit texts of Mahiśāsaka Vinaya. On his return journey an Indian monk Devadatta followed him to Paikche Korea where they translated seventy-two books of the Vinaya texts with the collaboration of eighteen eminent monks under the patron of King Song of Paikche. He founded a Vinaya school in Korea.

From the eighth century, the Korean Buddhists began to take keen interest in India and Indian culture. In I-tsing's *Ta-T'ang Hsi-yu Ch'iu-fa Kao-seng-chuan* (*Biography of Eminent Monks Who Went to the Western Region in Search of the Law During the Great T'ang Dynasty*) in the seventh century, as many as eight monks out of fifty-six in his biography went up to India.

The unification of the three kingdoms by Silla brought high progress of economic condition and social stability maintained by sharp demarcation of the ruler and the ruled. Among the ruling elites of the society, Buddhists were the most prominent one. The state patronized Buddhism with a good amount of land grant to Buddhist monasteries for the purpose of leading the Buddhists to develop the idealistic ethos of the religion. Thus various schools of idealism prospered. This finally encouraged the monks to go to the advanced countries — China and India — to study their sect ideology.

Hye-ch'o was a prominent one who went not only to China but as far as India and left a valuable record, *Wang-o-Chon-Ch'uk-Kuk-Chon* (*Memoir of a Pilgrimage to the Five Regions of India*). He left his mother land in his early age for China where he met and became a disciple of Vajrabodhi, a renowned master of Tāntric Buddhism, reached China in CE 719. He left for India sometimes shortly before 724. Hye-ch'o approached India through sea-route across South China Sea. Hye-ch'o started his travels in India from the eastern part of the country. He made pilgrimages to holy places such as Sārnāth, Kuśinagara, Rājagṛha and Bodh-Gayā as well as important places such as Varanasi and Kanauj. From here he went down southward up to the capital of "South Indian Kingdom" which was identified as the kingdom of Cāḷukyas.[1] Later he continued his travels and approached to western India which has been identified as the Valabhi kingdom of the Kāṭhiāwāṛ peninsula. Hye-ch'o headed for northern part of India and visited Jalandhara, Indus area, Kashmir Valley, Gandhāra, Kapiśa and several Central Asian states. He arrived at An-hsi, the frontier city of the T'ang Empire, which is identified by himself as Kucha.

From the eighth century, Korea witnessed rapid economic progress. Koreans exported to T'ang China several items such as several kinds of luxurious silks, gold and silver and their handiworks, etc. They imported mostly luxurious items such as emeralds, glass vessels, carpets, balm of Gilead and peacock feathers. Some of the luxurious items were handed over by Indian merchants but mostly done through Arabian traders who got the power of trade in the Indian Ocean and in West-South Asia in the pre-Turkish period.[2] The Indian traders are not reported anywhere in Persia and Central Asia, although we hear of Indian settlers in Alexandria in the beginning of the Christian era.

---

1 Yun-hwa Jan, "South India in the VIII Century Hui-Ch'ao's Description Re-examined", *Oriens Exremus*, **XII**(1) (1968): 169-77.

2 Kwangsu Lee, *Buddhist Ideas and Rituals in Early India and Korea*, Delhi, 1998, p. 45.

India was not the land of historical contacts but that of mythical contacts. And such was based on the ideology of the "Buddha Land" which was created in Sri Lanka as a way of legitimization of political power. In the case of Korea, the counterpart of the myth of the Buddha's visits to Sri Lanka is the myth of "Buddha Land". The myth related with the Buddha or *bodhisattva*s and sometimes "Aśoka" or "India" supplied a great ideological background to the political authority sometimes including king's violent acts too.

In the *Samguka-Yusa* it is represented in one place that in the second month of the fourteenth year of King Chin-hung's reign, a large ship arrived all of a sudden at Sapo, Hagok-hyon. An official letter was found there reading King Ayuk of Soch'uk has set a boat adrift laden with 570,000 *kun* of iron and 30,000 *pun* of gold since he tried to cast three of Buddha's images but in vain praying for "wherever may, let the country take these materials to cast images". And with this, were there models of one of Buddha's and two of *bodhisattva*'s images. An official of this county reported this, and the king sent an envoy to build a monastery named Tongch'uksa Temple where the three images were kept safe. And the materials were sent to the capital city and were successfully casted into the images. Silla, is a divine place where Śākyamuni Buddha and Kaśyapa Buddha had their abode and discoursed lectures. Their stone pedestal still stands there.

In this myth, we find remarkable conception of political legitimization through Buddhism. King Chin-hung was not simply depicted as ideal Buddhist king but as the one superior to the King Aśoka whom they admired as paradigm of ideal *cakravartin*, for the former accomplished the work that the latter failed to do. Silla was designed as the land of Kaśyapa Buddha that simply denoted that Silla existed as the land of Buddha much earlier than India, the land of present Buddha. Therefore, the monastery built in the place where the ship of Aśoka arrived safe was named as Tongch'uksa literally meaning monastery of East Chon-ch'uk, with upgrading their home country as superior or equal to India, which was degraded as So-ch'uk, West Chon-ch'uk. In this context, Silla was depicted as the land of *bodhisattva*s, Avalokiteśvara, Mañjuśrī, Kṣitigarbha, Amitāyuṣ and Vairocana. Raksan and Mt. Odae are the places where Avalokiteśvara and 50,000 Mañjuśrī and so on made their permanent abodes, respectively. The myth with the idea of Buddha Land became the ideological background for Buddhist kings' legitimization of their kingship. It clearly embodies the message that the country belonged to the Buddha. Whatever they might be, Korea's contacts with ancient India through the Buddha, *bodhisattvas*, Aśoka and so on in various myths and legends, they should be some invention of political legitimization. And it was a way of Buddhist historical thinking developed in India and Sri Lanka and passed into China, Korea and Japan. Now, nobody may say it logical to explore some historical fact in Buddhist myths and legends on Korea's contacts with India.

At the time between eighth and tenth century BCE, the Buddhist texts translated into Chinese language were widely introduced into Korea through China. And the explanation on the place is that the place had probably been some of the Buddhist temple which was the only place to contact the Buddhist Tripiṭaka containing the word "Ayodhyā" and to make some myth following the tradition of "Buddha Land" after sixth century onward.

The way of finding something with old inscriptions or writings as a testimony for the historicity or authenticity of monuments such as temples, tombs, pavilions, bells, Buddha/*bodhisattva* statues and so on is quite well known at this time. No doubt the real reason for adopting such way of finding secret inscriptions by small Buddhist temples/shrines in the eighteenth century laid in the poor economic conditions of the Buddhist temples. In the impoverished conditions of the post-war period, the Buddhist monks of the small temples/shrines had probably been trying to attract lay devotees for donations. It was the legend of princess Huh which played a good role of Buddhist syncretism in south-western area of Korean peninsula. In the process, Buddhist temples never hesitated to distort the history of the temple/shrine for the purpose of expanding their religious and economic power especially in the air of frustration after the two wars.

Though the legend of princess Huh was elaborated and expanded by Buddhist temples, it was mostly popularized by a novelist, Lee

Jongki, who created a story in 1977.[3] He maintained the "twin fish" of the paintings of main gate of King Suro's tomb is the evidence of princess Huh historical advent. According to him, the "twin fish" is national emblem of ancient Ayodhyā kingdom. However, the paintings of the main gate of King Suro is at best eighty years old that can say nothing on the 2,000-year old historical fact. Moreover, it is absurd to say that the kingdom of Ayodhyā had "twin fish" as its national emblem. Following the novelist's creative idea without any sincere approach, Kim Byongmo, a renowned archaeologist, revised and elaborated his idea and broadcasted in major newspaper and TV programme. And his works played influential roles in advertising legends as historical facts in Korea.

While no historian paid any attention to his essay, many writers, journalists and those who wanted to establish hoary history of Korea–India's historical contacts began to blow horns without any sincere analysis on the legend. Moreover, some scholars on folklore, archaeology and literature of "Great Korea" spirit, tried to confirm it as historical fact without any scientific research.

In this respect, Bruce Lincoln rightly points out, "if myth is ideology in narrative form, then scholarship is myth with footnotes". In turn, some most powerful and influential newspapers, like the *Chosunilbo* or TV programme armed with nationalism give full accounts on the legend wherein the values are firmly embedded, it used to be accepted as a historical fact amongst the mass. Moreover, the legend of Princess Huh was exported into India, the imagined home of the Princess Huh, by the Association of Kimhae Kim clan. Politicians from Kimhae Kim clan thought the myth to be a good source of legitimizing and upgrading the clan's dignity and played as useful channel for winning votes among the mass belonging to Kimhae Kim clan. In 2002, they set up a memorial stone by the river Sarayū of Ayodhyā in Uttar Pardesh, India. The memorial stone of black marble bears "This is the birth place of Princess Huh to become a queen in Karak kingdom of Korea" in Korean language. The construction of this memorial stone

---

[3] Lee Jongki, *Karakkuktamsa*, Seoul, 1977.

was supported by the Bharatiya Janata Party, the ruling party of Uttar Pradesh government and central government at that time. The myth of a princess of India to be a queen in Korea was so good source for Bharatiya Janata Party to propaganda Indian nationalism of Great India.[4]

History is not a science of historians any more, but a weapon of those who try to establish their ideological power. For them history is no more science arguing what happened in the past, but a weapon trying to fabricate the past according to an ideology. And the mass never listened what happened in the past, they are likely to believe the myth which priests and scholars created, and politicians and journalists broadcasted for their own interest.

References

Bakker, Hans, *Ayodhya*, Gröningen, 1986.

Gunawardana, R.A.L.H., "The Kinsmen of the Buddha: Myth as Political Charter in the Ancient and Early Medieval Kingdoms of Sri Lanka", in Bardwell L. Smith (ed.), *Religion and Legitimation of Power in Sri Lanka*, Chamsburg PA, 1979.

Lahiri, Latika (tr.), *Chinese Monks in India*, Delhi, 1986.

Lee, Jongki, *Karakkuktamsa*, Seoul, 1977 (Korean).

Lee, Kwangsu, *Buddhist Ideas and Rituals in Early India and Korea*, Delhi, 1998.

———, "Legend of Princess from Ayodhya and Myth-Making of Buddhist Temples in Korea", in Anita Sharma (ed.), *Buddhism in East Asia: Aspects of History's First Universal Religion Presented in the Modern Context*, Delhi, 2012.

Samguksagi, ed. and tr., Yi Pyong-do, rep., Seoul, 1988.

Samgukyusa, ed. and tr., Yi Min-su, rep., Seoul, 1987.

Sarkar, H.B., "The Ramayana in South-East Asia: A General Survey", in K.R. Srinivasa Iyengar (ed.), *Asian Variations in Ramayana*, Delhi, 1983.

---

4 Kwangsu Lee, "Legend of Princess Huh from Ayodhya and Myth-Making of Buddhist Temples in Korea", in Anita Sharma (ed.), *Buddhism in East Asia: Aspects of History's First Universal Religion Presented in the Modern Context*, Delhi, 2012, p. 197.

Yang, Han-Sung, et al. (tr.), *The Hye Ch'o Diary: Memoir of the Pilgrimage to the Five Regions of India*, Berkeley and Seoul, 1987.

Yi, Ki-baek, *Silla Sasangsa Yongu*, Seoul, 1986.

Yun-hwa Jan, "South India in the VIII Century Hui-Ch'ao's Description Re-examined", *Oriens Extremus*, **XII**(1), 1968.

———, "West India According to Hui-Ch'aos Record", *Indian Historical Quarterly, Oriens Extremus*, **39**(1-2), 1963.

12

The India–Korea Dynamic Relationship
Some Reminiscences

Ravinder Gargesh

THE relationship between India and Korea is growing day by day. It is poised to achieve still higher levels of mutual co-operation. The present paper, largely in the form of some reflections and reminiscences, focuses on five aspects (i) the strong historical links between India and Korea, (ii) some personal experiences in Korea (2006-07 and 2009-11), (iii) some aspects of language teaching based on my experience of teaching Hindi and Indian culture to Korean students in Korea and in India, (iv) some information about the teaching of Korean in India, and (v) to present some thoughts about the present economic and political relationship between India and Korea.

Historical Links

There are many differences between India and Korea such as geographical distance of location with no point of contact. Also Korea is culturally a homogeneous country while India is largely heterogeneous. Despite such differences there appears to have been historical and cultural contacts between the two countries in ancient times. A major connection has been the spread of Buddhism in Korea. Although Buddhism in Korea came from China in the Chinese variety, none the less there were some subsequent contacts between the Korean and Indian Buddhists.

Korea that we know today consisted of three kingdoms — Koguryo, Paikje and Silla — that flourished around the same time from about CE 313 to 668. Since Koguryo was the closest to China it became the first to adopt Buddhism in CE 372. In CE 374 the first Indian monk Ahdo came to Korea and in CE 384 Buddhism spread to Paikje. In CE 540 many teachers and Buddhist scriptures were sent to Paikje from China. Another monk named Kyumik brought from India sacred Buddhist texts and translated them into Chinese. A third monk from India named Mukhoja visited Silla in CE 417. Later another Indian monk named Jigong visited the Korean peninsula during CE 1313-30. I-Chang, a Korean scholar, came to India in CE 673 and stayed at Nālandā for about a decade to study Indian scriptures. He collected many Sanskrit texts and returned to Korea in CE 659 with as many as 400 Sanskrit texts.

The printing of the *Daejung-gyung*, the Buddhist scriptures in Chinese brought to Korea by Mukhwa in CE 981 translated from the Pāli and Sanskrit texts, was an achievement of the Koryo dynasty.

The study of Buddhism had necessitated the study of scriptures in Pāli and Sanskrit, and Korean did not have its own script. In 1446 King Sejong of the Yi dynasty developed a script for Korean known as Hangul. It is widely believed that one of the motivating factors behind this 28-letter script was the Sanskrit language. A Buddhist monk Uichun brought to Korea from China around 3,000 commentaries on Buddhist scriptures and these were preserved in the Hungchunsa Temple and 1,010 copies of the 4,740 volumes were printed in 1096. Although these were destroyed by the invading Mongols in 1232, these were reprinted in 1236 from some surviving volumes. The 81,658 blocks used for printing are known as the "Eighty Thousand" and these are preserved in the Hawinsa Temple.

Korean literature of this time has the Indian influence through Buddhism. In the fifteenth century an important work *Kumo Sinhwa* was composed and it contained five independent stories and one of these was "Manboksa Chap'o Ki" (Game with Buddha). Indian tales and fables also made their way to Korea [for the spread of Buddhism see http://www.esamskriti.com/essay-chapters/China-Korea-Japan-2.aspx].

Another legend often cited in Korea is the one narrated by a Korean monk, Iryon (CE 1206-89), in *Samguka-Yusa*, a Korean text, about an Indian princess from Ayodhyā who came to Korea and married Prince Kim Suro and who came to be known by the name of Queen Hur Hwang-ok in the Gaya kingdom in the first century CE. The legend is treated quite seriously in Korea. Keeping this legend in mind, in modern times, Gimhae, the city where the Indian princess from Ayodhyā is supposed to have landed and married Kim Suro, has signed an Memorandum of Understanding establishing a sister-city relationship with Faiẓābād–Ayodhyā in India. A monument in memory of the princess was erected in March 2001 by the administration of the two cities. The rationale for a close relationship between India and South Korea has been reinforced in modern times by political and economic imperatives. Busan and Mumbai had signed an MoU on mutual co-operation in 1977. Gyeonggi Province signed an MoU for mutual benefit with the State Government of Maharashtra in March 2007. Seoul has a sister-city relationship with Mumbai and has expressed interest in establishing a sister-city relationship with Delhi.

Apart from the above-mentioned legendary and historical facts some similarities between the destinies of the two countries can also be highlighted. Both Korea and India suffered as colonies at the hands of powerful countries like Japan and England, respectively. Subsequently both the countries have undergone a phase of transformation. Korea, the much smaller country has, however, by now become a part of the developed world while India is still part of the developing countries that are on the path of fast growth. Incidentally, both the countries won their freedom on the same day, i.e. on 15 August and after achieving freedom got divided into two parts — Korea into South Korea and North Korea, and India into India and Pakistan. During the Korean War of the early 1950s India had rendered valuable medical help to South Korea.

Personal Reminiscences

My experiences related to Korea and Koreans have been quite prolonged. I have spent three valuable years in Korea, i.e. September

2006 to August 2007 and once again from September 2009 till August 2011. Looking back in retrospect, it appears that the Korean connection has been quite intense. In fact, my first interaction with Koreans was in 1982 when I was a liaison officer with the Asian Games Organizing Committee that had organized the Asian Games in Delhi in 1982. My duty was to guide and look after Chung Ju Young, the then chairman of the Hyundai Corporation, and he was the President of the Korean Olympic Association. He was sixty-five at that time but was extremely energetic and played tennis with verve. During that time I met many Koreans. Chairman Chung had invited me to visit Korea for one month, i.e. in May 1983. I could not avail this opportunity for at that time I was in Italy on a Government of India scholarship. The next interaction with Koreans and Korea began when an MoU was signed between our university and the Hankuk University of Foreign Studies, Seoul, for the mutual exchange of students and faculty in 1992. The active relationship between our Department of Linguistics, University of Delhi, and Hankuk University of Foreign Studies (HUFS), Republic of Korea, commenced in 1993, a relationship that has become stronger with each passing year. Initially it began with a three-week Hindi course (Winter Programme) conducted once in a year. So far we have hosted eighteen such batches. Since the last five years the relations have become far stronger. In addition to the three-week Winter Programme, now every year one batch of students arrives at the end of February and studies in the department till June, i.e. for one semester course under the BRICS and the 7 + 1 programme of HUFS, and another one arrives at the end of August to remain with us for another semester, i.e. till the end of December. After the four-month programme the students undertake a one-month internship with a reputed Korean company in Delhi. Sometimes along with students of HUFS, students from the Busan University of Foreign Studies also come to our Department. In addition to this, since 2006 one faculty member from our department has served as a visiting professor at the Department of Indian Studies at HUFS, and incidentally I was the first one to go. I had also represented my university in signing an MoU between our university and Gangneung University at Gangneung in Korea in 2007 for scientific and technological exchanges.

I travelled almost all over Korea from Jeju island and Busan in the south of Korea to Gangneung and Suraksan mountain in the north-east of Korea. Korea is largely a hilly country with four distinct seasons — winter, spring, summer and autumn. The winter season is very cold and the trees get leafless exposing the strong nests of the "Kachi" birds. The Korean winters are unique because they are largely sunny though one cannot feel the warmth of the sun. In spring the nature appears to be rejuvenated and the trees begin to get their leaves and buds once again. There is also a brief period when the beautiful cherry blossoms appear, particularly along the Han River near "Building 63". The summers are warm and later become wet and humid. It is the autumn season that appealed me the most. This is the time when the natural vegetation on the hills changes hues from green to light reddish brown before the trees lose all leaves as a prelude to oncoming snowy weather. At the same time the Korean maples leaves take on hues of red and the leaves of the *ginko* trees turn golden before they all drop to the ground creating a golden "carpet". Here is the English version of one of the poems composed during this season:

Eunhang Namu

The Eunhang trees in a row
Lush green, straight and gentle
With green robed arms held up
Constantly praying towards the sky
The gentle green shimmering in the light
Changing time, cooler clime
Green giving way to golden yellow
Riot of yellow intoxicating the eye
With its colours from paradise
Golden coin-like leaves
Dancing in the breeze

Changing time, more cooler clime,
Golden yellows pave the path
For heavenly walks
Leaving the bare arms to pray
Constantly for regeneration.

Korea's prowess in the field of sports is well known, in fact. There is much love for sports all round. I was lucky to find that many professors in Korea loved to travel, play tennis, and have good food and drinks. During my sojourn in Korea I was struck by many cultural similarities between India and Korea, the most important being respect for the elders and eating food while sitting on the ground. It is visible in the form of Buddhism in the Buddhist monasteries in Korea. There are some similarities between the Korean festivals of *chuseok* and the Indian rituals of *śrāddha* where some rituals are performed for the well-being of the dead members of the family. The traditional Korean system of medicine based on herbs reminds us of the traditional Indian medical system of Āyurveda. It is to this intellectual side of Korea which even gave itself a script that was appropriate for its spoken form of language that Tagore refers to in his poem written at a time when Korea was passing through its difficult phase in 1929:

The Lamp of the East

In the golden age of Asia
Korea was one of its lamp-bearers
And that lamp is waiting to be
Lighted once again for the
Illumination of the East.

— *Rabindra Nath Tagore 1929*

South Korea has emerged strong after getting freedom from the Japanese occupation and from the painful division of their country. Today's Korea is a shining example of progress out of extreme adversity.

It is shocking to see that mostly Indian history that we study in school is largely from a Western perspective where the events are described and interpreted in terms of India's relationship with the West while our successful and peaceful and more lasting spread towards the East is hardly researched and recorded.

Teaching Hindi to Korean Students

I have been teaching Hindi as a foreign language to Korean students since 1993. In our department we focus on the four skills —

listening, speaking, reading and writing. Our teaching method keeps the basic linguistic knowledge about the Korean and Hindi languages in the backdrop. This information pertains to the domains of phonetics and phonology, morphology, syntax and pragmatics. Some examples are as follows:

> The first thing that we tell our students is that the writing systems are not exactly the same as spoken language, whether we compare Korean speech with the letters of Hangul or those of Hindi speech with the letters of Devanāgarī or the speech sounds of English with the letters of their alphabet. The spoken sounds many times sound differently for the same written consonant letter, e.g. the same letter of the alphabet in Korean stands for both the /*l*/ and /*r*/ sounds, while in Hindi generally the letters standing for /*š*/ and /*ś*/ respectively are articulated as the [*š*] sound. Once the teacher knows the differences and similarities between the sounds of Korean and Hindi better training can be given for articulating the words with different sounds, e.g. the Korean students find it difficult to articulate words with retroflex consonants of Hindi. Similarly a speaker of Indian languages finds it difficult to articulate Korean sounds due to the large number of allophonic variations.

One common thing is that Korean language shares with Hindi the SOV syntactic structure:

1. *Hana nun banana rul mogsupnida*
2. *Hanā kelā khātī hai*
3. Hana banana eats

In Korean and Hindi, verbs occur at the end of a sentence. In Korean, while the subject and the object are movable the verb remains fixed in the final position. In Hindi all these can be moved within the sentence structure and remain within the boundaries of acceptability. Let us take a Korean example, consider the expression — "Kim Do Young eats lunch at home":

김도영이 집에서 점심을 먹어요.

Kim Do Yong ichib e sau jom sim ul mok au yo

किम दो यंग घर पर खाना खाता है

Kim Do Young home-at lunch eats

김도영이 점심을 집에서 먹어요.

किम दो यंग खाना घर पर खाता है

Kim Do Young lunch home-at eats

집에서 김도영이 점심을 먹어요.

घर पर किम दो यंग खाना खाता है

home-at Kim Do Young lunch eats

집에서 점심을 김도영이 먹어요.

घर पर खाना किम दो यंग खाता है

home-at lunch Kim Do Young eats

점심을 김도영이 집에서 먹어요.

खाना किम दो यंग घर पर खाता है

lunch Kim Do Young home-at eats

점심을 집에서 김도영이 먹어요.

खाना घर पर किम दो यंग खाता है

lunch home-at Kim Do Young eats

From the above it is clear that similar movements of constituents are permissible in both Korean and Hindi.

Another similarity between Korean and Hindi is in the use of honorifics. Prestige forms of language are used for people of higher social status, elders, teachers, etc. Non-honorific forms are used for people of inferior status and among equals with close bonds of friendship, etc. The relationship between a speaker or writer and his or her audience is important in both Korean and Hindi, and the grammar reflects this use of polite forms.

Students can also be made aware of some differences between Korean and Hindi, e.g. Korean has particles like {+*ga*} and {+   n} that are suffixed to nouns whereas in Hindi no such particles are used. Hindi on the other hand has a single ergative construction {*ne*} in the perfectives with a transitive verb.

The point that is being emphasized here is that a prior linguistic knowledge does help a teacher to create interest in the students by trying to show them that the study of Hindi is easier for Koreans and vice versa.

The teaching of Hindi as foreign language has at its centre the development of communicative skills in the learners. This involves a focus on context-based language use, the kind of language used in the marketplace, at railway stations, while introducing oneself, in meeting strangers, etc. Special care needs to be taken to develop listening and speaking skills for there are many sounds of Hindi that non-existent in Korean, e.g. there are no retroflex sounds in Korean and there is no high central vowel in Hindi that Korean has, etc. All reading and writing is enjoyed by students if these are contextualized.

My other academic experiences in Korea include the completion of the *Korean–Hindi Dictionary* under the chief editorship of Kim Woo Jo, which was published by HUFS, Seoul, in 2008. The dictionary gives Hindi equivalents of Korean words which are very useful for the Korean students of Hindi since their Hindi vocabulary is limited. Another useful dictionary for Korean students was the *Hindi–Korean Dictionary* compiled by Jeong Ho Lee.

In addition to the teaching of Hindi, the Institute of South Asian Studies in HUFS provided opportunities to write articles on diverse subjects of South Asia and my contributions ranged from writing about co-articulation in Kashmiri language to the various stylistic analyses of Hindi and Punjabi poems and it included a paper on Sufism in Punjabi too.

Teaching Korean to Indian Students

Another impetus to the relationship between our university and Korea was given by the introduction of the teaching of Korean language and literature in our university in 2003 under the leadership of Kim Do Young. Although the teaching of Korean language began earlier in Jawaharlal Nehru University (JNU) in 1974 as one-year course, however, from 1995 onwards the teaching of Korean language in India is largely associated with the name of Kim Do Young. It was through his efforts that JNU began to have a 3 + 2 programme in Korean from 1995 onwards. After the successful graduation of three batches at JNU, he shifted to the University of Delhi in 2002 where he initiated the certificate, diploma and advanced diploma courses in Korean language. He is now trying to initiate a PG course in University of Delhi as well. Around 2006 the Indo–Korean Cultural Centre, with the help of TVS and Hyundai, began a three-four months certificate course in Korean language for working employees of companies like Hyundai. Jadavpur University had also commenced a certificate course around 2006 but that was closed down and then re-opened in 2008. Magadh University too began a certificate and a diploma course in Korean language in 2007-08.

Coming to teaching of Korean to Indian students the *Korean–English* and *English–Korean* dictionaries compiled by Kim Do Young for his Indian students are quite helpful. For the teaching of Korean the *Bharati–Korean* series by Kim Do Young have been found to be useful. It must be highlighted that at the University of Delhi Kim has introduced the aural–oral approach which is supplemented by the *Bharati–Korean* (parts 1, 2 and 3), *Reading Comprehension* (parts 1, 2 and 3), and a *Workbook* (parts 1, 2 and 3). His *Korean–English Dictionary* has the pronunciation of Korean words in Devanāgarī script. In fact, Kim uses Devanāgarī script to teach Korean in India. This makes Korean easy for speakers of Hindi but some Korean sounds which are non-existent in Indian languages become difficult to acquire since the learner will be misguided by the orthography's fixed Hindi pronunciation. Hence sounds like / ɨ / and short / ə / will be mispronounced.

What has attracted me to Prof. Kim's work is the title *Bharati–Korean*. What Kim has in mind is the teaching of Korean in India from an Indian perspective, and the closest and most widespread is the Hindi language through the Devanāgarī script. However, there is another dimension which Kim can keep in mind. Even the best of speakers of a foreign language manifest elements of their mother tongue in their use of the foreign language. Hence, some elements of sound or grammar may not be like that of the native speaker of the foreign language but that of the mother tongue of the speaker, a phenomenon termed as the Joseph Conrad phenomenon. The Korean spoken by Indians with some amount of Indianism can be termed as *Bharati–Korean*. I am sure Kim may be very happy with the Korean output of his students but still there will be something which will make it *Bharati–Korean* and not exactly the Korean of Korea. We Indians are very good at Indianizing languages and we find nothing wrong with it. We have done this many times before. We had done it to Persian in the past (*Sabke-Hindi*) and now we have done it to English (*Indian English*) (Abidi and Gargesh 2008). For a similar reason when the Korean students do the same to Hindi in our classes we don't mind that too, for it is all part of the learning process and self-identity. This course is now very popular in our university. So much so that one of our students is now doing his PhD in Korean language from Seoul National University.

Economic Co-operation Between India and Korea

A remarkable feature of South Korea is its transformation from a developing country in the 1950s to a high-income country with a substantial per capita income today. The economic reforms of the 1990s in India were influenced by East Asian successes and South Korea was among the chief countries to have an impact on Indian policymakers' thinking process. Though consular relations between India and South Korea were set up in 1962, it was in 1973 with the establishment of formal diplomatic ties that a new chapter was opened in the history of Indo–Korean co-operation. Both India and Korea contribute significantly to the world GDP. Korea is among the few Asian countries that are counted among the developed countries of the world; India, too, has a growing stature and increasing role in international affairs.

The socio-economic development of Korea has been remarkable, for in a short span of time the country has been able to achieve spectacular economic growth. It is a small country with an area of only 98,445 sq. km and a population of 50,112,000 as on 1 January 2011. The real GDP growth in 2012 has been 2.6 per cent and the inflation rate has been 2.8 per cent in the same period. The annual gross income for 2012 has been US $ 813,403.6 million, the annual disposable income for the same period has been US $ 628,742.8 million and the consumer expenditure US $ 597,573.4 million. This shows that the economy is much under control. The economic growth is matched by the higher living standards of the Koreans and by the almost uniform development of infrastructure in the whole of Korea. The country has a one of the largest spread of broadband internet and also has a very efficient system of plastic money. The country is a popular destination for tourists and in 2011 it earned US $ 12,345.5 million from tourism alone. The country is dotted with restaurants where food is available at an affordable price, and Koreans love to eat in restaurants where food is delicious.

Given the present geopolitical situation when many countries of the world do not realize the ancient Indian dictum of (the world is one family), it is natural for Indians and Koreans to become natural allies to safeguard their interests as well as for world peace. There is a convergence of interests today between the greatest power USA, India and the countries of the far-East which gives credence to India as a middle power aligning with South Korea, Taiwan and Japan in order to protect themselves from the expansionist tendencies of another super-power — China. This was made possible by the "Look East Policy" of the 1990s.

During the Cold War, India's relations with its South-East Asian neighbours were not very strong. After the end of the Cold War, the Government of India realized the importance of redressing this imbalance in India's foreign policy. Consequently, the Narasimha Rao government in the early 1990s unveiled the Look East Policy. Initially it focused on renewing political and economic contacts with the countries of East and South-East Asia. At present, under the Look East Policy, the Government of India is taking advantage of the huge market of ASEAN as well as of the energy resources available in some of the member countries of ASEAN like Myanmar. India became a sectoral dialogue partner with ASEAN in 1992, a full dialogue partner in 1995, a member of the ASEAN Regional Forum (ARF) in 1996, and a summit level partner (on par with China, Japan and Korea) in 2002. Since the beginning of this century, India has given a big push to this policy by becoming a summit level partner of ASEAN (2002) and by getting involved in some regional initiatives such as the BIMSTEC and the Ganga–Mekong Co-operation and since 2005 it has also become a member of the East Asia Summit (EAS). The first India–ASEAN Business Summit was held at New Delhi in October 2002. Since then this business summit has become an annual feature before the India–ASEAN Summits, as a forum for networking and exchange of business experiences between policymakers and business leaders from ASEAN and India.

The EAS is a pan-Asian forum held annually by the leaders of sixteen countries in East Asia and the region, with ASEAN in a leadership position. The summit has discussed issues including trade, energy and security. The members of the summit are all 10 members of ASEAN together with China, Japan, South Korea, India, Australia and New Zealand who combined represent almost half of the world's population. Russia has applied for membership of the summit and in 2005 was a guest for the first EAS at the invitation of the host country — Malaysia.

Narasimha Rao was the first Indian Prime Minister to visit Korea in 1993, and strengthen political and trade relationships. The same year the President of Korea became the chief guest at India's Republic Day celebrations. The countries signed some agreements for the progressive opportunities in the near future. Manmohan Singh became the second Indian Prime Minister to visit Korea in March 2012 in order to strengthen ties with the Asian economic partner and also participate in the Nuclear Security Summit. The aim of the visit was to sign an agreement on simplifying issuance of visas in order to strengthen people-to-people contact between the two countries, to strengthen co-operation in the field of science and technology, and also to co-ordinate the thinking on matters relating to regional security and international events. The visit also aimed at giving depth and greater meaning to the strategic partnership and to the comprehensive economic partnership agreement between the two countries. The main aim of the Nuclear Summit was to strengthen nuclear security and take measures to prevent terrorists getting access to atomic weapons. [See http://www.indianexpress.com/news/pm-embarks-on-fourday-south-korea-visit-tomorrow/927435/1].

During the visit of President A.P.J. Abdul Kalam in 2006, the first by any president of India to the Republic of Korea, the signing of a Joint Ministerial Statement on the Launching of a Joint Task Force to develop a Comprehensive Economic Partnership Agreement (CEPA) between the two countries was held. Two other agreements — Agreement on Co-operation in the Fields of Science and Technology and Agreement on Co-operation and Mutual Assistance in Customs Matters — were also signed during the visit. An MoU on Scientific and Technological Co-operation between the Department of Science and Technology and the India and Korea Industrial Technology Foundation (KOTEF) was also signed separately.

India's relations with South Korea show that India is increasingly looking for its influence in North-East Asia, and South Korea's relation with India is an effort at looking for a big new market as well as for an all-weather friend. This relationship will not only provide economic benefits to both the countries but will also enable both of them to create space for themselves in a region dominated by China. With respective governments support to the business community in a positive way and with the growing amount of globalization and liberalization, not only Korean companies are making their big role in India, Indian firms too are establishing themselves in Korea.

CEPA, a free trade agreement, was signed on 7 August 2009 in Seoul and it was ratified by the Indian and the Korean parliaments and came into force on 1 January 2010. Some of the highlights include the fact that the CEPA binds South Korea to phase out or reduce tariffs on 90 per cent of Indian goods over ten years, while India is to eliminate tariffs on 85 per cent of South Korean exports within the same period, which is longer than what is written in other FTAs South Korea has signed. In addition to tariff reduction, South Korea will be able to move into various industrial sectors of the Indian economy, such as food processing, textiles, garments, chemicals, metals and machinery. The deal also opens the service and investment sector, with India accepting South Korean company inflows in its telecom, accounting, medical and advertising markets, as well as allowing South Korean financial firms in the investment market. With respect to rules of origin, both countries agreed on the allowable level of foreign contents to be up to 65 per cent. South Korea expects massive inflows of Information Technology (IT) workers, engineers and English teachers as both sides agreed to allow temporary migration of professional workers.

Today South Korea is the fourth largest investor in India in terms of actual inflow of FDI into India. During the first three quarters of 2008, for which data is available, 164 investment proposals from fifty-two Korean companies for a proposed total investment of $ 243 million approved. The cumulative investment from South Korea in India has been $ 1.46 billion in terms of actual flow from 382 Korean companies for over 900 projects.

The Korean's investments in India have largely taken place in the transportation industry, energy (power and oil refinery), electrical equipment (including computer software and electronics), chemicals (other than fertilizer), commercial, office and household equipment, metallurgical industries and food processing industries. Major South Korean companies active in India include Hyundai Motor, Samsung Electronics, LG, Lotte Group and Doosan Heavy Industries. Now, major South Korean companies like Samsung, Hyundai and LG are expanding production facilities in India and smaller companies are focusing on technical collaborations. The Lotte Group acquired Parry's Confectionery Chennai in 2004. Samsung Electronics opened a mobile phone plant in the state of Haryana in March 2006. Samsung Engineering has opened its Global Engineering Centre in New Delhi. An Indian company Mahindra & Mahindra Motors acquired a majority stake in Korea's SsangYong Motor Company in 2011. Tata Motor's purchase of Daewoo Commercial Vehicles at the cost of $ 102 million also highlights India's investments in Korea.

Trade between India and South Korea was $ 15.6 billion in 2008 and it crossed the $ 20 billion in 2011 and is expected to reach $ 40 billion by 2020. This is a major increase from 2002, which had a total trade amount of $ 2.6 billion.

The countries are becoming a part of the larger connect in terms of movies too. There is a movie called *Finding Kim Jong Wook*, starring popular lead pair Gung Yoo and Im Soo-Jeong, based on love story about two Korean tourists who meet in India. On the other hand, an Indian movie called *Gangster* has Korea as the primary locale for the enfolding of its action.

Conclusion

Korea and India are both beautiful countries that not only have ancient links but also need to link up in the present times. Despite ecological and cultural diversity, philosophical, economic, political and military needs are reasons strong enough to bring the two countries together. The ancient legend of Prince Suro and the legacy of Buddhism prevalent in the country along with some common socio-cultural traits are the foundation on which this relationship is built. The convergence of interests between the two countries, as reflected in a major pact like the CEPA which covers wide domains like economic, scientific, defense, cultural and educational cooperation, shows the political will of the two countries to come together for the common of mutual benefit. This relationship is destined to grow further in today's complex world.

References

Abidi, S.A.H. and R. Gargesh, "Persian in South Asia", in B. Kachru, Y. Kachru and Nelson (eds.) *Language of Asia*, Cambridge: Cambridge University Press, 2008.

Chang, Suk-jin, *Korean*, Philadelphia: John Benjamins Publishing Company, 1996.

Indian Express, 2012, "PM Embarks on Four-day South Korea Visit

Tomorrow". http://www.indianexpress.com/news/pm-embarks-on-fourday-south-korea-visit-tomorrow/927435/1 (downloaded on 18 November 2012).

Lam, P.E. and T.W. Lim, *Introduction: China, India and the New Asian Drama*. http://www.worldscibooks.com/etextbook/7381/7381_ch01.pdf (downloaded on 30 October 2012).

Lee, Ki-Moon and S. Robert Ramsey, *A History of the Korean Language*, Cambridge: Cambridge University Press, 2011, 352 pages.

Mahbubani, Kishore, *The New Asian Hemisphere: The Irresistible Shift of Global Power to the East*, New York: Public Affairs, 2008.

Nayyar, S., 2002, "Indian Influence Abroad", http://www.esamskriti.com/essay-chapters/China-Korea-Japan-2.aspx (downloaded on 30 October 2012).

Sohn, H.-M., *The Korean Language*, Cambridge: Cambridge University Press, 1999.

———, *Korean Language in Culture and Society*, Boston: Twayne Publishers, 2006.

Song, J.-J., *The Korean Language: Structure, Use and Context*, London: Routledge, 2005.

13

Literature of "Beyond" Towards "out of" Eurocentrism

A Political Detonator in Korean Literature, Boundary/Minority/Orality

Ko Myeong-Chel

Korean Literature Imprisoned in Eurocentrism

WE need to thoroughly reconsider some apocalyptic discourses that have charmed us since Fukuyama's *The End of History and the Last Man* (1992). One cannot deny that those discourses have alerted us to the supremacy of modernity and driven us to seek the post-modernity as an alternate to overcome such a modernity. This post-modern project has not been easily accepted and accomplished, of course. Under the justification of pursuing its project, the West that already tasted the sweet modernity has naturally imposed their modern accomplishments on the non-Western world, i.e. colonial modernity. Since this colonial modernity is rooted in the Western epistemology, the West has been able to manipulate the level of the modernity by its own will. As generally noticed, the (post-)modern project situated in between quasi-periphery and periphery of world capitalism permits only itself. This is a critical issue that we cannot overlook.

My argument starts with this very point. Are there indeed any other social and cultural systems outside the Western capitalism? What is the role of the literary imagination against capitalism? If there is not such an imagination, do we have an urgent agenda to discover it? Or, do we have it as merely a potential, not as a fully developed one? To do so, how Korean literature should participate in this political and literary imagination against Eurocentrism. In other words, we are now confronting a critical question of how Korean literature as a new literary and political framework can be an "alternative" to overcome Eurocentrism and the (post-)modernity. Or finally, can we hope a literary revolution towards "different (post-)modernity (or, -ies)" that has (have) been ignored and distorted by the West: such a revolution is another counter-path against the Western (post-)modern project.

Consideration of Korean Literature on "Geopolitics of Colonialism": From Margins to Frontiers

What strategy of the non-Western criticisms or theories can rightly reverse Eurocentrism? Whenever this bold and challenging question appears, we first need to investigate a sociological term, "geopolitics of colonialism",[1] which was initiated by the West. Doubtless, starting with the Renaissance and reaching the Enlightenment as its apogee, and based on the Christian cosmology, the West had recognized itself as the origin of civilization that was set in motion by the universal reason.[2] Accordingly, it has claimed that the savagery of the non-

---

1 The concept of "geopolitics of colonialism" has not been fully developed, and should be thoroughly investigated. The notion in this paper is indebted to Latin-American theorist, Walter Mignolo's term, "geopolitics of knowledge". Walter Mignolo, *Latin-America, the Continent that Has Been Made*, tr. Kim Eunjoong, Seoul: Greenbee, 2010.

2 Kant and Hegel are the most influential philosophers on this thought. Their philosophy has been normally appreciated to open a new ground about the universality of human mind. However, Kant and Hegel (and Enlightenment) offer various doctrines of geopolitics that justify the purposiveness of colonialism over non-Western worlds since the sixteenth century. Hegel's Eurocentic understanding of world history serves the same justification. See Susan Buck-Morss, *Hegel, Haiti, and Universal History*, tr. Kim Youngho, Seoul: Moonhakdongnae, 2012. Mignolo, by drawing the study of Kant's geography (1756-96), argues that Kant was not free from the rampant Christian cosmology at his time. He also critically maintains that some aspects of racist recognition appear in Kant. Walter Mignolo, "The Darker Side of the Enlightenment: A De-Colonial Reading →

Western worlds (Asia, Africa and Latin America) has to be enlightened. Such a desire for the Westernized way of enlightening over the non-Western worlds presupposes a dichotomy between the West (or the centre) and the non-West (or margins), so-called "geopolitics of colonialism" towards the non-Western worlds.

In this geopolitical point of view, however, once we see the non-Western worlds not as the other but as another origin of the subject, an urgent issue can be brought about: a task to rediscover the true values of non-Western worlds that have been distorted and reduced by the Western knowledge system, wherein orientalism appears. Kim Hyoungsoo's novel, *Zode* (2012), among the most recent novels in Korean literature, is a good way to find one of the values. One must carefully look at the contrast between "plains and deserts of Mongolia" in his novel. Kim understands the Mongolian plains without an orientalist standpoint, but also his Mongolian plains are not depicted from the (post-)modern view. By representing the plains as self-salvation or an escape (or flight) from monotonous and base routines in cosmopolitan life, he clearly keeps distance from "road's narrative" which visits the intact nature preserving its cosmic mystery. His novel differs from Western narratives that largely consume non-Western literary sources only within the limit of the Western framework, in order to make a contrast to the Western values, or a little sarcastically speaking, in order to pursue the (post-)modernity.

The Mongolian plains in *Zode* are not damaged yet because the novel's time frame was before Genghis Khan established his empire in the twelfth century. This draws an attention to the question of why Kim Hyoungsoo focuses on that era: why he chooses the pre-modern time. First of all, his interest is in the wisdom of nomadic life that conforms to "the Great Earth",[3] the earth that was once forgotten in the West. He is amazed by an innate nature of the nomadic life to survive wolfishly, and at its religious precepts on *Zode*'s life of "bloody

→ of Kant's Geography", in *Reading Kant's Geography*, ed. Stuart Elden and Eduardo Mendieta, Albany: State University of New York Press, 2011.

[3] Kim Hyoungsoo, *Zode I*, Seoul: JaumguaMoeum, 2012, p. 183.

cold of plains and deserts, not going away until all the things in the world disappears in air".[4] He desires to represent a non-Western narrative depicting coexistence with the earth, not the (post-)modern narratives, wherein people have moved away from the earth. Therefore, what *Zode* requires of us through its aggressive reading is the question of how the nomadic people live along with "the great earth": how the people nurtured by the earth had relationships with others and nature, and in those relationships what is the value of "old newness". Furthermore, in what manner are all these relationships narrated? If we focus on these questions, we can realize the true meaning of humanity's foolishness that "he, the best sibling of the nature cannot understand his mother' words",[5] and the connotation of "crossing the border" and deterritorialization through "scattered, if we are hungry or amiss, we go somewhere to find [food and shelter]".[6] If we take "geopolitics of colonialism" as an analytic tool for *Zode*, it cannot help us to perceive Mongolia and its nature as she is. Instead, Kim overturns the concept of "geopolitics of colonialism" through his literary imagination on the Mongolian plains.

Then, an issue followed is how to recognize the non-Western worlds (or other places outside the West) not as the margins of the West but as "frontiers" or "in-betweens", where Western values conflict against the non-Western worlds. For instance, *Soonyee Uncle* (1978) dealing with an episode of the April Third Resistance, *A Bird Chirping on the Border* (1983) about Jeju island in the modern transformation era and so on, are the works related to Hyun Kiyoung's thematic stage, which is Jeju island. Such an idea of "frontiers" or "in-betweens" requires different analyses, in understanding Hyun's works, from "anxiety narrative" about Cold War ideology and "resistance narrative" against this ideology, which are commonly known as a key method to analyse this kind of works. His narratives, in spite of their variations, have the values of "anxiety" and "resistance" only through Western theories.

---

4 Kim Hyoungsoo, *Zode I*, Seoul: JaumguaMoeum, 2012, p. 65.

5 Ibid., p. 48.

6 Ibid., p. 280.

Throughout the geopolitical history of Jeju, on the one hand, the island had been regarded as a subordinate territory of Korea, and on the other hand, as an important military spot for the political dominance over East Asian countries by Western empires. Regarding this twofold understanding of the island, we need to situate ourselves in seeing the history of Jeju as "double colonialism",[7] one colonial oppression from the Korean government, the other from the dynamics of world powers. However, one should see that this understanding of Jeju as a part of a unitary state is just a residue from Western "geopolitics of colonialism", which reduces Jeju into a margin. Therefore, the political narrative to be considered in Hyun Kiyoung's works is: (1) the revealing of "double colonialism" in Jeju history, and (2) the re-illumination of anti-civilization that was executed by Western values. This reconsideration can contextualize and transform the geopolitics of knowledge of "Jeju-island-border (or margin)" formula into that of "Jeju-island-frontier (or in-between)". What remains is to expand this reframing method to Korean literature located in a frontier away from the West. By occupying the position of "frontier (or in-between)" where Western values severely conflict, Korean literature should develop its literary imagination of the "frontier", instead of just surviving in the framework of world literature.

Ethics of Minority in "Korean Literature as Frontier"

One cannot deny the literary struggles in the modern history of Korean literature in the first half of the twentieth century: a literary endeavour to establish an independent country from Japanese empire by using "resistant narratives" and "literary practice" to constitute a united nation from two governmental systems in one country during the time that the global capitalism has dominated. The literary practice is best achieved by the people (Realism) and damaged individual (Modernism). It is not unfair to say that various individual literatures consist of Korean literature. Yet, it also needs clarification. All the key researches of who has led Korean literature until now are

---

7 Ko Myeong-chel, "Outrage at the Becoming of Violent People by State Power", *Realist*, Seoul: Samchang, 2011, n. 5, pp. 22-27.

imprisoned within Eurocentric frameworks. Whether pan-progressive literature as social participation or pan-liberalist literature for its aesthetic autonomy, they set in motion only to realize the (post-)modern project. A politically positive and meaningful aspect in Korean literature is that its literary imagination has been developed to complete the country's political and economic democracy in the sense of Western modernity.

However, in the twenty-first century the subject in Korean literature is not the one who is indulged in the imported (post-) modernism. Korean literature is not the "margin" but the "frontier" of the geopolitics of colonialism any more, and it is "minority" as the subject of "frontier". This minority is not referred to socially weak people excluded from social powers. It is a new subject that cannot be recognized from the viewpoint of Western political economy, in which the (post-)modern values fiercely conflict each other. The emergence of this subject in the recent Korean literature is very encouraging. Migrant workers in novels are dealt with in such as Park Bumshin's *Namaste* (2005), Kim Jeayoung's *Elephant* (2005) and Son Hongkyu's *Islamic Butcher*'s (2010). Hwang Seokyoung's *Baridaegi* (2007), Jung Dosang's *Wild Rose* (2008), Kown Lee's *Mystery of a Left-Hander* (2007) and Lee Eungjoon's *Privacy of State* (2009) focus on various narratives about North Korean refugees. In poetry, Paek Moosan, Song Kyoungdong, Lim Sungyoung and Kim Sayi have produced realism poems. Laborious works by Ha Jonghoin specific, *Factory Without Border* (2007), *Asian Korean* (2007), *Immigrants* (2009), *Empire* (2011) and *Dictionary of North and South Korean Symbols* (2011) are good works.

These writers investigate the life and reality of immigrant workers, including North Korean refugees from Democratic People's Republic of Korea for survival. They accuse of, witness, and criticize nationalism and racism which are rampant in the Korean society. They suggest that many problems of modern nationalism cannot be overcome through the Western modernity. Rather, they create a new literary ethics of multi-cultural era, meaning that the minority such as immigrant workers shares their happiness together.

Literacy and Orality (or Performance)

The characteristics of non-Western literatures should be noted, which were used to be excluded, extorted and ignored by (post-)modern doctrines. Among these characteristics, I am interested in orality that is supposed to entail performance. As generally agreed upon, oral literature is understood as an old one initiated before the modern period, in institutionalized education of literature, in terms of the privilege of written literature over oral one. In this sense, the modern cultural history takes written literature as its own property, and the (post-)modern literature can achieve its own purpose through this written literature. This understanding of literacy highly pertains to the overcoming of memory-dependent orality, and to the fact that it expands the artistic foreground of enabling thoughts to be more accurately expressed than orality does. Furthermore, mass circulation of written words resulted in prosperous written literature, and then played a key role in proliferating democracy by decentralizing the privilege of written words. However, it should be noted that the political oppression of written literature is hidden behind the ability of reading and writing. As the education and achievements in Korean literature are accumulated, Eurocentrism has been instilling in our daily life without consciousness. Other non-Western literatures translated from the institutionalized Western literature go through the same process.

It is the problem, as emphasized from the beginning, that Eurocentrism cannot maintain the happiness of human life but drive us to ruin. Then how is it possible to stop this ruin? An answer to this question is orality that has not been remarked. What if orality is delicately arranged within texts, although written literature or literacy has long been familiar to us? Or, can we create a new form of literature that, through nullifying the binary concept of literacy and orality, can replace written literature of the literacy-oriented and Eurocentric values?

Kim Hyoungsoo's *Zode* can give us some convincing answers. For example, the first lines in the novel start with: "Once upon a time, lands first shaped themselves. The sun rose, leaves woke up. The moon set, arises became blue. Then the event occurred."[8] This description seems as if the grand narrative on the origin of cosmos is told vividly right before our eyes. *Zode* is not read as one of Western narrative heroes which are familiar with us. Songs that had passed down to the nomadic as an oral form are inserted in the novel: the barren nomadic life for Taemujin to grow up to Khan, the life and death of all creatures living in Mongolian lands, and symbiosis with *Zode* which is a disaster of land and measurable to that of sea, and so on. The oral history of the nomadic life handed from the pre-historic era is related to Mongolian lands, and it is expressed through not only mystic epics on the musical performance triggering the soul by a Mongolian guitar, but also the language of dance and body. By focusing on the description of the oral tradition, *Zode* presents its holy resonance and pattern between human being and nature, which cannot be fully understood from Eurocentric knowledge. The novel realizes a disparate form of narratives from most Western ones, through *sensus communis* beyond mere audio- and visual-harmony. It is an experiment of a narrative form.

Such an experiment can be also found in Korean poetry. The experiment of its form, to put it more exactly, can grasp the non-Western literary qualities, not of the (post-)modern literature. In this regards, Moon Moobyoung's *Gut Poem* draws our attention. This poem is created through the chemical interaction between a form of folklore, namely shaman exorcism and modern poetry. For Moon, *Gut Poem* is a narration executed by a shaman, and an expression of a rigour for the afterlife. This narration is holy, but at the same time, the holiness comes from people's ordinariness. In other words, the shaman's narration crosses the borderline between the religious and the secular, and finally, reinvigorates people. Moon's interest is in merging the key characteristics of shaman narration and modern poetry. Here we can experience a pleasure of shaman exorcism, and this performance politically relieves the tragic history of modern Korea that had been suffered by the twofold colonial oppressions mobilized by geopolitical

---

[8] *Zode I*, p. 8.

colonialism. Successive literary attempts to overcome the limit of Eurocentric literature, absorbing East Asian literary forms actively, prove *Gut Poem*'s significance and its political meaning.

An Adventure Towards "out of" Eurocentrism

It is not deniable that Eurocentrism has dominated the world's intellectual and cultural history since the fifteenth century, but at the same time, it cannot be everlasting. This is because the capitalist mode of production as the economic foundation of the Western values also will be substituted for an alternative, as the feudal mode of production had transformed into the modern capitalism. The mode of production cannot help but to follow the Eurocentric understanding of modern history. An urgent suggestion regarding an alternative framework would be finding the true values of non-Western artistic practices, and continuous arguments against the Western literature and its geopolitical colonialism will be followed. The whole arguments would be an intellectual adventure for reversing the old routines of Eurocentric ways of understanding in the global era, which would be seen as a severe interrogation. We need to begin theoretical practice and practical theory together, with patience of anxiety. It is the Korean literature's politics in the twenty-first century: the politics that I should pursue and achieve as a Korean critic.

14

Two Different Metaphysics of Language
Bhartṛhari and Diṅnāga

Kyung-Hee Lee

Introduction

FROM the most ancient of times, language has been thought as being marvellous and magical. The power of the word to denote the referent has especially been regarded as being quite mystic and, hence, it has been deified. No one would deny that were it not for language none of the achievements of any of the civilizations such as their sciences, arts, and even their religions could have been successfully established. It is apparent that the power to realize these exists in language.

It is language that gives humans the power of communication and of archiving. It seems, however, that the research in Western linguistics has been focused on communicative aspects such as morphology, semantics and syntax, till recent times. The recent trend of research is not only directed towards the study of articulated sounds spoken by human beings, but also the realization of artificial intelligence towards machines having the faculties of analysing and recognizing the natural speech sounds of human beings and of responding to them with a meaningful purpose along with human being's verbal commands.

In the field of linguistics, there has forever remained the unanswered question of how and where language originates. This question remains unanswered because it is impossible to provide an answer to it even with the help of all the scientific methods available to us.

One, nevertheless, always thirsts for an answer to the question. The unslakable desire to answer this question seems to stem from the hope that would the answer shed light on the nature of language, but it would also possibly shed light on such ontological questions as to who or what being is.

There are however, in this regard, two great ancient Indian philosophers who seem capable of fulfilling this hope — Bhartṛhari (CE 450–510) who was a king, a poet, a grammarian and sometimes known as a Buddhist, and Diṅnāga as a Buddhist monk (CE 480–540).

India has always maintained a peculiar tradition that regards the Veda or master's teaching as the source of knowledge. Due to this, the importance of language has been greatly recognized. The flow of sacred knowledge from master to pupil was neither to be interrupted, nor distorted. Moreover, the Indian tradition of oral transmission made it possible to develop the divisions of linguistics into phonetics, or the science of grammar and so on so as to memorize and transmit the knowledge held sacred without any distortion and omission.

The linguistics which had been growing in this advanced tradition came to full bloom as linguistic metaphysics during the period of Bhartṛhari and Diṅnāga. They had a common understanding that language is a means of awakening, since it is related with both existence and cognition, even though they belonged to two conflicting schools of philosophy.

For Bhartṛhari, language is the *Brahman*. The grammatical study of language becomes the ladder to obtain union with the *Brahman*. On the other hand, Diṅnāga asserts that one is able to achieve awakening only by abandoning linguistic thought. He considered linguistic thought as the cause of differentiated cognition and thought, and thereby as the origin of illusion.

These two conflicting theories were originated from the dispute as to whether language derives from a permanent universal or whether it is the product of ephemeral conventions. Hence, many other Indian scholars after them have also concentrated on the deductive or inductive study of the cause of language and how it comes to denote meaning.

An enquiry into these earlier studies is desired not only to attain an understanding of the ancient Indian metaphysics of language, but also, as was said above, for a grasp of the nature of human beings. And furthermore, in a narrow sense, it will also stimulate our scholarly imagination regarding modern linguistics, since it has a thread of connection with the studies of modern linguistics.

The Nature of Language: Śabda-Brahman and Vikalpa

ŚABDA-BRAHMAN

Bhartṛhari defines the nature of language in the first verse of his *Vākyapadīya* as follows.

> *anādinidhanaṁ brahma śabdatattvaṁ yadakṣaram* |
> *vivartate 'rthabhāvena prakriyā jagato yataḥ* ||1||

> The *Brahman* who is without beginning nor end is the nature of language which is indestructible. It manifests itself into *artha* (object/meaning). From it, the word is produced.

This is the most important verse in understanding Bhartṛhari's philosophy of language. According to it, the word or language is not simply a tool of communication that is made by any being. It is *nitya* (the given). Rather, it is a substratum that is without beginning and is indestructible. Thus it is also without end.

This is not the definition of ordinary languages (*bhāṣya*) about which we have known. It is rather the basis of all practical languages which have been used in different times and spaces. According to Bhartṛhari, there exists a substratum of all the sounds available to human beings.

Why does Bhartṛhari suppose this ultimate language as the basis of all particular languages?

Some insist that language is produced by the convention laid down between human beings. Thus, it is due to the convention of associating the word "book" with the object "book", established between members in a community, that they are able to understand the reference to the real object in the external world, once the word is heard. According to them, it is clear that there does not exist an innate and indivisible relationship which the word "book" has to refer to the object "book". The object of "book", hence, is denoted by the articulated sounds, *chaek* in Korean, *kitāb* in Urdu, and "book" in English. On the basis of the fact that the real object of "book" is referred to by different articulations in different times and places, they reach the conclusion that languages are only the accidental products created by the conventions of the members in a given community.

Moreover, it is commonly observed that when one teaches a word to children, one points one's finger to the object. Citing this practice as an example they insist language is produced by convention. By learning the convention that a heard word and an object are related to each other by the action of pointing a finger, it is made possible for children to acquire and use language.

According to Bhartṛhari, this theory of the language acquisition, however, is no more than a false viewpoint that lacks deeper observation. The convention itself is not possible without a premise of language. For example, animals that do not possess language are not able to relate words and objects, even though they hear the word "book", and see the object "book" that is being pointed to by a finger. The understanding and premising of the relation of a word and the object to be denoted are not obtained only by the action of pointing a finger itself, but on the basis of the understanding between a speaker and a hearer of what the action of pointing means. The action itself, therefore, premises a meaning and a language. No one can establish the relationship of the language and the object (meaning) through convention. Therefore, it has to be presupposed that there exists the essential and permanent language to denote meanings.[1]

On the other hand, Bhartṛhari proves the existence of the ultimate language, which is eternal, as a basis of our particular languages such as Korean and Hindi, in another way. For instance, we use such words as "past" or "future" and have ideas of what they mean.

---

[1] *nitye 'nitye 'pi vāpy arthe puruṣeṇa kathañcana* |
saṁbandho 'kṛtasaṁbandhaiḥ śabdaiḥ kartuṁ na śakyatekhanda ||
— *Vākyapadīya* III.3.38 (Sampurnanand,1991 edn.)

Perception does not perceive the object in the past and the future. The object in the past does not exist for the perceiver, because it has passed away, and the one in the future does not exist yet because it has not come into being.

But verbal cognition (*śābdabodha*) is quite different from perception. In verbal cognition, one has cognition of the past, whenever one hears of it even though its object has disappeared. This is why Bhartṛhari asserts that language roots secondary being in the mind which is different from primary being located in the outside world. Secondary being is like something from which meanings come. It is the basis of meanings, or, rather, a unity of meanings. Primarily, a word denotes an object in this secondary being and it is then correlated with a real object in the outside world, when a word is uttered. In verbal cognition, primary being is secondary and secondary being is compulsory. Without it, verbal cognition cannot be achieved. This is clearly shown by use of the example of the "rabbit's horn" for which there is no primary being corresponding to the word in the actual outside world.

According to Bhartṛhari, this secondary being is what mediates between the word and object in the outside world. Without it, the acts of pointing at an object and of speaking its word are useless as far as the relation between the two is concerned. Secondary being, therefore, is the universal, the *Brahman*, and the *Śabda-Brahman*. It is eternal, without beginning and end, and was not created by any being.

Bhartṛhari insists that this *Brahman* is the origin from which the world emanates. It is through *Brahman* that there exists the world which is various, differentiated and sequential, since the *Brahman* transforms itself in such ways. Moreover, the nature of the *Brahman* is precisely *śabda* and the inverse is also true that, the nature of *śabda* is precisely *Brahman*. And thus we arrive at the concept of *Śabda-Brahman*.

Bhartṛhari reaches the conclusion that the *Brahman*, *Śabda-Brahman*, and the world are the same through an ontological and epistemological analysis in the following manner.

He shows in the first verse of *Vākyapadīya* I, that the *Brahman* is the indestructible being which is without beginning and end. That which is without beginning implies that which is not produced, and therefore, it means that its destruction does not exist and it is without end. Only the thing which is with beginning, i.e. which is produced is destroyed and ceases to exist.

Brahman is the absolute. It is free from any relativity. It does not admit any limitation and restriction. Even the world should not be regarded as being relative with the *Brahman,* though it is seemed to be created by the *Brahman*. Otherwise, it causes the loss of the absoluteness of the *Brahman*. In fact, the *Brahman* does not create the world, but manifest itself into it, from which emerge its diversity, sequence and differentiation. Therefore, the *Brahman* is the cause of the world maintaining its absoluteness and non-distinction. It should be kept in mind that the *Brahman* and the world are said by Bhartr̥hari, to be different and not different from each other. The relation between the *Brahman* and the world is compared to the relation of the water and the waves formed upon it. The waves also, in the final analysis, belong to the ocean as do the waves and the two are indistinct, although they are perceived as being different from each other by virtue of being differently named.

All the diversities are, therefore, only our mental constructions by *avidyā,* i.e. *parikalpa* or *vikalpa.* They are not real, but illusions. However, they are a means to reach the *Brahman*. The relationship of the *Brahman* and the world is described in the second verse of the *Vākyapadīya* as follows:

> *ekam eva yad āmnātaṁ bhinnaṁ śaktivyapāśrayāt* |
> *apr̥thaktve 'pi śaktibhyaḥ pr̥thaktveneva vartate* ||2||

> Although the mentioned is the one, it is diversified depending upon its powers. Although it is not different from its powers, it appears to be different.

The Absolute reality, the *Brahman,* manifests itself into the world. Bhartr̥hari calls it *vivarta*. Essentially, *vivarta* is not different from *Brahman*. It only appears as being different from *Brahman*. As shown in the example of the water and its waves, the waves are not, in essence, different from the water on which they are formed, but they only appear as being different from it.

The *Vṛtti* says that *vivarta* (manifestation) has two aspects of *mūrti* (form) and *kriyā* (action). The *Brahman*, which is the non-segmental and all-pervasive one, emanates itself in multiplicity by the influence of the two powers of space and time. It is like the moon reflected on different surfaces of various objects such as a lake, a crystal, or on metal. The moon only appears as being different by seeming to have assumed the properties of the objects on the surface of which it is reflected, although in essence it is the same one.

Similarly, the *Brahman*, which is one, is modified into many, in the world by being reflected in space and time. Therefore, space and time, which are the powers of the *Brahman*, are the cause of differentiation, sequence and multiplicity. And they are the source of the perception of difference.

Mūrti-vivarta is realized by space and *kriyā-vivarta* is realized by time. According to *Kārikā*, the six *vikāra*s (modifications) of *jāyate* (birth), *asti* (existence), *viparivartate* (change), *vardhate* (growth), *apakṣiyate* (decay) and *vinaśyati* (destruction) are caused by the power of time which is the most important of the powers of *Brahman*.[2]

Bhartṛhari argues that the world manifested from the *Brahman* is of the nature of the *śabda* and the *Brahman*, hence, it is the *Śabda-Brahman*, by virtue of the relation established between the *Brahman* and the world along with analysis of the cognition of the world.

The first verse of the *Vākyapadīya*, as quoted above, states that the *Brahman* manifests into *artha*. Here, *artha* has dual meaning of object and of meaning. As was mentioned earlier, the *Brahman* manifests into the object, and the object and it, are not different from each other. Now, Bhartṛhari asserts that *Brahman* manifests itself into the meaning too. The meaning is secondary being and is not different from the universal. Secondary being, which is the basis of the conventions and the foundation of language usage, is the transformation of the *Brahman*.

---

2 *adhyāhitakalāṁ yasya kālaśaktim upāśritāḥ* |
janmādayo vikārāḥ ṣaḍ bhāvabhedasya yonayaḥ | |
— *Vākyapadīya* I.3 (Sampurnanand,1988 edn.)

As it was mentioned above, the world appears as *mūrti-vivarta* and *kriyā-vivarta*. These are the two aspects of the world, i.e. form and action. In these two aspects, in the purview of language, the difference in form is represented by names or nouns, and that of time (of the action) through verbs. In other words, it is through these linguistic elements that one understands and expresses the world.

Thus cognition is intertwined with language. No cognition is obtained without the intervention of language. According to Bhartṛhari, even the cognition of a newborn baby and the cognition in a dream are equally impossible without language and the possibility of indeterminate cognition (*avikalpa jñāna*) is completely rejected.

For Bhartṛhari, if it is knowledge at all, it has to be intertwined with a word, not, of course, the specific name of the object but a very general word such as the pronoun.[3] Also, Bhartṛhari asserts the identity of language and consciousness, or awareness from the way in which *Vākyapadīya* I.118 [126] is worded.[4]

Consciousness in all beings never goes beyond language, it is never different from the fact of having the form of language. Therefore, when Bhartṛhari says that *Brahman* is *śabda-tattva*, the word-principle, he implies that it is consciousness.

According to Bhartṛhari, therefore, the world comes from the *Brahman*. Such world is cognized only through language. This shows that the world is of the nature of language. He, thus, arrives at the conclusion that the cause of the world, the *Brahman* is also of the nature of language and *Śabda-Brahman*. The *Śabda-Brahman* is the supreme reality which is devoid of any diversity, differentiation, and

---

3 K.A. Subramania Iyer, *Bhartṛhari*: Poona: Deccan College 1969, p. 103.

4 *saiṣā saṁsāriṇāṁ saṁjñā bahir antaś ca vartate* |
tanmātrām avyatikrāntaṁ caitanyaṁ sarvajātiṣu ||
— *VP* I.118 [126] (Sampurnanand,1988 edn.)

(The consciousness of all beings going through transmigration is in the nature of the word. It exists within and without. The consciousness of all types of beings does not go beyond this essence.)

sequence, though it is the cause and source of all diversities. Bhartṛhari calls this level as *paśyantī* of three stages of *vāk*.[5]

In this context, Bhartṛhari classifies language into three stages from the essential nature of language, which is free from all differences and equal with the *Śabda-Brahman* itself, to actual audible languages.

The most external of all the stages — the *vaikharī* — is described first. In this stage, it is uttered by the speaker and heard by the hearer. It is, therefore, closely associated with the organs of articulation. It is also associated with *prāṇa* which is what strikes against the organs of articulation at the time of utterance and brings about temporal sequence. As the *Vṛtti* describes it, *vaikharī* is not merely the name of the fully externalized form of human speech. Such sounds as that of the axle of a cart, of a drum, of a flute and of a lute (*bīṇa*) are also included in it according to Vṛsabha. In this way, the *vaikharī* is said to have infinite varieties. Its chief characteristic is that it has fully developed temporal sequence. Going inwards, the next stage is called *madhyamā*. Its association is chiefly with the mind, *buddhi* (the intellect), not with the organs of articulation. It is the word as conceived by the mind before its actual utterance. As there is no actual utterance, there is no real temporal sequence in *madhyamā*. But it is not absolutely without it. It is there in a subtle form. As it is *prāṇa* which brings about fully developed sequence in the *vaikharī* stage, where sequence is only in an incipient subtle form, the *prāṇa* also must be presumed to be functioning in a subtle form. *Prāṇa* is gross and physical when it strikes against the organs of articulation. When it does not do that, it may still be there in a subtle form. The description of the next and the innermost stage, the *paśyantī* is more detailed but also more obscure. It is also said to have infinite varieties (*aparimāṇa bheda*). It is also described as being of a lower and a higher kind and we are told that the higher kind (*paraṁ rūpam*) is beyond the range of verbal usage.[6]

5 *vaikharyā madhyamāyāś ca paśyantyāś caitad adbhutam* |
anekatīrthabhedāyās trayyā vācaḥ paraṁ param | |
— *VP*. I.142 (Sampurnanand,1988 edn.)

6 *prantu paśyantīrūpamanapabhraṁśamasaṁkīrṇaṁ lokavyavahārātītam* | —The *Vṛtti* of *VP* I, p. 216 and K.A. Subramania Iyer, *Bhartṛhari*, Poona, 1969, p. 144.

Vikalpa and Anyāpoha

Diṅnāga (CE 480–540) who was a founder of Buddhist's logic-linguistic philosophy was a contemporary of Bhartṛhari. He asserted views which are very contrary from Bhartṛhari's monism of *Śabda-Brahman*, although he was influenced by Bhartṛhari in many parts of the theories of language.

Diṅnāga established his own peculiar theory of language by analysing language on the basis of Buddha's teachings of impermanence and non-self which are the essence of Buddhism, while Bhartṛhari did it in a deductive way from the point of view of the absolute, the *Brahman*.

Buddhism considers everything as being of "dependent arising" (*pratītyasamutpāda*) from impermanence and non-self. Diṅnāga derives this theory of impermanence and non-self from epistemology and applies it to the theory of language.

According to him, everything in this world, arguing the Vedic viewpoint of the absolute self, or of the eternal and unchangeable nature and the like, is no more than being transient and constantly changing. They are the existences that are being destroyed every moment. Even one object "A" does not have the identity between "A" in the first moment and "A" in the second moment, since they are changing. Therefore, no one is able to put one's foot twice in the same river. Such a Buddhist's ontology of impermanence and non-self becomes the basis of a peculiar epistemology and theory of language in Buddhism.

In Buddhism, there are no subject and object which are permanent and thing as itself. The subject of cognition is also impermanent and changing. Therefore, it is to be answered how cognition between the two is obtained.

Diṅnāga says as follows in the second verse of the first chapter of his own work *Pramāṇasamuccaya*:

> The means of cognition are [immediate and mediate, namely,] perception (*pratyakṣa*) and inference (*anumāna*).

The object to be cognized has [only] two aspects.[7]

According to this verse, there are only two kinds of valid cognition which we have. The reason is that there are only two aspects in the object which one cognizes. The one is "unique particular (*svalakṣaṇa*)" which is peculiar in object. It exists in the outside world and is not expressed by language as it is constantly changing. It is cognized only by perception. Therefore, the object expressed by any language after perceiving it is not the real object as it was, because the unique particular of an object obtained by perception is never described by language.

The object expressed by language is universal/general property (*sāmānya lakṣaṇa*) which Diṅnāga mentions as the second object of cognition. According to him, this universal is in essence not the permanent and the absolute. It is not real in the outside world. It is the conceptual construction of our minds. It is, hence, illusionary and unreal. It does not belong to an object but is the creation of mind depending on the perception of the object. Its nature is the differentiation of the other and is combined with language. Therefore, it is expressed through language.

Diṅnāga asserts that the "unique particular" does not have any power to differentiate between this and that at all. Therefore, the differentiation between this particular and that particular is possible not by perception but by conceptual constructions which are produced after perceiving them.

From this point of view, the only one reality which an object possesses is precisely "unique particular". Diṅnāga's theory originates in an observation of the world in a thoroughly inductive way. He completely ignores the unseen being — the *Brahman*, the universal, and the like which may hide behind phenomenon. Hence, for him,

---

7 mṅon sum daṅ ni rjes su dpag
tshad ma dag ni
gñis kho na ste, gaṅ gi phyir. (k.2 a-b1)
mtshan ñid *gñis
gṣalbya. (k.2 b2-c1)

only unique particulars are real and constantly changing, and furthermore, there is no any commonness in them. Seeing them as being common is no more than the function of a concept, a mental product of human being, and the illusory creation of *anyāpoha*. It is the ground on which language stands.

In this context, it has to be answered how a word is able to denote whole objects which are subsumed under the same class of it. Here, a traditional answer available is that the basis of language usage is but the universal, the general property, and concept.

However, Diṅnāga completely rejects all bases of language which had been traditionally accepted in Vedic schools, i.e. that of the universal and the general property which were regarded as homogeneous with the *Brahman* in its permanence.

The verses in *Pramāṇasamuccaya* refute their validity and offer instead the concept of *anyāpoha* which is no more than a kind of mental function or construct.

Everything is changing and impermanent, as are the conceptual construction, the conceptual mind, which are derived from it. They too are impermanent. There is no space for the permanent and eternal in mental construction. Therefore, Diṅnāga has to explain the question of how the word always denotes the object or the meaning, without supposing of the permanent and eternal such as the universal. That is to say, how is a constant relation between the word and the meaning (the object) possible? In addition to this, as it was mentioned earlier, there remains another question to be answered by him as to how whole objects under the same class are denoted by a word.

Diṅnāga's reply lies in the concept of the *anyāpoha*. He asserts that verbal cognition, *anyāpoha* is the same as inference in the process of obtaining cognition. That is why he classifies verbal cognition under the inference.

For example, hearing a word causes the understanding of the meaning which the word denotes, as one validly infers a fire in the mountain by seeing "a smoke" which is the inferential mark. Therefore, here, the word is the same with the inferential mark of inference. In this context, it is natural to question how the word calls the meaning, the referent, i.e. how the concomitant relation between the word and the referent is established.

Regarding it, Diṅnāga discusses in *PSV V* (*Pramāṇasamuccaya Vṛtti*, chapter 5): 50b towards the very end of the chapter, how the connection between the word *panasa*, breadfruit tree, and a prototypical instance of a breadfruit tree is taught. This paragraph addresses the process of *vyutpatti*: teaching the denotation of a word by ostentation (*hastasaṁjñā*). Diṅnāga's description of *vyutpatti* assumes that someone points to a prototypical example of a breadfruit tree, and explains "this is a breadfruit tree" (*ayaḥ panasa*). Thereby the learner understands the connection between the term *panasa* and the thing it denotes. Diṅnāga puts weight on the deitic function of the demonstrative pronoun "this" (*ayaḥ*) which accompanies the ostentation because the syntactical agreement between the pronoun and the term *panasa*, the name of the object, secures the grammatical validity of the reference. In *PSV V*: 50c Diṅnāga continues explaining that the connection (*sambandha*) between the word and its referent is mentally constructed at the thought "this is the word for that thing". *Vyutpatti* thus implicates two separate moments: first, the moment of learning how a term is used by observing its application to its referent, and second, the subsequent moment of constructing the connection in the mind (*manas*). Diṅnāga closes the paragraph by pointing out that the connection between any word and the thing it denotes is similar to the connection between inference and inferred (*anumānānumeyasambandha*).

The person who is learning the denotation of a name like the word *panasa* or any other term through *vyutpatti* must ascertain that it refers to all instances of the breadfruit tree and not only to the prototype.[8] However, it is impossible to justify the invariable connection of the term *panasa* and its referent, the breadfruit tree, by showing how it applies to every single instance as instances are infinite.

---

8 Ole Holte Pind, "Dignāga's Philosophy of Language: Dignāga on Anyāpoha", PhD dissertation, University of Wine, 2009, pp. 48-50.

Concerning this matter, Diṅnāga approaches in a very scientific way, three valid characteristics of the inferential marks: a property of the subject of the inference (*anumeya-sadbhāvaḥ*), observation (*darśana*) in what is similar (*tat-tulya-eva-sadbhāvaḥ*), and non-observation (*adṛṣṭi*) in what is dissimilar (*astināstitā eva*). The relation of the word and the referent to be denoted is established in case of non-observation of the application of another word to that referent.

Stating its non-application to what is dissimilar is possible, even though it is infinite (*atulye saty apy ānantye*), through mere non-observation (*adarśanamātreṇa*); and just therefore (*ata eva ca*) it has been explained that [the word's] denoting its own referent (*svārthābhdhānam*) is an inference from [its own referent's] exclusion from these [other referents] (*tadvyavacchedānumānam*), from its not being observed [to apply] to other [referents] than its own relata (*svasambandhibhyo 'nyatrādarśanāt*).

Diṅnāga's presentation shows that the feasibility of the connection (*sambandhasaukaryam*) depends on the fact that the word is observed to apply to an instance of its referent and not observed to apply to the referents of other words. It is noteworthy that Diṅnāga's use of non-observation does not address non-observation of things that have been temporarily removed from their expected place, but rather the universal non-existence in time and space of other things in the locus of the thing to which the indicator refers. The absence of other referents is substantial: no non-tree (*avṛkṣa*) is ever observed where a tree (*vṛkṣa*) is found.

An inferential rule has to be established which makes it possible to infer that the word "tree" denotes the referent tree irrespective of its individual character. Whatever is dissimilar to the prototypical object is characterized by a single property (*ekadharman*) which is its being non-x.

Therefore, for Diṅnāga, verbal cognition inevitably is the inference. Diṅnāga equates verbal cognition to inference by means of joint absence (*vyatirekamukha*), which explains why commentators compare *apoha* to *vyatireka* and unanimously refer to Diṅnāga's *apoha* theory as "having joint absence as the chief thing" (*vyatirekapradhāna*).

Classical Indian scholars interpret *vyatireka* as characterized by non-existence (*abhāva lakṣaṇa*) and Diṅnāga assumes that joint absence of word (*śabda*) and referent (*artha*) is equivalent to mutual non-existence of any speech unit and non-speech unit, and any referent and non-referent, which is implied by his claim that existence of the nature of one thing presupposes the non-existence of the nature of other things.

For Diṅnāga, therefore, it is not inherent real general properties in things or words that are the causes of application of words and identity of words, but rather non-existence or preclusion of other, whether things or words. Thus Diṅnāga attributes the properties of real general properties to exclusion of other referents.

Conclusion

This presentation has investigated the metaphysical backgrounds of the theories of language maintained by two great Indian philosophers of language — Bhartṛhari and Diṅnāga.

Their theories of language were amazingly developed in highly profound forms. As we can see in their theories, the study of language is not confined only to the phenomenon of language usage. It is a science of demanding the Copernican conversion of mankind by a study of epistemology, ontology and the philosophy of grammar, and moreover, of the awakening, the ultimate, the *Brahman* and the *Śabda-Brahman*.

The recent trend of unifying various sciences seems to be a reflex action against the sciences having bound and shackled humanity through categorization, even though they were divided and differentiated for helping the increase of mankind's happiness.

The ancient Indian scholars and sages are seen to have already known and have by themselves realized how all kinds of sciences could contribute to the freedom and awakening of human beings, even in a speculative and sophistic thoughts arising from highly subdivided and deepened studies of each sciences.

References

Bhartṛhari, *Vākyapadīyam Part I (Brahma-Kāṇḍam)*, with the Commentary Svopajñavṛtti by Harivṛṣabha and Ambākartri by Pt. Raghunātha Śarmā, Sampurnanand Sanskrit University, 1988.

———, *Vākyapadīyam Part II (Vākyakāṇḍam)*, with the Commentary of Puṇyarāja and Ambākartri by Pt. Raghunātha Śarmā, Sampurnanand Sanskrit University, 1980.

———, *Vākyapadīyam Part III (Pada-Kāṇḍam) (Jāti, Dravya and Sambandha Samuddeśa)*, with the Commentary of Prakāśa by Śrī Helārāja and Ambākartri by Pt. Raghunātha Śarmā, Sampurnanand Sanskrit University, 1991.

———, *Vākyapadīyam Part III, vol. II (Bhūyodravya-Guṇa-Dik-Sādhana-Kriyā-Puruṣa-Saṁkhyā and Liṅga Samuddeśa)*, with the Commentary Prakāśa by Śrī Helārāja and Ambākartri by Pt. Raghunātha Śarmā, Sampurnanand Sanskrit University, 1997.

———, *Vākyapadīyam Part III (Padakāṇḍa) (Vṛttisamuddeśa)*, with the Commentary Prakāśa by Śrī Helārāja and Ambākartri by Pt. Raghunātha Śarmā, Sampurnanand Sanskrit University, 2000.

Diṅnāga, *Pramāṇasamuccayavṛtti*, translated into Tibetan by Vasudhararakṣita and Seng rgyal, Text 5701 in *Tibetan Tripiṭaka*: Peking Edition, kept in the library of the Otani University, ed. by Daisetz T. Suzuki, Tokyo and Kyoto: Tibetan Tripitaka Research Institute, 1957.

———, *Pramāṇasamuccayavṛtti*, translated into Tibetan by Gser gyi go cha and Dad pa shes rab, Text 5702 in Tibetan *Tripiṭaka*: Peking Edition, kept in the library of the Otani University, ed. Daisetz T. Suzuki, Tokyo and Kyoto: Tibetan Tripitaka Research Institute, 1957.

———, *Pramāṇasamuccayavṛtti*, translated into Tibetan by Vasudhararakṣita and Seng rgyal, V.1490: Sde dge Bstan 'gyur Series, V.174-193, Delhi Karmapae Chodhey, Gyalwae Sungrab Partun Khang, Delhi, 1986.

Hattori, Masaaki (ed. & tr.), *Dignāga, On Perception: Being the Pratyaksapariccheda of Dignāga's Pramanasamuccaya*, Harvard University Press, 1968.

Hayes, R.P. (ed. & tr.), *Dignāga on the Interpretation of Signs*, Dordrecht and Boston: Kluwer Academic Publishers, 1988.

Iyer, K.A. Subramania, *Bhartṛhari*, Poona: Deccan College 1969.

Pind, Ole Holten, "Dignāga's Philosophy of Language: Dignāga on anyāpoha: Pramāṇasamuccaya V Texts, Translation, and Annotation", PhD dissertation, University of Wine, 2009.

15

Aesthetic Experience in Jeong Ji Yong's Poetry

Ravikesh

Introduction

COMMUNITIES of different cultural backgrounds have marked aesthetics which defines beauty in terms of their cultural influence on the viewer or the reader. What constitutes beauty is different from one culture to another, which produces difference in the aesthetics of communities. Aesthetics identifies the effect of art, its enjoyment and seeks to elucidate or account for the ground of this enjoyment. The emotion, which is evoked by enjoyment, softens the harsher instincts of human beings. In Indian aesthetics this emotion is compassion (*karuṇa*), the selflessness of the human heart. And this selflessness is beauty — human goodness, not necessarily ethical rightness, but a goodness of feeling and instincts, the inherent possession of the universal being.

The Korean world-view, influenced also by Buddhist philosophy, is very close to the Indian world-view at the philosophical level. Korean aesthetics forms a part of what may be termed as Asian aesthetics. This is evident in iconography, the Buddhist iconography in which the state of being can be understood by Buddha's image which appears placid and calm, meditative and deeply aggrieved if viewed from three different angles. The tranquillity is viewed and felt differently with change in the perspective. In Korea, the static mountains with moving water provide perfect state of bliss especially to the Buddhist monks who used to leave city life and meditate deep in the mountains.

In Buddhistic figural sculpture, the body, arms and particularly the face, are full and gracefully modelled, and unbroken lines run from the head to the tip of the toes. The drapery folds are depicted in animated realism, and the sensitive, human approach is immaculately perfected by technical excellence with an overall effect and pattern, definitely Korean. This idealistic naturalism has been the basic undercurrent in Korean art throughout the ages (Kim 1996: 4).

Like other oriental civilizations, living in harmony with nature has been a basic Korean trait and, therefore, the Koreans have always been in harmony with the nature. Traditional Korean aesthetics reflected in its literature has greatly adhered to this principle. It is influenced by its geographical environment along with religious or spiritual sentiments and signifies a harmony between human beings and nature. Primarily there are two major themes of traditional Korean aesthetics that are reflected in poetry: "love of peace" which is based in the religious belief and is also based on five moral standards as — loyalty to the king, filial piety, seniority, friendship and chastity and the "love of nature" which is about kinship with the various elements and attributes of the nature (Zŏng 1983). Yanagi Muneyoshi, a noted art critic, observes in his book *Korea and Her Art* (1922) that the beauty (in Korea) is not made by man, but endowed by nature. It is born as a result of Korean artists' complete trust in nature of their freedom from a worldly ambition for human perfection.

In this background, this paper attempts to analyse some of the representative poems of Jeong Ji Yong, as one of the significant literary figures in Korean literature, in Indian framework. In order to understand the Korean poetic sensibilities and aesthetic consciousness, this paper underlines the basic aesthetic values of India and Korea.

Indian Aesthetics

The word "aesthetics" does not have an exact parallel in the Indian tradition. The term *saundaryaśāstra*, used by some contemporary Indian thinkers to stand for something that is analogous to Western concepts and theories about art, comes closest to what one understands as "aesthetics" in the Western context. However, one does not come across this term in either philosophical or non-philosophical context in classical Indian literature. There is no particular branch of Indian philosophy which has developed under this nomenclature. Nevertheless, whatever is brought as a subject of study under this name of "Saundaryaśāstra" has been discussed under different names such as *rasa* the "Kāvyaśāstra", "Alaṁkāraśāstra" and others. This proves that the concept of *rasa*, which is considered to be at the base root of aesthetics, is embedded in the most ancient literatures of India. These literatures, as ancient as the Vedic texts, are the ones which compare the highest spiritual bliss with aesthetic enjoyment.

Before taking up the case of *rasa* theory in further detail, it is important to pose the question whether a philosophical approach to art has a special identity of its own in different parts of the world. Is it proper to talk about Western, Indian or Chinese aesthetics and approach them differently? One thing that can be said with surety is that every culture has its own traditions and cultural determinants, which can be called the contributing factors of art practices. Every culture possesses a certain world-view which is common to its members and, in most cases, is quite distinct from other cultures. Therefore, Indian (as well as Korean) art and aesthetics have a unique identity of their own, determined by their long cultural and intellectual traditions and world-view. These can be seen as a distinct entity from Western aesthetics on these very grounds.

In the Western tradition, as Kapil Kapoor (1998) encapsulates that the carpenter is the paradigm artist. The artist is seen as a "maker" who can segment, measure and quantify reality. In the Indian tradition, the potter is the paradigm artist who is not a maker but a "manifestor". The artist manifests and gives *rūpa* (form) to *dravya* (substance). In Indian world-view, reality is continuous, simultaneous and non-segmental. In accordance with this world-view, beauty is also seen as a quality. Western philosophers have always considered beauty as a question of right proportion and quantity. He further explains that experience shapes us and art, as surrogate experience, shapes us more effectively by virtue of its aesthetic mode, its appeal of "beauty". But what is "beauty"? Aesthetics is the science of the beautiful. As such, it is the science of perceptible forms and accounts for nature, source, purpose and creative process of art (*kalā*), its central concern being the nature and source of art experience. Different meanings of the word *kalā* are available in some other texts. In the Śaiva literature, *kalā* has been associated with that element which limits the prefecture of *ātman*. The reason for this is again the connection between *kalā* and *kāma* and so long the self is not free from the desire for sensuous pleasure, it cannot reach the level of perfection it is capable of realizing.

Some further implications of the concept of beauty and the concept of art can be made clear in the following manner. The supreme beauty according to the Upaniṣadic way of thinking can be traced only in the aesthetic state of the realization of the harmony between *ātman* and *Brahman,* a perfect state of *rasa* or a detached state of delight and enjoyment (*ānanda*). However, the representation of such a harmonious relation in the gross natural objects has been called *lavan* or *susama.* Art has been considered as a limiting element of the perfection of the reality on the one hand, and a technique of upgrading the matter by bringing it in close unity with mental concepts on the other hand. Art is, thus, viewed as a medium for establishing reconciliation between mind and matter in this way.

Korean Aesthetics

Korea's natural environment (three sides surrounded by sea and 70 per cent of the land is covered by the mountains) has nurtured the aesthetic and intellectual minds of its people. It has nurtured the Korean consciousness as a homogeneous ethnic group throughout its history. However, its strategic geographical location has also caused the Koreans pain with numerous foreign attacks. In the passage of time, the Koreans, however, have learnt the art of responding and resisting the external invasion. There are times when they were finding it hard to preserve their identity, ethnicity, homogeneity and freedom with a lot of resistance with the neighbouring countries, particularly China and Japan. Thus, the history of Korea is full of struggles to preserve and save the country from the colonial hands. There have been influences of West that are more evident in modern times. Korean literature mirrors these changes in the course of its own development.

The Korean literati tried various techniques to convey their mind, directly or indirectly. The writers and poets looked for a distinct style and modes for thought and expression.

Korean aesthetic consciousness has sound foundations of the philosophy of Confucianism, Buddhism, Daoism and the folk belief. Korean people believed that all creatures are divided into *yin* and *yang* and this belief became the bases of time and space world (Yang et al. 2003: 2). Korean aesthetic concepts are believed to be predominantly influenced by China owing to its own historicity and cultural and geographical proximity. As "there was no clear position concerning the subjectivity of Korean art, Korean art theory has been considered poor in substance, and even more so when compared with China" (Kim 2002: 187). However, the extent/scale and validity of this is contested by many Korean scholars. Kim Jae Sook believes that though aesthetic concepts were borrowed from China, a uniquely Korean aesthetic sense was well established within the Korean aesthetic sensitivity prior to the adoption of formalized theories. He further says that though these theories are influenced by the Chinese sources, they were articulated from Koreans' point of view.

> Korean theories of art were not simply imitations of their Chinese counterparts, but developed with a specifically Korean aesthetic subjectivity, centred on Koreans. Korean aesthetics was broadly established within the universality of the East Asian aesthetic system. — Kim 2002: 187

In order to understand the Korean aesthetic sensibilities, it is imperative to understand the concepts of "Han", which binds all Koreans together with a feeling (*jeong*).

"Feeling" and the "Jeong"

Traditionally Koreans enjoy song, dance and drink. They are believed to be having "Jeong" in abundance in their heart. There are numerous examples of "Jeong" manifested in various modes and forms in the daily life of a Korean. Yi Gwang Su is regarded as one of the first modernist poets whose literary composition and contribution is widely recognized in Korea and abroad. He strongly believes in the importance of "feeling" (*jeong*) rather than only knowledge or morality in a literary composition. He defines literature as "those who write books which stimulate feeling of beauty and pleasure in people", he further adds "literature has the objective of satisfying feeling". He describes feeling as "an independent mental effect and not a slave to cognition and ill." Therefore literature too, being based in feeling, is an independent phenomenon, not a slave to politics, morality or science, but equal to them and even closer relation with us (Yi 1979: 509).

In Korean literary works, there is a fusion of feelings with the natural scenes whose beauty often influences the poetic sensibility. A certain kind of feeling is evoked with visual images. As a dominant theme of Korean literature, the nature's image has influenced the Korean *maaum* (mind and heart). This can be said to be influenced by the Chinese theory of "fusion of feeling and scene" (*ch'ing-ching chiao-yung lun*) of Wang Fu-chih (1619-92) (Shin 2002). This theory shows the facet of selflessness derived from the mental state that the self and things merge with each other to become one. In spite of the difference that one of them rests in mind and the other lies in things, the feeling and the scene do engender each other. Whether the feeling is joy or sorrow, and whether the scene thrives or withers, they are reserved for each other in their confidential house. Here, the feeling is something inside the mind, as it was, something emotional and subjective; the "scene" is something outside, that is, objects or things — chiefly referring to nature. In this sense, as Shin explains, the feeling and the scene can be replaced with the self and things, or humans and nature. Likewise, the idea of "fusion of feeling and scene" can be replaced with that of "unity of things and the self" or "things and the self become one" (Shin 2002).

The interconnectedness of the "empty mind" and the "minimum in ordinary life" is most explicit in the literary theories around "freedom in peace" or "detachment" (*han*). Yi Sang-jong (1711–1811) opines that poems are based on nature and feeling, and if uttered, they become chants and songs. After one cuts off the reeking of the blood of worldly life, poems become lofty. On the contrary, if one respects the gaudy and luxurious, poems become unworthy, and if one respects the arrogant and unrestrained, the reckless and dissipated, all of these are not sufficient to be called poems (Yi 1987).

AESTHETICS OF "HAN"

Karuṇa Rasa and Han

Korean poetry mostly evokes the sentiment of *han* in the reader's mind. *Han* can be characterized as an aesthetic — a cultural root of expressed beauty and meaning in visual arts, dance and music; or similarly, as a sentiment — an ideology, emotion and feeling — that can also be represented in or a motivation for the arts. Certain Korean philosophers and theologians describe *han* as "totalistic", "harmonious", "non-dualistic" and "non-orientable" — as derived from the topological Moebius strip theory (Kim and Ro 1984). Minjung's *Essence Korean–English Dictionary* defines the meaning of *han* as one, the same, the whole, the peak, or the middle. The dictionary contrasts that definition with another type of *han* which is "a grudge; resentment; a bitter feeling; spite; hatred; a mixed feeling of sorrow and regret (unique to Korean) and an unsatisfied desire" (*Minjung sorim* 1997: 2418).

Other scholars are more apt to defend the study of *han*, noting that it served as a motivating factor in the *Minjung* social movements and other economic or political activities (Ablemann 1996). When used in this sense Abelmann states:

> *han* refers obliquely and variously to anger and resentment that build over time and under the weight of hardship . . . (It) connotes both the collective and the individual genealogical senses.

Suh Ji-moon, who compiled and translated a collection of Korean short stories, came to the realization that literature displays the full and true record of the nation's life (Suh 1998). She states:

> Koreans having suffered many abuses at the hands of fate and the social structure, the dominant mood of their verse literature (is) regret and longing . . . naturally reflecting the

> circumstances of the nation, much of the literary output of Korea in colonial times dealt with the suffering and sorrows of the Korean people, and comprises a chronicle of the nation's survival.
> — Suh 1998: xi

A close study of the character and nature of *han* indicates the commonality that it shares with concepts of the Indian *rasa* theory in general and *karuṇa rasa* in particular.

Jeong Ji Yong's Poetry

Jeong Ji Yong (1903–?), a poet of the early twentieth century, is a lyricist whose themes are predominantly the sea, the mountains and the village life (different facets of nature). He is one of the significant literary figures of the modern Korean poetry. He was one of the members of Shimunhakpha (The Poetry School). Most of the members belonging to this school were those literati who founded the journal *Shimunhak* (new poetry) with an aim to promote pure poetry. Jeong Ji Yong entered the literary world during 1930s when the Korean society was passing through a very critical and crucial phase as Japanese militarism was getting strengthened and new ideologies were imposed.

Reading of Jeong Ji Yong's poem is an enriching aesthetic experience in the true sense of the term. The knowledge of *rasa* helps a *sahṛdaya* (an empathetic reader) to fully realize how an understanding of Jeong Ji Yong's message comes forth only in moments of one's enjoyment of the poems. Such a statement has rich and very complex implications. In terms of *rasa,* the literary meaning is imminent in the aesthetic experience of the spectator/reader (Kapoor 1998).

Indian literary theorists, like Korean literati, strongly believe that no poetic meaning is possible without sentiments (*rasa*s). Korean scholars also regard "feeling" to be a major constituent of poetic sensibilities as discussed in the previous sections of this chapter. To understand how various shades of human "feeling" evokes aesthetic beauty in Jeong Ji Yong's poetry, there is a need to evaluate and examine the course of aesthetic experience in the framework of cross-cultural studies.

A closer look at the *rasa* theory helps to understand the effect of literature and other artistic forms on the spectator/reader. The object of art is knowledge. But this knowledge is imported through experience — the aesthetic experience of *rasa*. Therefore, in Indian theory as well as Korean aesthetic tradition, it is emotion and not reason (or in most of the Western theories except Aristotle) which is the chief component of art. Since the beginning of literary theories, there has been arguments as to where lay the meaning of a literary composition — in the author's mind, the life that the text imitates, the linguistic features of the text or in the reader? The *rasa* theory dilutes all speculations and claims that meaning has to be seen in the psychodynamics of the spectator/reader of poem. The artistic endeavour does not leave him/her indifferent. S/he is moved and s/he shows some instinctive responses. The beauty of art, thus, communicated through language would stir her/his emotions, and render her/his to infer the meaning of the text in her/his way of invoking *rasa*s. Jeong Ji Yong's poetry is abounding in a variety of emotional states, which are presented through a range of expressions. It is interesting how a better understanding of his aesthetic viewpoint becomes possible through a reading of his works in the light of the *rasa* theory. This reinforces the tie between Indian and Korean lines of thought and thus, in the process, shows the close connection that the artist of the east shares with his readers and listeners.

Jeong Ji Yong's poems evoke various *rasa*s. While reading Jeong Ji Yong's poems, a *sahṛdaya* reader would experience varied aesthetic delights like *śānta rasa*, *karuṇa* (pathetic) *rasa*, *bībhatsa* (odious) *rasa* and *bhayānaka* (terrible) *rasa* in her/his true understanding of the poetic piece. We will examine two dominant *rasa*s, i.e. *śānta rasa* and *karuṇa rasa* in the poetry of Jeong Ji Yong and their effect on the reader.

ŚĀNTA RASA

In Indian tradition, one of the important qualities of aesthetic experience is stressed in the concept of *śānta rasa*. *Śānta* connotes tranquillity, repose and serenity. The Central Tradition upholds this *rasa* and even declares that *śānta* is the great basic *rasa* (*mahārasa*). All feelings in aesthetic experience merge out of the icinta and are in the end submerged in it (*Nāṭyaśāstra*, pp. 334-35).

As Jeong Ji Yong's poems are mostly focused on nature and its various manifestations, the reader gets the aesthetic experience of *śānta rasa* (the blissful state). As discussed in the earlier section, this state of being can be understood by Buddha's image, which appears placid and calm, meditative and deeply aggrieved if viewed from three different angles. The tranquillity is viewed and felt differently with change in the perspective. In Korea, the static mountains with moving water provide perfect state of bliss especially to the Buddhist monks who used to leave city life and meditate deep in the mountains. Reading Jeong Ji Yong's poem provides the reader with a similar tranquil and meditative imagery.

In Jeong Ji Yong's poem, the poet expresses his loneliness in nature and he tries to find a solution from nature. He fondly remembers his hometown which is located in the lap of nature. In "Hometown", the poet expresses his loneliness through a place which is not the home where he wanted to live. In the state of utter helplessness, he tries to console himself. The word "Hometown" (*kohyang*) holds a significant meaning for a Korean. Irrespective of huge economic development that the peninsula has witnessed in modern times which has caused the Korean people to move into new places of living (in cities), their hearts still beat for their native place where "Wild pheasants brood eggs/And cuckoos call in season". "Hometown" does not simply represent a physical embodiment, but, is rather an extension of the inner self which instigates a person to feel in a certain way, i.e. innate desire. The onomatopoetic word *kohyang* is present twice in the first line to stress the poet's utmost desire and tireless love for his hometown. He comes back home, a place which he wished to come back to for a long time, but to his disappointment he finds it not the same as he dreamt of. The first line suggests returning to the hometown at "present" (tense) with a desire to fulfil the long cherished "past" mentioned in the second line. In the third line the poet goes down the memory lane and recalls the pheasants brooding eggs and the cuckoos who call in season. The "phesant" and "cuckoo" are sourccs of inspiration as the memory of the "brooding pheasant" invokes in him a feeling of compassion, carefulness and a sense of being protected while the sweet voice of the cuckoo creates a harmonizing effect on his psyche. The poet comes back to the "present" state in the third stanza and even then his inner self is not satisfied.

Jeong Ji Yong expresses his deep inclination towards nature where sea and mountain are the dominant images and constitute the core of his poetic sensibility. In his poetry these two images complement each other thematically as well as aesthetically. Most of his poems have sea and mountain settings, some of them have the setting of night as well. He discovers his poetic voice in the solitude of night. Two-third of the poems of his third period (1936-42) is related to the mountain. In the words of Kim Gi-Rim, who himself is regarded as the father of modern Korean literature, Jeong Ji Yong is considered as a master of metaphor. The stylistic features of his metaphors blend naturally with the suggestion and description of landscapes. For achieving the emotional effect, he relies mostly on visual descriptions and metaphorical formulations. To achieve the desired aesthetic effect on the mind of the reader, Jeong Ji Yong often employs figurative language like similes, metaphors and personification. Some of the examples are illustrated hereafter which evokes *sthāyibhāva* of *śānta rasa* in reader's mind.

(1) 전설 바다에 춤추는 밤물결 같은
검은 귀밑머리 날린 어린 누이와…. – (향수)

The place where little sister, dark ear locks
flying like nighi waves dancing in a fairy-tale sea . . .
— "Nostalgia"

(2) 보고 싶은 마음
호수만 하니
눈 감을 밖에 – (호수1)

But the longing heart,
Large as a lake —
can only shut the eyes.
— *"Lakel"*

In this poem, the poet suggests the limitations of human beings. The mood is tranquil and "shut the eyes" evoke *sthāyibhāva* of *śānta rasa*

(3) 물먹은 별이,반짝,보석처럼 백힌다
아아.늬는 산ㅅ새처럼 날러 갔구나! - ('유리창1')

Drenched stars, agleam, are set like jewels . . .
You've flown away like a wild bird.
— "Window-1"

Jeong Ji Yong uses onomatopoetic language to recreate a vivid landscape in words.

(1) 줄 다름질 처가쟈
바람은 휘잉.휘잉. - ('새 밝안 기관차')

Come on, scoot along!
Whee — Whee — the wind.
— "A bright red locomotive"

In these lines, the poet calls upon the reader to enjoy the serene natural environment.

(2) 달이 이리 창백한 밤엔
풍설을 잡아타고
화분 날리는 하늘로 둥둥 떠오르기도 하려니… - ('피리')

On a night like this,
the moon so wan,
Riding a balloon
And floating, floating
towards a pollen-strewn sky . . .
— "A Reed Flute"
(tr. Danial A. Kister)

"Moon" evokes *ālambana vibhāva* whereas "floating, floating" evoke *uddīpana vibhāva*. When one reads the poem, *sthāyibhāva* of *śānta rasa* is awakened in the reader's mind.

KARUṆA RASA

Jeong Ji Yong's poetry mostly evokes the sentiment of "han" in the reader's mind. To understand his poetic creations and the processes

of the *sthāyibhāva* of *karuṇa rasa* in the individual is awakened by the perception of *vibhāvas*, *anubhāvas*, *vyabhicāribhāvas* and *sāttvika-bhāvas*.

In "Breakfast" (1941) the poet says "I become a heartsick bird/ And peck grains of white rice". In "Grace" (1933), the poet is in the state of remorse as he says

Remorse, too-
A sacred grace. . . .
For whom do ardent sighs
pierce the heart?
In a stifled soul
again settles love's dew
Ah, to sink my bones
in remorse!
just to ache!'

In "Pierce the Heart", the pain evokes *sthāyibhāva* of *karuṇa rasa.* Similarly in "Café France" (1926), he expresses his sorrow over the pathetic condition of his motherland, which has been annexed by Japan. Though the poet never visited any foreign countries (except Japan where he studied), he used it as a symbol to bring about freshness and freedom.

나는 나라도 집도 없단다.
대리석 테이블에 닿는 내 뺨이 슬프구나!
오오, 이국종 강아지야
내 발을 빨어다오.
내 발을 빨어다오.

No country, no home —
Against the marble table
My cheeks, sad!
O-oh, foreign Puppy,
Lick my feet!
Lick my feet!

Similarly, in the poem "You Return" (1946), the poet commemorates Korean Independence from Japanese rule at the end of the Second World War.

At every still suddenly waiting village —
How should you tread flowers?
Make a path in tears through thorns!
— tr. Danial A. Kister

After reading these two poems, the question that arises is what happens to a *sahṛdaya* when s/he reads and meditates upon these lines? How does s/he get the intended meaning? Is she not really moved? According to Abhinavagupta, the reader would cease to remain his own self. Abhinavagupta claims that an empathetic reader would abstract the particularities associated with the emotion and universalize it to enjoy the aesthetic experience. The predominant emotion here is that of *karuṇa* (pathetic sentiment). The reader would raise his self to nobility and enjoy the felt sense of violence and chaos in one's society. There is a visible change and a transformation of his "being".

The *rasa* is evoked through the orderly configuration as enumerated by Bharata Muni. *Vibhāva* is the condition, the external condition that produces *bhāva*s. In this context, *vibhāva*s relate to the external data that has been perceived and which is meditated on by the reader. According to Abhinavagupta, *vibhāva* may have different manifestations, on the basis of *viṣaya* (subject), *āśraya* (substratum) and *uddīpana* (context which arouses dominant feeling or emotion). *Vibhāva* would lead to *bhāva* (the dominant state of mind). *Bhāva* conjured in the poetic lines is that of *śoka* (grief). While reading the poem, the reader will be spell-bound by the emotional experience of grief, which arises on account of chaotic events and the violence taking place within the scope of the poem. Once *bhāva* (*śoka*), which has been latent, is evoked by *vibhāva*s, its effects are clearly manifested in *sahṛdaya*'s physical reactions. These reactions or responses are called *anubhāva*s. *Bhāva* (*śoka*), here, arises due to the loss of human lives in colonized Korea, which has led to the loss of any feeling of happiness. *Anubhāva,* thus, evokes *vilāpa* (mourning).

*Bhāva*s are always accompanied by ancillary psychological states. In this case the ancillary psychological states of *cintā* (painful reaction), *āvega* (agitation, flurry), *trāsa* (great fear or alarm), *viṣāda* (despondency) and *dainya* (depression) are present. A disinterested or detached observer would not experience them. These psychological states are momentary and ephemeral, but they do exert a considerable influence on establishing *bhāvas*. A reader would undergo *cintā* when s/he may feel for the loss of an ideal or happy state in life. As would feel so involved in the crisis represented, and become concerned, would thus, be feeling *āvega*. The sorry state of affairs may drive her/him to *viṣāda* and *dainya*. All these determinants and consequences would together evoke *sthāyibhāva* of *karuṇa rasa*.

In another poem "A Train" (1932), the poet is in a state of grief. As if he is consoling his grandma, his inner self is in pain which expresses his longing for his hometown.

Grandma,
What's so sad that makes you cry?
Crying, crying, and headed for Kagoshima.

A handkerchief of tattered home spun
Drenched with tears.
No! though I lean this way and that,
Haunted by memories,
I never shall sleep.

I, too-my teeth ache
To seek my home town.
— tr. Danial A. Kister
할머니
무엇이 그리 슬어 우십나?
울며 울며
녹아도**鹿兒島**로 간다.

해여진 왜포 수건에
눈물이 함촉,
영! 눈에 어른거려
기대도 기대도
내 잠못들겠소.

내도 이가 아퍼서
고향 찾어 가오.

In "A Short Piece of Music" (1938), Jeong Ji Yong describes the life circle of water bird who

On a morning
When field birds fly in
and shed tears of sorrow.

Conclusion

The Korean world-view, influenced also by Buddhist philosophy, is very close to the Indian world-view at the philosophical level. As one of the representative poets of modern Korean poetic sensibility, Jeong Ji Yong reconciles and reconstitutes indigenous and "contemporary" streams of thought around the issues involving aesthetic theories and issues. At the heart of this discourse, nature in her various hues and forms, particularly in the Korean scenic set-up, serves as a rich source of imagery and symbolism. Nature in Korea is tranquil, meditative, self-contained and overarching principle of Korean life, philosophy and art.

Jeong Ji Yong's poetry underlines the basic principle of harmony between man and nature as microcosm and macrocosm. In his poems, nature serves as a medium through which the poet fondly remembers his beloved. Though he is alone, as soon as he identifies himself with nature, he starts enjoying its benevolent beauty. In his poem the self and the universal self exist face-to-face (like the image and counter-image in a mirror) and identities each other as one (*advaita*, non-dual).

Based on the literary qualities in his composition, Jeong Ji Yong seems to be a *kāvya kavi* who excels in craft language and aesthetic effect. He qualifies to be also called as *racanā kavi* as he excels in choice and arrangement of words. As his poems evoke different states of mind/*rasas*, he may be designated as a *rasa kavi*. His poetic excellence is reflected when he employs various figurative devices making him an *alaṁkāra kavi.* As already discussed, Jeong Ji Yong's inner self transcends from the narrow "self" towards the universal humanity and attains peace and *ānanda* (blissfulness) by unifying himself to *Brahman* (the Supreme self). His subconscious self reflects upon the fundamental belief of Korean culture in particular and Asian culture in general. There is also a need to further explore and study such Korean literary works in the Indian framework that will promote a better understanding between the two countries.

References

Abelmann, Nancy (1996), *Echoes of the Past, Epics of Dissent: A South Korean Social Movement*, Berkeley: University of California Press.

Abhinavabhabhāratī (GOS), *Naṭyaśāstra of Bharatamuni with the commentary Abhinavabhbhāratī of Abhinavagupta*, vol. II, 2nd edn., revised and critically edited by V.M. Kulkarni and T. Nandi, Gaekwad's Oriental Series, no. 68, Vadodara: Oriental Institute, 2001.

Alford, C. Fred, *Think No Evil: Korean Values in the Age of Globalization*, Ithaca and London: Cornell University Press, 1999.

Choe, Dong Ho, *Modern Korean Poetry and the Aesthetics of 'San-su (Landscape) Poetry*, The Korean Comparative Literature Association, vol. 28, 2002.

Churaumanie, Bissundyal, *Indian Aesthetics Can Add Flavor and Strength to Western Writing*, 2011 (http://www.suite101.com/worldliteratures)

Hwang, Jong-yon, "The Emergence of Aesthetic Ideology in Modern Korean Literary Criticism: An Essay on Yi Gwang-su in Korean Literature: Its Classical Heritage and Modern Breakthroughs", New Jersey, USA: Hollym International, 2003.

Kapoor, Kapil (in Collaboration with Nalini M. Ratnam), *Literary Theory: Indian Conceptual Framework*, Delhi: Affiliated East-West Press, 1998.

Kim, Jae Sook, "Reading Traditional Korean Artistic Sensibilities Through the Concept of Jin-gyeong", *Korea Journal*, **42**(4), Winter 2002.

Kim, Kwang-Myung, "Korean Aesthetic Consciousness and the Problem of Aesthetic Rationality" presented at State University of New York/Buffalo, Colloquium, Department of Philosophy, 22 October 1996.

Kim, Sang-il and Ro, Young-chan (eds.), *Hanism as Korean Mind: Interpretation of Han Philosophy*, Los Angeles: Eastern Academy of Human Sciences, 1984.

Kim, Heung-gyu, "*Joseon hugi yesul-ui hwan-gyeong-gwa sotong gujo* (The Environment and Communication-Exchange Structures Surrounding Late Joseon Art)", in *Hanguk sahoeron (Theories of*

Korean Society), ed. Jeong Chang-su, Seoul: Sahoe Bipyeongsa, 1995.

Kiyoharu, Aizawa, Yuichi Nakamura and Shin'ichi Satoh, *Categorizing Chinese Painting Images*, Advances in Multimedia Information Processing-PCM, Berlin, Heidelberg, New York: Springer 2004.

Michael, J. Seth, *A Concise History of Korea: From the Neolithic Period Through the Nineteenth Century*, Rowman & Littlefield Publishers, 2006.

Minjung's Essence Korean-English Dictionary, Seoul: Minjung sorim, 1997.

Munhak-iran hao in *Yi Gwang-su Jeonjip*, vol. 1, Sam jung Dang Co, 1996.

Peter, Hyun (1987), "5000 Years of Korean Art", *Koreana*, **1**(2), Summer 1987.

Shin, Eun-kyung, *Taoism and East Asian Literary Theories: Chuang Tzuis Theory of Selflessness and the Poetics of Self-effacement*, Korean Studies, vol. 26, 2002.

Suh, Ji-moon (ed.), *The Rainy Spell and Other Korean Stories*, M.E. Sharpe: Unesco Publishing, 1998.

Yang, Eun-Hee et al., "A Study on the Colors in Korean Traditional Wedding Dress at the Period of Joseon Dynasty", in 6th Asian Design International Conference, Japan, 2003.

Yi, Jong-muk, "*16 segimal 17 segi hansisa yeon-gu* (A Study on the History of Korean Classical Chinese Poetry from the Late Sixteenth to Seventeenth Century)", *Jeongsin munhwa yeon-gu* (Korean Studies Quarterly, Academy of Korean Studies), 2000.

Yi, Sang-jong, "*Cheongnak-chae Kim-gong Sijip So* (A Preface to a Collection of Poems by Chongnak-chae Kim)", *Taesan Sonsaeng Munjip* (An Anthology of Master Taesan), Seoul: Kyeong-in Munhwa-sa, 1987.

Yu, Bong-hak (2002), *Gyeonghwa sajok-gwa jin-gyeong munhwa* (Gyeonghwasajok and Jin-gyeong Culture), in Jin-gyeong sidae (Jin- gyeong Era), Seoul, 2002.

Zõng, In-sob, (1983) *A Guide to Korean Literature*, Elizabeth, NJ: Hollym International Corp.,

16

Feminism in Yi Moon-Yeol's Novel "Seontaek" (Choice)

Kim Young Soon

Introduction

CHOICE became a sensation even before it was published. What perhaps makes it particularly special is the strong antagonism generated towards *Seontaek* by feminists.[1]

This novel consists of four parts. It is the story of one woman, Lady Jeong who lives in the Joseon dynasty. It starts with the description and admonition of contemporary women from her own eyes, but essentially Lady Jeong's story of her life as it unfolds in its different stages. The first part is narrated as a daughter, the second, as a wife, the third, as a mother, and the last as a big mother to her relatives. This story criticizes contemporary women, who have strong ideas on self-identity, free sex, freedom to divorce, sexual immorality and avoiding having children. As a reader, I too, am one of those contemporary women who are living in this world and especially in India.

The protagonist consistently emphasizes the fact that it was "her" choice and therefore that she and only she was responsible for the direction her life had taken.

In the novel, Lady Jeong was a very intelligent and talented woman. Her father educated her, unlike most women in that society. She used to write poems with difficult Chinese characters. But she said she had given up her desire to study and instead had

1 Moon-Yeol Yi, *Choice*, 1997, p. 223, http://ask.nate.com/qna/view.html?n=8379443

taken up the choice, to lead her life of that of a housewife, who could develop the capacity to look after growing children, serving her husband, and any guests that visit the house. She insists it was fully her choice, and that there was no force involved in the decision.

One is led but to question if this truly was the case. If indeed it was her free choice, then why does she stress the choice she makes for her life direction so insistently in that manner? From one point of view she seems as though she wants to deny her choice for the life direction, preparing herself for what was never to be. I highly doubt that she had the freedom to accept any lifestyle, thus irony of the title of the novel *Choice*, when in fact she had none.

As men and women, we are born into different roles we are supposed to play in this society. This adjusts as we grow. For the women, the roles are complicated. Our society is a patriarchal one, where women are forced to be "women". Feminism is a reaction to patriarchy, some stances of which follow the line where the woman refuses to follow the set role and spend time just giving birth to children and supporting the logic of the family organization. I am not making emotional judgements here. Personally I am against it. But after having lived in India for so long, I feel women should be stronger than the stereotypes we are meant to follow.

Therefore, my question to the protagonist, the lady who lived 300 years ago in Korea, who chose to dedicate her life to her husband, and praised her sister-in-law, who killed herself after her husband's death[2] (in a situation similar to that of *satī* in India), is, was her choice made by herself or was it an inevitable decision made under the tacit direction of society.

Main Subject

ABOUT THE AUTHOR, YI MOON-YEOL

Yi Moon-Yeol is one of the best selling novelists of Korea, with the largest number of readers, practically making him a representative novelist of South Korea. But before his debut, his life was very tough.

[2] Moon-Yeol Yi, *Choice*, 1997, pp. 126-30.

Why has the author written such an anti-feminist novel?

Yi Moon-Yeol is the descendant of an orthodox Confucianist aristocratic family in Korea. His father was an elite who studied in UK and became a professor. He was a Marxist intellectual and abandoned his family to go to North Korea. The remaining family members suffered a lot and were left with great scars because of the absence of the father and furious government investigation and trials. Such an environment made him obsessed about his genealogy and family background. Uncertain about his future, poverty and anxiety caused him to form an attachment with his glorious aristocratic background. He tried to build himself an identity based on family lineage.

Based on his background, his writing *Choice* also follows the same trend. He traced his family lineage and found out about lady Jang and embellishing on her life making it into a novel.

SUPPORT FOR CONSERVATIVE TRADITION

Since the 1990s, the status of women and society the world over has changed tremendously. Women's role in politics, culture, economics, and even in literature has increased. After the economic recession in 1997, women just couldn't stay at home anymore. The situation drove women to the frontline of survival activity. This brought about a necessary change of the fixed idea about the role of women into one that was progressive and open-minded.

The fact remains that although the woman's position has somewhat been uplifted, the woman who stays at home as a housewife still is and feels powerless. A woman who works outside and handles housework is what is ideal. Thus, further complicating matters with the creation of the "Super Woman Complex".

It is in such a situation that the author has written this novel, to talk about his ideal of a "true and happy life" through a lady from the aristocratic group in the Chosun dynasty. The author wants to reveal the lady's strong identity as a high status woman in the Confucian Joseon_dynasty, in an attempt to show the generation of women today what is truly the "right way". It starts in this manner:

> I am the one with no name who lives in King Sukjong's time in Joseon dynasty. In this world, I am called by my father's family name, Jang, and country has given me the title of nobility, Madam Jeong.[3]

But from the beginning itself, the author's critical attitude towards feminism became a very big issue. The author reveals his deep faith in his roots of the traditional noble family. I feel that he showed his conservative ideology by openly portraying that Korean traditional women's virtue and cultural sense are more valuable than contemporary postmodernism in women. He portrays nostalgic feelings towards Korean women's traditional noble beauty, as compared to modern women who have a strong sense of identity. According to the author due to globalization and strong Western ideology that are sweeping through Korea, we Koreans have forgotten our identity. Western lifestyle and ideas have driven Korean traditional lifestyle out.

The Conflict of Feminism and Traditional Confucianism

Confucianism is based on the three fundamental principles and the five moral disciplines of human relations. The Chosun dynasty particularly, was built on this doctrine. The core of Confucianism is patriarchy — that is its crux consisted of a father, the first son, and men in general. In such a male-centred society, a women's role in the house of an illustrious official was to maintain the ancestral rituals and various kinds of family matters. Women in lower classes were to give labour for their farming. In academics, politics, economy, and culture men held power and women were simply helpers who were supposed to help men to make their work more comfortable. Men were to be served, women are to serve men, and they are not equal. Men's physical desire too could be fulfilled easily, but women were forced to keep their fidelity and remain locked within the trappings of the seven grounds for divorce, i.e. "Chilgeojiak". Chigeojiak was meant to describe the women who were eligible to be thrown out of

---

3 Moon-Yeol Yi, *Choice*, 1997, p. 7.

the house because of disobedience to parents-in-law, lack of a son, jealousy, anger, having a disease, talkativeness, or thievery.[4] Even today, women are treated badly, and they only serve as instruments for production of sons, and objects of fulfilment of men's physical desire. Such a situation may not be different in Western society, but Korea is especially very influenced by Chinese Confucianism. Society demands that women have more morality, endurance, and a yielding spirit.

But now, in Korean society, things are changing. Women are insisting upon integral equality against the man-centred social systems and ideas. In the time of strong angst against social structural discrepancy, *Choice* was treated as a ridiculous, senseless anachronistic idea. The author's value of beauty of traditional women's morality based on Confucius patriarchal ideas hurts feminist ideology, which arose as a slogan of gender equality.

The author tried to obviously try and replace the space of women's radical idea of free sex, family disorganization with the merits of traditional Confucianism.

But I feel that the author, for whatever reason has shielded his ideals from the situation of the victims of gender disparity, inequality etc. Women are victims of such men like Yi Moon-Yeol.

Lamentation on Disappearing Tradition and Culture

> Among relations between humans, husband and wife's relationship is instinctive, deep and long. Instinct should be controlled by etiquette. If not, selfishness and violence will follow. The relation between husband and wife lasts for the longest time and is exposed to selfishness and violence. The only difference between coupling of animals and humans is propriety. — *Choice*

Such are the ethics of husband and wife in a traditional Confucian aristocratic family. They had a beautiful tradition and culture. But

[4] Moon Hyun-A, A Reinterpretation of the Late Choseon Wife Murder Cases in Chugwanji (The Record of Justice) Through Discourse Analysis, 2011.

Western materialism and pragmatic idea drove out traditions and cultures in the name of discomfort. The author was also worried and warned about the trend of the contemporary generation to easily replace uncomfortable and unnecessary things. Traditional festivals, Korean dress, Korean food, Korean house, Korean style marriage, funeral ceremony have already disappeared. We can find those things in museums only. They enjoy Western style fast food and instant food. Fashions from New York and Paris arrive within a day in Korea. People treat "Samgang Oryun" the three fundamental principles and the five moral disciplines in human relations and "Chilgeojiak" as relics of the past.

Nowadays, "the wife" in a family also makes income for the family and the father is the nearest friend among friends to the children. And if the father shows authority to the children, children will ignore their father. Now, husband and wife, parents and children, teacher and students, are all at the same level and their relationship is not vertical but horizontal. In the situation of globalization, minimalism, postmodernism, people have lost their identity. For the author, Yi Moon-Yeol's nostalgic childhood and ideas of women's virtue motivated the novel.

Conclusion

A FEMINIST OBJECTION

Through the novel *Choice*, the author has reprimanded women in this society. He stressed the role of a woman to be only that of a sacrificial mother and wife without her own identity. Feminist Yu, Sook-Yeol pointed out an infringement of human rights. She said that in the novel, women are described as castrated, whose meaning lies only in the existence of being a mother.[5] People criticized the author, saying that he has the "Choice" of commerce. He regards feminists as women with ideas of free sexuality and as patients of sexual perversion. He doesn't understand the meaning of feminism.

---

5 Yu Sook-yeol, one of the famous feminists and journalists in Korea http://www.sisapress.com/news/articleView.html?idxno=12117

The author's extreme prejudice against women made people angry especially women in Korea. Finding out about Yi Moon-Yeol's family background and his life has allowed readers to understand his work. But, a strong strain of feminism can't accept his work, and they treat his novel as an outdated one in this generation. In his work he has shown his personal preference, which has greatly angered readers. Most of the women readers and I, too, don't criticize the protagonist Madam Jeong, but the author's negative attitude towards contemporary women's ideas on women and family.

References

Kim, Hee-Kang, *Trands and Issues in Western Theory and Their Implications to Korean Feminist Scholarship in the Global Content,* Seoul: Hakjisa, 2006.

Kang, Chan-Mo, "Study on Confucian Humanism in Novels of Lee Moon-ku and Lee Moon-Yeol", *Bipeong Munhak* **30**: 159-78 (2008).

Kim Haeyoung, "The Familism and Woman's Rights in Korea", *Asia Women's Research*, **42**: 9-46 (2003).

Kang Sook-Ja, "Reinterpretation of Women in Coufucian Thought", *Dongyang Jeongchi Sasangsa*, **3**(3): 7-48 (2003).

Moon Hyun-A, A Reinterpretation of the Late Choseon Wife Murder Cases in Chugwanji (The Record of Justice) Through Discourse Analysis, 2011.

Lee Moon-yeol, "Byeongeong", *Munhakgwa Jiseongsa*, 1998.

http://terms.naver.com/entry.nhn?docId=955884&mobile&categoryId=

http://terms.naver.com/entry.nhn?docId=333733&mobile&categoryId=

http://kin.naver.com/open100/detail.nhn?d1id=3&dirId=307&docId=324078&qb=7J2066y47Je0IOu5hO2PiQ==&enc=utf8&section=kin&rank= 12&search_sort= 0&spq=0

17

The Unification Policies of the Republic of Korea
From 1988 to the Present

Alokka Dutta

THROUGHOUT most of the twentieth century, the Korean people have yearned for the establishment of an independent and unified Korea. Before the Second World War, this was denied to them by Japan's annexation of the Korean peninsula in 1910. With the defeat of Japan in 1945, hopes of a unified independent Korea were again raised but soon dashed by the partitioning. Ostensibly a temporary division to expedite the surrender of Japanese forces, as wartime co-operation between occupying powers quickly developed into post-war competition, the division of Korea became permanent and reunification hopes faded.

Throughout the subsequent Korean War, both sides attempted to achieve reunification by force without decisive result, and although after 1953 reunification nominally remained on the agenda of both Koreas, in the increasingly tense environment of the Cold War, the issue received little more than token attention. The Korean desire for reunification is based on a long and proud history of unity that saw Korea develop into a culturally and ethnically homogeneous country with a deep sense of national unity. This, combined with significant Chinese influence, has resulted in Korean people with a strong adherence to the ties of family, culture and history. Because of this background and despite decades of tension and animosity between North and South, Koreans harbour a powerful desire for reunification.

To most Koreans, the current division of the peninsula is a temporary aberration that, with time, will be resolved.

Attempts during the Cold War to overcome hostilities and obtain some degree of reconciliation as a first step toward reunification were not successful. In 1972 both Pyongyang and Seoul philosophically agreed that reunification would occur peacefully without foreign interference. Divergent views on how this was to be achieved stalled further progress. In 1984 similar attempts were again made but failed amid the mutual distrust and acrimony characteristic of Republic of Korea (RoK)–Democratic People's Republic of Korea (DPRK) relations throughout the Cold War. However, in the wake of German reunification, the death of Kim Il Sung in 1994 and the Korean Peninsula Summit of 2000, there was a raft of predictions by scholars, commentator and officials of not if but when reunification would occur.[1] Most of these assessments assumed that reunification would be achieved by the absorption of North Korea by the South.

Over the past few years, enthusiasm for such predictions have faded, and although the underlying assumption of eventual reunification remains, forecasts of when this will occur have been fewer and more subdued than the confident predictions of the 1990s.

Eventual reunification poses two distinct yet interdependent conundrums: reunification itself, which represents the most immediate challenge; and the strategic landscape that emerges from reunification, in which the prospect of a unified Korea has the potential to fundamentally transform strategic relationships in North-East Asia.

Within this context this paper examines the prospects from Korean unification from the administrations of 1988 to present. The commitment to unification, as measured by a willingness to assign high priority to it has varied from regime to regime in South Korea. And this level of commitment ostensibly peaked during the sixth republic.

---

1 Unification Board, T'ongil Chongch'aek-sil, ed., *T'ong'il paekso* (1990 White paper on Unification), 1990, pp. 300-02.

The Unification Policy of the Sixth Republic

The inauguration of Roh Tae Woo as president of the RoK on 25 February 1988 marked the first peaceful transfer of power since the founding of the republic in August 1948. Roh was the first popularly elected president in sixteen years. Having won the presidential election of December 1987 with less than 37 per cent of the effective vote, however, Roh could claim neither a solid mandate nor indisputable legitimacy. The need to produce tangible results, therefore, was no less pressing for Roh than it was for his predecessors.

He seemed to have decided to place top priority on both democratization and inter-Korean relations. Having committed himself to the goal of democratization in the historic declaration of 29 June 1987, as well as during the presidential campaign, Roh was honour-bound to press ahead with that task. Improving inter-Korean relations, preferably achieving a breakthrough, was a goal Roh apparently set on his own. He made that plain in a series of acts, beginning with his inaugural speech and culminating in the unveiling of the "Korean National Community (KNC) unification formula" in September 1989.

In his inaugural speech in February 1988, Roh proclaimed the beginning of an "era of dialogue and co-operation between South and North Korea". He indicated a willingness to "visit anywhere in the world and to engage in a sincere dialogue with anyone" in order to ensure peace on the Korean peninsula and expedite its reunification.

He also vigorously stated his intention to pursue "northern diplomacy" with a view toward creating an environment conducive to Korean unification. Two months later, during his first press conference as president, Roh made explicit his determination to "pave the way for peaceful unification through reconciliation and co-operation between South and North Korea" during his term of office.

Then, on 7 July 1988, Roh took the first significant step toward achieving his goal: in a special statement, he outlined a policy aimed at transforming inter-Korean relations from confrontation to co-operation. Stressing the need for the two parts of the divided peninsula to work together to build a genuine *minjok kongdonch'e* (national community), Roh declared that South Korea would take a series of measures:

1. It would pursue an exchange of people in all walks of life between North and South;
2. it would redouble efforts to assist separated family members to locate, communicate and reunite with one another;
3. it would encourage inter-Korean trade, treating the latter not as interstate trade but as trade within the same nation;
4. it would no longer oppose trade involving non-military goods between its allies and friends on one side and North Korea on the other;
5. it hoped to replace counterproductive diplomatic competition with North Korea in the world arena with co-operation in pursuit of common interests; and
6. it would be willing to assist North Korea to improve relations with the United States, Japan, and other states that are friendly with Seoul.

Seoul, for its part, would seek improved relations with the Soviet Union, China, and other socialist countries.[1] The Korean National Community (KNC) formula set forth a number of basic guidelines that mildly govern the unification process. First, unification shall be guided by three principles: independence, peace and democracy. Second, the unified Korea shall be "a single national community in which every citizen is his own master, that is to say, a democratic nation that guarantees the human rights of every individual and his right to seek happiness". The unified Korea, moreover, must be a single nation in every sense of the word, not a confederation of two states with differing ideologies and political systems. Third, the legislature of the unified Korea shall be a "bicameral parliament composed of an upper house based on regional representation and a lower house based on population".

To no one's surprise, North Korea has categorically rejected the KNC formula, asserting that its own formula — the proposal for the establishment of the Democratic Confederal Republic of Koryo — is the only realistic and reasonable blueprint for unification.

In December 1991, Seoul and Pyongyang signed two agreements that may well have momentous consequences. A product of five rounds of "high-level talks" in which both delegations were headed by their respective prime ministers — the first agreement, known as "the Agreement; on Reconciliation, Non-aggression, and Exchanges and Co-operation Between the North and the South", laid the groundwork for the inter-Korean dialogue, spawning many structures that are not too dissimilar from those envisaged by the KNC formula. The second agreement, the Joint Declaration on the Denuclearization of the Korean peninsula, complements the first. Both entered into force in February 1992.[2]

The first agreement, which is usually referred to as the North-South basic agreement, resembled an international treaty, for it contained a preamble and numbered articles, and was signed by the prime ministers of both sides, and calls for an exchange of instruments of ratification before its formal entry into force.

But very little progress has been made in terms of substantive issues. The most intractable of all the issues was the nuclear inspection issue — namely, whether and how to conduct mutual inspections of each other's nuclear facilities. That impasse fuelled the suspicions, shared by Washington and Seoul, about a clandestine North Korean programme to develop nuclear weapons, prompting them to announce that they would resume their annual joint military exercise, code-named Team Spirit, in 1993 after suspending it in the preceding year.

This in turn angered North Korea, leading it to suspend the high-level talks and all negotiations with South Korea under the rubric of the various sub-committees and joint committees. It should be noted that the unfolding of the dispute over special inspections coincided with the political transition in Seoul. While the decision to resume the

---

[2] National Unification Board, Nambuk Taehwa Samuguk (The Office of the South–North Dialogue), ed., *Nambu Taehwa* (South-North Dialogue), no. 54, 1992.

Team Spirit exercise was made during the Sixth Republic, its actual implementation did not occur until after the inauguration of Kim Young Sam's civilian government.[3]

Kim Young Sam's Unification Policy

In his inaugural address on 25 February 1993, the new RoK president Kim Young Sam pledged that he would spare no effort to realize national reconciliation and unification. He then called on his counterpart in North Korea, using the latter's official title "President Kim Il Sung", to assume the posture of genuine co-operation. Noting that the world is entering an era of peace and co-operation in which multifaceted co-operation is occurring between different nations, Kim Young Sam reminded Kim Il Sung that neither allies nor ideology can surpass the bonds of ethnicity; he used the Korean word *minjok*, which is usually translated as "nation".[4]

Kim Young Sam expressed confidence that he and the North Korean president could "solve all the problems" by approaching them from the standpoint of the same nation or common ethnicity. The new administration also explicitly reaffirmed its predecessor's policy of linking economic co-operation to the nuclear issue. Signs of change, however, were not totally absent. In some ways, in fact, notable changes began to occur. In a word, the Kim Young Sam government initially struck a more conciliatory posture toward North Korea than its predecessors. Two examples will suffice. First, one of the first acts it took was to allow the repatriation of Yi In-mo to North Korea. Yi was a seventy-six-year-old former North Korean soldier who had spent over thirty-five years in South Korean prisons. Yi's refusal to renounce communism had been a key factor in his prolonged detention. After his plight was reported in the South Korean press, the North

---

3 The joint statement of the Twenty-Fourth Security Consultative Meeting between the United States and the RoK held in Washington on 7 and 8 October 1992 in *Korea Herald*, 9 October 1992.

4 *Hanguk Ilbo*, 25 February 1993, evening edition. The full text of Kim's speech appears on p. 2.

Korean authorities located his wife, daughter, and grandchildren in the North. North Korea's demand for his repatriation had been a contentious issue in the Inter-Korean dialogue.

Given this background, the Kim Young Sam government's decision to allow Yi's return to North Korea was a goodwill gesture of major proportions. Another example of the Kim government's conciliatory posture concerns its initial handling of the crisis precipitated by Pyongyang's announcement on 12 March 1993, that it would withdraw from the Nuclear Non-proliferation Treaty. The Kim Young Sam government's blueprint for unification, first unveiled in July 1993, was all but indistinguishable from the KNC formula of the Sixth Republic. It embraced a "three-phased approach to unification" guided by three principles. The three phases wore:

1. Reconciliation and co-operation,
2. the Korean Commonwealth, and
3. one state, one nation.

The three guiding principles were:

1. Democratic national consensus,
2. coexistence and co-prosperity, and
3. national well-being.[5]

In August 1994, President Kim Young Sam introduced a slightly modified version of his government's unification formula. Renamed the "three-stage unification formula for the creation of Korean National Community", the new version retained the three stages but omitted any explicit reference to the three principles.[6]

If we construe unification policy broadly so as to subsume the entire gamut of the two Korean states' policies toward each other, then there were other developments bearing on the Kim Young Sam government's unification policy worth noting as well. In a departure from the generally conciliatory approach it had taken toward the

---

[5] *Nambuk Taehwa* (South–North Dialogue), no. 58, October 1993, pp. 5-20.

[6] Ibid., no. 60, October 1994, pp. 47-72, 127-38.

North, the Kim Young Sam government struck an unmistakably hard-line posture toward Pyongyang in the wake of Kim Il Sung's death in July 1994.

Not only did Kim Young Sam fail to issue any statement of condolences but dealt harshly with South Korean citizens who attempted to pay their respects to the deceased North Korean leader.

The death of Kim Il Sung had a chilling effect on inter-Korean relations. Were it not for his sudden death, an unprecedented summit meeting between him and Kim Young sam would have materialized, which might have opened the way for a new era of amity and co-operation in Korean peninsula.

In June 1995, a stunning development occurred, a first in the annals of inter-Korean relations. Pyongyang requested Seoul to provide free rice to deal with serious food shortages.

It was quickly followed by a Tokyo–Pyongyang agreement, signed in Tokyo, under which Tokyo would supply Pyongyang with 300,000 tons of rice, of which a half would be free and the remainder would be sold on a deferred payment basis.[7] During the implementation of the Seoul–Pyongyang rice deal, however, two incidents erupted that nerved to dampen the prospects for a flow inter-Korean rapprochement. First, a South Korean ship carrying the first shipment of rice to the North was forced by the North Korean authorities to replace a South Korean flag with a North Korean flag before entering the port of Ch'ongjin. After North Korea apologized for the incident, South Korea resumed its shipment of rice. Then, a month later, North Koreans perpetrated another incident in Ch'ongjin. A South Korean ship that had just delivered rice was detained, with its entire crew, on grounds that a crew member had taken photographs of Ch'ongjin harbour, an act defined by North Korea as espionage. This time it was South Korea that was compelled to wire an apology to North Korea in order to obtain the release and return of the ship and its

---

7 *Nambuk Taehwa*, no. 62 (December 1994 – June 1995), p. 30; *Japan Times* Weekly International Edition, 3-9 July 1995, p. 3.

crew. These incidents triggered an avalanche of outrage and criticism on the part of politicians, journalists and ordinary citizens in the South.[8]

In the aftermath of a severe flood which, according to Pyongyang, adversely affected 5.2 million people and caused damage estimated at US $ 1.5 billion, North and South resumed dialogue in Beijing in late September. Seoul, however, set preconditions for discussing the issue or additional supply of rice and aid to flood victims: the release of a South Korean fishing vessel and its crew being detained in the North as well as an inquiry into what the South suspects is a kidnapping of a South Korean clergyman from Yanbian, China by North Korean agents. Pyongyang's refusal to meet these conditions led to an impasse.[9]

In sum, the unification policy of the Kim Young Sam government was a continuation of its predecessors. If any change was detectable it was a movement in the direction of moderation, reconciliation and responsiveness *vis-à-vis* the North. The bottom- line, however, was that the civilian government was no less committed to the overriding goal of national security and peace than any of its predecessors.

The "Sunshine Policy" of the Kim Dae Jung Government

The emergence of the Kim Dae Jung government in February 1998 marked a new watershed in South Korea's transition to democracy. For the first time in the fifty-year history of the RoK, power was transferred from the ruling party to the opposition camp in a peaceful fashion. Not only did this stunning development trigger a metamorphosis of the structure and dynamics of power in South Korea but it also paved the way for change in South Korea's posture and policy toward the North.

Kim Dae Jung was and remains proponent of a "three-stage unification" formula. Upholding three principles of "self-reliance, peace, and democracy", the formula posits the stages of

---

8 *Hankuk Ilbo*, 30 June-3 July, 9-10 August 1995.

9 Ibid., 28-30 September 1995.

(1) confederation, (2) federation, and (3) the formation of either a centralized system of government or several autonomous regional governments on the model of the United States or Germany. The first stage in this formula resembles the Korean commonwealth in the proposals of Kim's predecessors, while the second stage has some similarties with Pyongyang's proposal for the establishment of a Democratic Confederal Republic of Koryo.[10]

Against this background, Kim Dae Jung unveiled his "Sunshine Policy" — a policy aimed at inducing change in North Korean policy toward the South through conciliation and displays of goodwill. Such a policy is clearly distinguishable from one of trying to force change in North Korean policy by pressure, display of force and other hard-line measures. The idea and phrase are derived from an Aesopian fable in which, in a contest to determine which was the stronger, the Sun, not the Wind, succeeds in getting a man to take off his heavy coat. The policy, according to Kim Dae Jung, is guided by three principles. First, we will never tolerate armed provocation of any kind. Second, we do not have any intention to undermine or absorb North Korea. Third, we will actively pursue reconciliation and co-operation between the North and the South beginning with those areas which can be most easily agreed upon.[11]

Any arguments that the sunshine policy was a continuation of the policy of Kim's predecessors was quickly dispelled when the Kim Dae Jung government took steps to facilitate non-governmental exchanges between the North and the South. It began to lift or reduce restrictions on travel and investments in the North by South Korean citizens. The most dramatic example of such policy was a sharp increase in the number of South Korean visitors to the North. With the opening

---

10 Kim Dae Jung, *"Three Stage" Approach to Reunification: Focusing on the South–North Confederal Stage*, tr. Rhee Tong-chin, Los Angeles: Center for Multiethnic and Transnational Studies, University of Southern California, 1997, pp. 1-5.

11 *Chong Wa Dae* (The Inaugural Address by the Fifteenth President: Let Us Open a New Era in Which We Overcome Our National Difficulties and Make a Leap Anew), 25 February 1998.

of the scenic Kumkang (diamond) mountain to South Korean tourists, tens of thousands of South Korean citizens are visiting the North every month. The North is in a huge financial stake in the tourist programme operated by Hyundai group, for it earns $ 25 million a month — which may well be the largest single source of foreign exchange earnings for the cash-starved DPRK.[12]

Official contacts between Seoul and Pyongyang, however, remained minimal. And direct negotiations have not produced any tangible results.On 9 October 2006, following the nuclear and missile tests, South Korea suspended aid shipments to the North and put their military on high alert status. There was much concern regarding how South Korea can maintain a co-operative policy towards the North when such provocative acts occurred. None the less, the government of South Korea insisted that at least some aspects of the Sunshine Policy, including the Mount Gumgang Tourist Region and the Kaesong Industrial Region would continue. However it should be noted that among a few tangible result of the unification policy was that a unified Korean team marched in the opening ceremonies of the 2000, 2004 and 2006 Olympics, but the North and South Korean national teams competed separately. There were plans for a truly unified team at the 2008 Summer Olympics, but the two countries were unable to agree on the details of its implementation. In the 1991 table tennis world championships in Chiba, Japan, the two countries formed a unified team.

Lee Myung-Bak's Guiding Principles

On 10 May 2007, Lee officially declared his intention to run for the Grand National Party (GNP) its presidential candidate. On 20 August 2007, he defeated Park Geun-hye in the GNP's primary to become its nominee for the 2007 presidential election. From March 2008, however, the new president of the South, Lee Myung-bak and his party took a harsher stand towards North Korea, and the South Korean

---

[12] Ministry of Korean Unification, "98 nyondo Taebuk Chongch'a p'yongka" (An Apprasisal of the Policy Toward the North During 1998), 4 January 1999.

government stated that any expansion of the economic co-operation at the Kaesong Industrial Region would only happen if the North resolved the international standoff over its nuclear weapons. Relations have again chilled, with North Korea making defensive moves such as a series of short range ship-to-ship missile tests.

After the 2009 North Korean nuclear test the relationship between Seoul and Pyongyang was again strained. According to Jungmin Kang writing in the *Bulletin of Atomic Scientist* , "Because of the post-1998 'Sunshine Policy', many South Korean non-governmental organizations and the public weren't concerned about North Korea's threats, believing that Pyongyang would never use nuclear weapons against them". South Korea's response to the nuclear test, although dampened by the death of its former President Roh Moo-hyun, included signing the Proliferation Security initiatives to prevent the shipment of nuclear materials to North Korea. In November 2010, the South Korean unification ministry officially declared the Sunshine Policy a failure, thus bringing the policy to an end.

The Lee Myung-bak administration is guided by four principles: pragmatic and result-oriented approaches; strict principles and flexible approaches; national consensus; and balance between inter-Korean co-operation and international co-operation.

1. It will be pragmatic and pressed for results based on a spirit of reconciliation and co-operation. It will move forward with a North Korea policy that the South Korean people desires; that improves the quality of life for North Koreans; that is cost-effective; that facilitates the economic development of North Korea; and that contributes to peaceful unification of the Korean peninsula.
2. The Lee government will strictly abide by principles but take flexible approaches. It will hold to the principles of achieving the denuclearization of North Korea and pressing for sincere and effective dialogue. Yet, it will be flexible in approaches in dealing with these objectives considering the reality of inter-Korean relations.

3. It will implement North Korea policy in a transparent manner based on a national consensus. It will reflect a wide range of public opinions and seek bipartisan co-operation as well as public participation in implementing North Korean policy.
4. The government will expand inter-Korean co-operation in harmony with international co-operation. It will pursue a peaceful resolution of the North Korean nuclear issue through the six-party talks and advance inter-Korean relations in co-operation with the international community.

In spite of these efforts in 2010, relations between the two Koreas were strained by the sinking of the RoK's Cheonan and the loss of its forty-six-man crew, which an official investigation concluded was due to the explosion of a torpedo several metres from the ship (North Korea denied any such action) and the bombardment of Yeonpyeong Island by North Korean forces, leaving two South Korean marines and two civilians dead, in response to regular South Korea artillery exercises (which North Korea had requested to be called off). The death of Kim Jong-il since 18 December 2011 has led to uncertainty regarding North Korea's future as the current transition of power may be questioned. This has led to fear of a crisis on the Korean peninsula.[13]

Conclusion

Eventual political integration of the Koreas under a democratic government from the South is generally viewed as inevitable by US and South Korea. However, the nature of unification, i.e. through North Korean collapse or gradual integration of the North and South, is still a topic of intense political debate and even conflict among interested parties, who include both Koreas, the People's Republic of China, Japan, Russia and the United States. Some political analysts even say the process of reunification has already begun, albeit at a

---

[13] Bruce Cumings, *Korea's Place in the Sun: A Modern History*, New York, Norton, 2005, p. 511.

very gradual pace, through the current process of reconciliation and economic co-operation between the two Koreas.

Bruce Cumings speculated that

> it seems to me that for all these reasons, and short of a catastrophic war, no reunified Korea will emerge before a prolonged period of regional sovereignty, perhaps under one national name and one flag, perhaps for years to come.[14]

---

14 "Seoul Reaffirms North Korea's Torpedo Attack in Final Report", *Korea Times*, 13 September 2010.

18

Analysing Deepening Strategic Partnership Among India, South Korea, the United States and Japan

Sanjeev K. Shrivastav

Introduction

In an increasingly interdependent and globalized world, the strategic partnership between India, South Korea, the United States and Japan has been constantly growing. This partnership between these four democracies is based on shared values as well as shared interests. Democracy, open economy and liberal society, and secularism bind these four nations together. The economic ties between these countries are constantly growing. However, it must be clarified here that this emerging partnership should not be viewed against any particular nation, for instance, China and North Korea. There must be constant efforts to establish better co-operative relationship between those countries which are important neighbours though they have non-democratic regimes. At the same time, it is also essential to promote deeper economic ties and people-to-people contact with such societies.

Meanwhile, it is essential to note that

> a strategic partnership between two countries may be defined in terms of shared values and areas of co-operation in the spheres of defence, foreign policy, economy, energy, human resource development, and environment by taking into account existing geopolitical realities and diplomatic practices. A strategic partnership should be viewed as a long-term commitment and it is essential that both partners develop a clear understanding and vision about its objectives and practices. It is also imperative that a strategic partnership be

based on mutual trust and respect for each other's sovereignty, territorial integrity and shared values.[1]

The nature of emerging strategic partnership between India, South Korea, the United States and Japan is mainly bilateral and in some cases trilateral as well. Now it is pertinent to discuss emerging partnership with these countries bilaterally and then multilaterally.

India–South Korea Ties

India–South Korea relation has been historical in nature and dates back to ancient times. According to *SamgukYusa* (*The Heritage History of the Three Kingdoms*) which was written in the thirteenth century, a princess from Ayodhyā (Suriratna) visited Korea in the year CE 48 and married King Kim-Suro. She was known as Queen Hur Hwang-ok. The influence of Buddhist thoughts and practices binds two societies and cultures together. India's great litterateur and Nobel Laureate Rabindranath Tagore, in his poem "Lamp of the East" in 1929 wrote:

> In the golden age of Asia
> Korea was one of its lamp bearers
> And that lamp is waiting to be lit once again
> For the illumination of the East.[2]

India's role in establishing peace and stability in Korean peninsula has been significant. When Japanese colonial rule ended in 1945, India played an important role as the Chairman of the nine-member UN Commission which was set up in 1947 to hold elections in Korea. These efforts paved the way for the establishment of the Republic of Korea on 15 August 1948. During the Korean War (1950-53), India

---

1 Sanjeev Kumar Shrivastav, "Contours of the India–United States Strategic Partnership", IDSA Strategic Comment, 29 September 2009, available at http://www.idsa.in/idsastrategiccomments/ContoursoftheIndia-UnitedStatesStrategicPartnership_skshrivastav_290909

2 "India–Republic of Korea (RoK) Bilateral Relations", Embassy of India, Seoul, available at http://www.indembassy.or.kr/IndiaRoKBilateral.aspx?Cul=en-US

sponsored a resolution which was accepted by both the warring sides which led to the ceasefire, declared on 27 July 1953.[3] In fact, a special session of Indian parliament was convened on 31 July 1950 to discuss the Korean crisis which highlights the Indian commitment for peace and stability in the Korean peninsula. At the same time, India also sent a medical unit which included 60 Para Field Ambulances, to the multinational forces of the United Nations during the war. As the Chairman of the Neutral Nations Repatriation Commission (NNRC), India contributed its best to deal with the humanitarian issues which arose as a result of the war.[4]

India and South Korea (Republic of Korea (RoK)) established consular relations in 1962. In 1973, these relations were upgraded to Ambassador level. In the post-Cold War period, South Korean popular quest for democracy introduced in 1987 helped in creating a natural affinity between the two societies and nations since the Indian society and nation shared these values with that of South Korea. Similarly, South Korea's open-market policies gelled well with India's economic liberalization and the "Look East Policy". India, at the same time, has been a consistent supporter of a peaceful reunification of the two Koreas which has been welcomed by South Korea.[5]

In February 1996, India–RoK Joint Commission for bilateral co-operation was established, headed by the foreign ministers of both the countries. India and South Korea have established a Foreign Policy and Security Dialogue (FPSD) at Secretary (Vice-Ministerial) level as well.[6] India's Defence Minister A.K. Antony visited Republic of Korea in September 2010. As an outcome of this visit, both the nations signed a Memorandum of Understanding (MoU) on Defence Co-operation, as well as, between Defence Research and Development Organisation (DRDO) of India and Defense Acquisition Program Administration (DAPA) of RoK for co-operation in research and development (R&D).[7]

[3] "India–Republic of Korea (RoK) Bilateral Relations"

[4] Ibid.

[5] Ibid.

[6] Ibid.

[7] Ibid.

Major Korean companies such as Samsung, Hyundai Motors and LG have made huge investments in India and their products now have become household names. It is estimated that till March 2012, these companies have invested approximately $ 2.5 billion in India. On the other hand, Indian firms have invested over $ 1 billion in South Korea. It would be worth noting that Novelis, a subsidiary of Hindalco, acquired a Korean aluminium company. Mahindra & Mahindra acquired a major stake in SsangYong Motors of South Korea. Tata Motors acquired Daewoo Commercial Vehicle Company in March 2004.[8]

India's Prime Minister Dr Manmohan Singh visited South Korea during 24-27 March 2012 for deepening of the strategic partnership between the two nations. India and RoK had already concluded a bilateral Comprehensive Economic Partnership Agreement (CEPA), which was signed by the Minister for Commerce and Industry Anand Sharma at Seoul on 7 August 2009. CEPA came into force on 1 January 2010. As a result, bilateral trade between India and South Korea in 2011 reached beyond $ 20.5 billion which was a 70 per cent growth over a two-year period. On 25 March 2012, Dr Manmohan Singh and South Korean President Lee revised this trade target to $ 40 billion by 2015.[9]

India–United States Ties

India–United States strategic partnership is steadily growing since last decade and has gained momentum in the last few years. The future of this partnership appears to be bright. During the Cold War, relations between India and the United States were marred by mutual suspicion and mistrust. In the post-Cold War period, this relationship began to transform since the last years of the Bill Clinton presidency and this process continued in subsequent presidencies. After the attacks on America on 9/11, 2001, US National Security Strategy, 2002 noted that "U.S. interests require a strong relationship with India". Later,

---

8 "India–Republic of Korea (RoK) Bilateral Relations"

9 Ibid.

in a joint statement issued by India's Prime Minister Atal Behari Vajpayee and US President George Bush in January 2004 declared that India–United States "strategic partnership" included expanding co-operation in the areas of easing restrictions on dual use technology export to India, increase in civil nuclear and civil space co-operation, as well as expanding dialogue on missile defence. These steps were regarded as Next Steps in Strategic Partnership (NSSP).[10] India's Prime Minister Dr Manmohan Singh's visit to the United States in July 2005 and the significant joint statement issued after this visit as well as the visit by US President George Bush to India in March 2006 further paved the way for a stronger strategic partnership between India and the United States which are world's largest and oldest democracies, respectively. This emerging strategic partnership reached a major milestone after the signing of the historic India–United States civil nuclear co-operation agreement in October 2008, which marked the end of India's thirty-four years of isolation from the global mainstream in the sphere of civil nuclear energy technology.[11]

India–US economic co-operation has regained upward trajectory after the lull period in year 2009 which was the worst hit by the economic crisis. According to the US Census Bureau figures, India–US trade (in goods only) in 2010 was at $ 48.78 billion whereas in 2009, it was $ 37.61 billion which indicates a 29.72 per cent annual growth.[12] It also highlights that bilateral trade between the two nations is attaining upwards trajectory if right conditions prevail. During the third India–United States strategic dialogue, it was noted in the joint statement that bilateral trade between the two countries (in both goods and services) is continuously growing and is likely reach $ 100 billion soon.[13]

---

[10] Sanjeev Kumar Shrivastav, op. cit.

[11] Ibid.

[12] US–India Trade figures, *US Census Bureau*, http://www.census.gov/foreign-trade/balance/c5330.html

[13] "Joint Statement 2012 U.S.–India Strategic Dialogue", Ministry of External Affairs, 13 June 2012, available at http://www.mea.gov.in/bilateral-documents.htm?dtl/19917/Joint+Statement+2012+USIndia+Strategic+Dialogue

The defence ties between the two countries have grown over the years. In June 2005, the "Defence Framework Agreement" was signed which aimed at formalizing and providing a rationale and direction to the growing bilateral defence ties between India and the United States. It would also be worth noting that India has conducted maximum number of joint military exercises with the United States, compared with any other country. The Malabar series of joint naval exercises have become an annual feature. However, after rejections of bids of two United States aircrafts companies in the multirole combat aircraft (MMRCA) deal, many doubts were raised about the future of this partnership. Later, India's confirmed deal for ten C-17 Globe Master Aircraft worth $ 4.1 billion cleared doubts about India's aversion to defence deals with the United States. There are reports that India has plans to buy more C-17 aircrafts from the United States.[14]

Reports noted that according to a parliamentary committee on defence, India would be spending more than $ 100 billion in the next five to ten years for defence procurements.[15] This opens up a great space for the US companies to compete in India's defence sector. It may be noted that since 2008, India has signed more than $ 8 billion defence deals with the United States "up from effectively zero, less than a decade ago".[16]

Taking further steps on India–United States co-operation in the education sector which is of great importance, significant initiatives

---

14 "India to buy more than 16 C-17 airlifters", *The Economic Times*, 14 June 2011, at http://articles.economictimes.indiatimes.com/2011-06-14/news/29657247_1_kaveri-engine-jet-engines-aircraft

15 "Indian defence, aerospace and security sectors likely to receive $30 billion investment in 5-10 years", *The Economic Times*, 03 August 2011, at http://articles.economictimes.indiatimes.com/2011-08-03/news/29846591_1_indian-defence-aerospace-sectors

16 "The United States and India: A Vital Partnership in a Changing World", remarks by William J. Burns, Deputy Secretary, US Department of State, Center for American Progress, Washington DC, 26 October 2012.

are being taken. India and United States held first Higher Education Summit in Washington DC on 13 October 2011. Both the nations have also decided to have higher education dialogue each year in alternate capitals. The Obama–Singh 21st Century Knowledge Initiative which was launched in 2009 is making steady progress. Recently, under this initiative, proposals have been invited by both sides which will be reviewed by a joint working group for academic awards in support of university partnerships.[17]

It would be worth mentioning that among all international students in the US higher education institutions, 14 per cent students are from India. The number of enrolled Indian students in these institutions of higher learning during in 2010-11 was over 100,000. Meanwhile, in a notable development, the number of American students studying in India has grown by a whopping 44.4 per cent from 2,690 in 2009-10 to 3,884 in 2010-11.[18] Given the advanced state of education system in the US and enormous demand for quality education among young Indian society, co-operation between India and the United States could be very fruitful.

India and the United States held their first Homeland Security dialogue in May 2011 in New Delhi. This initiative was announced by Indian Prime Minister Dr Manmohan Singh and President Barack Obama in November 2010.[19] India–United States co-operation on

---

17 "US–India Joint Statement by Secretary of State Hillary Rodham Clinton and Minister of Human Resource Development Kapil Sibal", Embassy of India, Washington DC, 13 October 2011, at http://www.indianembassy.org/prdetail1809/u.s.-india-joint-statement-by-secretary-of-state-hillary-rodham-clinton-and-minister-of-human-resource-development-kapil-sibal

18 "Minor drop in number of Indians studying in the US", *The Hindustan Times,* 15 November 2011, at http://www.hindustantimes.com/News-Feed/OtherStories/Minor-drop-in-number-of-Indians-studying-in-the-US/Article1-769330.aspx

19 "India–US Homeland Security Dialogue — Joint Statement", 27 May 2011, Embassy of India, Washington DC, at http://www.indianembassy.org/prdetail1722/india-u.s.-homeland-security-dialogue—joint-statement

agriculture is expanding. Taking inspiration from Green Revolution in 1960s, both the nations are working for Evergreen Revolution.[20]

Expanding the horizon of their strategic consultations, India and the United States have "launched a Central Asia Dialogue in June 2011 in New Delhi and a West Asia Dialogue in July 2011 in Washington DC which to help them realize full potential of this global strategic partnership. Both the nations intend to expand strategic consultations to other regions, including Latin America and Caribbean."[21] India and the United States have already had three rounds of the East Asia Dialogue.[22]

India–Japan Ties

India–Japan Strategic Partnership is constantly growing. The relations between India and Japan believed to have started in the sixth century CE with the introduction of Buddhism to Japan. In the modern era, interaction between the two societies began only in the Meiji era (1868–1912), when Japan embarked on the process of modernization.[23] After the establishment of diplomatic ties between India and Japan in 1952, the two nations have strengthened their bilateral relations which are based on shared values and shared interests. India and Japan are committed to enhance their strategic partnership to a new level. In August 2000, Japanese Prime Minister Yoshiro Mori visited India to establish the "Global Partnership in the 21st Century". In April 2005,

[20] "India–US Strategic Dialogue Joint Statement", Ministry of External Affairs, Government of India, 19 July 2011, at http://www.mea.gov.in/mystart.php?id=530517853

[21] "India–US Strategic Dialogue Joint Statement", *Ministry of External Ajfairs*, Government of India, 19 July 2011 at http://www.mea.gov.in/mystart.php?id=530517853

[22] "Joint Statement on the Third US–India Strategic Dialogue", Media Note, Office of the Spokesperson, US Department of Defence, Washington DC, 13 June 2012, available at http://www.state. gov/r/pa/prs/ps/2012/06/192267.htm

[23] "India–Japan Relations", Embassy of India, Tokyo, Japan, available at http://www.embassyofindiajapan.org/new/documents/bilateral/India-Japan%20Relations%20%2017042012.pdf

Japanese Prime Minister Junichiro Koizumi visited India and it was decided that both nations would further strengthen their bilateral co-operation and would also explore a new architecture for closer regional co-operation in Asia. India's Prime Minister Dr Manmohan Singh visited Japan during 13-16 December 2006 and held meeting with the Prime Minister of Japan, Shinzo Abe. During the visit, a Joint Statement Towards India–Japan Strategic and Global Partnership was signed by the two prime ministers.[24]

In September 2010, India and Japan reached to an agreement in principle for an Economic Partnership Agreement (EPA) to liberalize trade and services between the two countries. The prime ministers of both the countries met several times in 2010 in different world forums. During 24-26 October 2010, India's PM Dr Manmohan Singh visited Tokyo for the Annual Bilateral Summit. During the visit, a joint statement titled as "Vision for India–Japan Strategic and Global Partnership in the Next Decade" as well as a joint declaration on the "India–Japan Comprehensive Economic Partnership Agreement" were signed. On 16 February 2011, the Comprehensive Economic Partnership Agreement (CEPA) was signed by the Commerce and Industry Minister (CIM) Anand Sharma and Japanese Foreign Minister Seiji Maehara. In the wake of the 11 March devastation caused by the magnitude 9 earthquake and the subsequent tsunami in north-eastern and eastern Japan, India's Prime Minister made a statement in Indian Parliament on 14 March expressing "full solidarity" with the people of Japan. A large quantity of Indian relief was sent to Japan. India also sent a forty-six-member team relief and rehabilitation from its National Disaster Management Authority (NDMA) to Japan.[25]

In continuation of a series of strategic dialogues between India and Japan, India's External Affairs Minister S.M. Krishna visited Japan during 28-30 October 2011 and participated in the 5th Annual Strategic Dialogue. This was followed by the visit of India's Defence Minister A.K. Antony for the India–Japan Defence Ministers' meeting on

[24] "India–Japan Relations".

[25] Ibid.

2-3 November 2011. Later, Prime Minister Yoshihiko Noda visited India from 27-29 December 2011.[26] After this visit, a joint statement was signed which was entitled as "Vision for the Enhancement of Japan–India Strategic and Global Partnership upon entering the year of the 60th Anniversary of the establishment of diplomatic relations".[27]

United States–South Korea Ties

The United States–South Korea strategic alliance was established during the Cold War. At the end of Second World War, when Japanese lost the control of Korea, the United States and the Soviet Union divided the Korean peninsula into two territories. The Republic of Korea (RoK), with its capital in Seoul, was declared as the only legitimate government on the peninsula by the United Nations in 1948[28] which was rejected by the Soviet Union. In 1950, war broke out between the North and South Koreas. The United States, led the UN forces came to the aid of South Korea. This war lasted until 1953, when a ceasefire was agreed at roughly the thirty-eighth parallel.[29] On 1 October 1953 in Washington, the mutual defence treaty between the Republic of Korea and the United States of America was signed which entered into force on 17 November 1954.[30] Article 3 of the 1953 Mutual Defense Treaty states:

---

26 "India–Japan Relations".

27 "Joint Statement: Vision for the Enhancement of Japan–India Strategic and Global Partnership upon entering the year of the 60th Anniversary of the Establishment of Diplomatic Relations", Ministry of Foreign Affairs of Japan, 28 December 2011, available at http://www.mofa.go.jp/region/asia-paci/india/pmv1112/joint_statement_en.html

28 Jayshree Bajoria and Youkyung Lee, "The US–South Korea Alliance", Backgrounder, Council on Foreign Relations, 13 October 2011, available at http://www.cfr.org/south-korea/us-south-korea-alliance/p11459

29 Ibid.

30 "Background Note: South Korea", Bureau of East Asian and Pacific Affairs, US Department of State, 12 April 2012, available at http://www.state.gov/r/pa/ei/bgn/2800.htm

> Each Party recognizes that an armed attack in the Pacific area on either of the Parties in territories now under their respective administrative control, or hereafter recognized by one of the Parties as lawfully brought under the administrative control of the other, would be dangerous to its own peace and safety and declares that it would act to meet the common danger in accordance with its constitutional processes.[31]

Under the US–RoK Mutual Defense Treaty of 1953, the United States is committed to help the Republic of Korea defend itself against external aggression. In support of this commitment, the United States has maintained Army's Second Infantry Division and several Air Force tactical squadrons. A Combined Forces Command (CFC) was established in 1978 to co-ordinate operations between these units and the over 680,000-strong Korean armed forces. The head of the CFC also hold the responsibility as Commander of the United Nations Command (UNC) and US Forces Korea (USFK) as well.[32]

However, the United States–South Korea security relationship is changing as the United States is moving from a leading to a supporting role. An agreement was reached in 2004 on the return of the Yongsan base in Seoul as well as a number of other United States bases to the RoK along with the eventual relocation of all United States forces to south of the Han River. This process is expected to be completed by 2016. Both the sides have also agreed to transfer wartime operational control from the US to the South Korean military on 1 December 2015.[33]

Economic relations are an increasingly significant aspect of the United States–South Korea strategic partnership. There has been a significant flow of manufactured goods, agricultural products, services

---

31 "1953 Mutual Defense Treaty", USFK SOFA Documents, United States Forces Korea, available at http://www.usfk.mil/usfk/sofa.1953.mutual.defense.treaty.76

32 "Background Note: South Korea", Bureau of East Asian and Pacific Affairs, US Department of State, 12 April 2012, available at http://www.state.gov/r/pa/ei/bgn/2800.htm

33 Ibid.

and technology between the two countries. Major American and South Korean companies have been investing in each other nations. By the end of 2011, the significant US–Korea Free Trade Agreement (KORUS FTA) was ratified by respective legislatures of the United States and South Korea which entered into force on 15 March 2012. According to an estimate by the US International Trade Commission, the tariff cuts in the United States–Korea trade agreement will enhance exports of US goods by $ 11 billion annually.[34]

US–Japan Ties

The United States–Japan alliance since the Second World War has been very strong. Under this alliance, there are about 36,000 US troops and other US military assets in the Asia-Pacific region. The United States also provides nuclear umbrella for Japan to help it dealing with threat perceptions from nations such as China and North Korea. During the 11 March 2011 earthquake and tsunami, the United States provided massive and immediate relief to Japan.[35]

In their relations, difficult issues such as relocation of stationed marines from Okinawa remain. In April 2012, both the governments agreed to relocate several thousand marines elsewhere in the region, but not much progress has been made so far. Japan is one of the key economic partners of the United States. It would be worth noting that Japan is US' second largest export market and second largest source of imports outside of North America. Japanese firms are the US' second largest source of foreign direct investment, and Japanese investors are the second largest foreign holders of United States treasuries.[36]

However, Japan has been severely affected by the world financial crisis and economic downturn. Japan's gross domestic product (GDP)

---

34 "Background Note: South Korea".

35 Emma Chanlett, William H. Cooper, Mark E. Manyin, "Japan–US Relations: Issues for Congress", Congressional Research Service (CRS) Report, 4 May 2012, available at http://www.fas.org/sgp/crs/row/RL33436.pdf

36 Ibid.

declined 1.2 per cent in 2008 and 5.3 per cent in 2009. However, it grew to 4 per cent in 2010 and then again it declined the 0.7 per cent in 2011. Japan has expressed interest in joining the Trans-Pacific Partnership (TPP).[37]

South Korea–Japan Ties

Although South Korea–Japan relations have not been so cordial because of bitter history between the two nations, Japan supported United States contingency plans to dispatch United States armed forces in Japan to South Korea in case of a North Korean attack on South Korea. At the appeal of the United States, South Korea and Japan normalized their relations in 1965 when the Treaty on Basic Relations between Japan and RoK was signed. After this treaty, Japan recognized South Korea as the only legitimate government in the entire Korean peninsula. Since then, South Korea and Japan have held series of foreign ministerial meetings. In 2002, Japan and South Korea jointly organized FIFA World Cup. Both the nations designated year 2005 as the "Japan–South Korea Friendship Year". However, in a recent development, Japan and South Korea were at loggerheads with each other over Takeshima islands. It would be worth noting that the Takeshima islands, comprising two small islands and more than ninety rocks and reefs, were made part of Japan's Shimane prefecture in 1905. In 1952, South Korea declared these islands as it own territory.[38] So, both Japan and South Korea have been making claims over these islands.[39]

Other than these growing bilateral relations between these four nations, there have been trilateral initiatives as well between these nations.

---

37 Emma Chanlett, William H. Cooper.

38 Profile: Dokdo/Takeshima islands, BBC News Asia, 10 August 2012, available at http://www.bbc.co.uk/news/world-asia-19207086

39 "South Korea and Japan face off over disputed islands", *The Guardian*, 10 August 2012, available at http://www.guardian.co.uk/world/2012/aug/10/south-korea-japan-disputed-islands

India–US–Japan Trilateral Dialogue

India, United States and Japan have had two rounds of trilateral dialogue on co-operation among themselves. The third round of trilateral discussion is scheduled on 29 October 2012 in New Delhi. According to reports, the United States "pivot-to-Asia" policy, Iran, China–Japan maritime dispute and South China Sea could be the issues to be discussed during this round. According to the official sources, the United States is expected to brief about its "pivot-to-Asia" policy. The United States is also expected to discuss about its policy towards Iran's nuclear programme. Japan is expected to brief about its maritime dispute with China and also the increasing Chinese influence in South China Sea. According to sources, the three nations will also explore the possibilities of co-operation in areas such as piracy and safety of sea lanes in the Asia Pacific region.[40]

The first India, United States and Japan trilateral meeting was held in Washington DC in December 2011. The second meeting was held in Tokyo in April 2012. After the first meeting, the Indian embassy in the United States said in a statement that these discussions mark the beginning of a series of consultations among the three governments, who share common values and interests across the Asia-Pacific and the globe. At their first ever trilateral dialogue the three sides "exchanged views on a wide range of regional and global issues of mutual interest". "All sides welcomed the frank and comprehensive nature of the discussions, and agreed the talks help advance their shared values and interests", it added.[41]

---

40 "India–US–Japan trilateral meet on Monday", *The Times of India*, 26 October 2012, available at http://articles.timesofindia.indiatimes.com/2012-10-26/india/34748822_1_maritime-dispute-chinese-influence-south-china-sea

41 "First US–Japan–India trilateral meeting", The Hindustan Times, 20 December 2012, available at http://www.hindustantimes.com/world-news/Americas/First-US-Japan-India-trilateral-meeting/Article1-784695.aspx

India–Japan–South Korea Trilateral Dialogue

The first India–Japan–South Korea trilateral dialogue was held in New Delhi in June 2012. Delivering the inaugural address during this dialogue, Secretary (East), Ministry of External Affairs, India, Sanjay Singh stated:

> This dialogue marks a milestone in the history of co-operation between our three countries. The foundation stone for this is indeed the robustness and dynamism of our respective bilateral relationships. Speaking for India, and I believe it holds equally true for Japan and Korea, it is the deeply valued strategic partnerships with both Japan and South Korea. In India today there is wide-ranging support for the strategic partnerships with Japan and Korea and it is indeed noteworthy that we have been able to constantly re-invent and re-invigorate the relationships. This has been possible because these partnerships are in turn based on something more profound, i.e. shared values and goals. These elements are the driving force for the synergy required to propel this trilateral framework. Japan and Korea are already involved in some trilateral processes.[42]

Shri Singh further noted that:

> We are also involved in a trilateral dialogue with Japan and the United States. Our experiences from these processes should inform this dialogue as well and we should from the very beginning calibrate this process to benefit the relationship amongst our countries and our peoples. We can never lose sight of the fact that this process has the unique character of a dialogue between three great democracies of Asia. Being leading democracies of the world we share a common commitment to democratic values, open society, human rights and the rule of law. These shared values provide us similar

---

42 "India–Japan–RoK Trilateral Diaiogue — Inaugural Address by Shri Sanjay Singh, Secretary (East)", Institute for Defence Studies and Analyses, 29 June 2012, available at http://idsa.in/event/IndiaJapanROKTrilateralDialogueInauguralAddress

perspectives and perceptions of the fast evolving regional and global environments. Similarly our strategic interests also coincide. We seek a peaceful and secure Asia free from the threats of terrorism, proliferation, piracy and conflict between states.[43]

Concluding Observations

It is evident that the partnership between India, South Korea, United States and Japan is steadily growing. However, this emerging strategic partnership between these four nations should not be viewed as a counterweight to the rise of China. It is noteworthy from above discussion that rise of China has caused concern for all these nations and it could be a factor for the emergence of partnership between these nations but this should not be viewed as the main factor. It is a fact that world is much more globalized today than ever before. It is much different from what it was during the Cold War period. Global economic interdependence as well as information and communication revolution have made this globe much more interconnected, interdependent and dynamic. With this growing strategic partnership, India, South Korea, United States and Japan would be able to establish much more co-operative relationship with each other and would also be able to deal with their various challenges efficiently and successfully. It needs to be clarified with regards to China that it is essential for these four nations that they closely engage with China as it is a major stake holder in the world affairs. There needs to be more people-to-people contacts between China and these four nations which will help in developing co-operative partnership with Chinese regimes as well as its society.

---

43 "India–Japan–RoK Trilateral Diaiogue — Inaugural Address by Shri Sanjay Singh, Secretary (East)", Institute for Defence Studies and Analyses, 29 June 2012, available at http://idsa.in/event/IndiaJapanROKTrilateralDialogueInauguralAddress

19

Reconstruction and Development
Relevance of the Korean Experience in Education

G. Balatchandirane

As a nation that embarked on modernization after its liberation from Japan and registered tremendous economic progress in a short span of time, the Republic of Korea (henceforth Korea) has a huge repertoire of lessons to offer to the late comers to development. Korea itself was well aware of the Japanese historical experience of modernization and did take a number of useful pointers by studying the Japanese model. What makes the study of the Korean case interesting is the fact that it was able to achieve much of what Japan did in a time-frame that was even shorter. A number of developing countries including India which have been assiduously studying the Japanese experience in rapid modernization have even more to gain by looking at the Korean experience.

Herein, I focus on education and attempt to see how the Korean experience can offer useful pointers for development for the currently developing countries in general and India in particular. The caveat at the outset is that there were certain features of the Korean historical experience with education which may not be desirable and need to be avoided — for example, the large financial burden borne by individual families in educating their children, the tremendous competition that youngsters face in getting to the higher education institution of their choice, the "examination hell" phenomenon and the like — but this does not negate the fact that much that is useful can be learnt from the Korean experience.

Why is education important when we talk of economic development? There are many pathways through which education impacts favourably on economic development. Tilak (1989) points out:

(a) There is significant contribution of education to economic growth as returns to education are comparable to those arising out of investments in physical capital.

(b) Education has significant poverty reduction and income distribution effects leading to reduced inequalities.

(c) Even the non-monetary contributions of education are positive.

Walter McMahon (1999) finds that the overall returns to investment in education are huge and can be seen in areas such as reduction of infant mortality, increase in life expectancy, reduction in fertility rates, promotion of democracy, human rights, political stability, reduction of poverty and inequality, reduction in pollution and lowering of crime. Detailed review of this literature is available (Balatchandirane 2007b).

Specifically turning to the Korean case, there is again ample evidence in the literature that highlights the important role that education played in its rapid economic growth in the last six decades or so. There was " . . . an abundant supply of low-cost, well-educated labour", and this was one reason that helped Korea in its industrialization — and this was a defining feature of twentieth-century development of later industrializing countries. The available labour was not just cheap and abundant but educated as well. This was an important reason that enabled Korea to turn competitive in world markets. Second, "Salaried engineers have performed especially well in Korea because society has invested heavily in education. . . ." Enough engineers were created leading to competition for jobs which drove up productivity. Korea was about to begin massive industrialization with a population that was more educated than Germany or the United States eighty years earlier (Amsden 1989: 8-18, 216). Three-fourths of the workers in the manufacturing sector had either secondary education or more in the early 1980s. Jison Lee (2001) contends:

> . . . Korea's experience clearly indicates that education, or more generally human capital accumulation, is indeed extremely important for rapid economic development. Rapid accumulation of human capital is a necessary condition for fast and sustained economic development.

After liberation from Japanese colonial rule in 1945, there was a spectacular expansion in the number of schools. They increased from 3,000 to almost 20,000 in the following half-century. The student population rose from 1.5 to 11.7 million. The Education Law of 1949, which was formulated under strong American influence, made six years of elementary education compulsory. This was implemented in right earnest after the Korean War of 1950-53. The Constitution stipulates in Article 31 that it is the responsibility of parents and guardians to ensure that an elementary school education for their children aged six to eleven is provided; it also states that this education would be given by the state free. In 1969 South Korea made nine years of education compulsory. The emphasis was on raising the educational standards of the whole population and not on the creation of an elite class (World Bank 2006).

Elementary education which is for six years starts when the child is six years old. Secondary education is for six years, with the first three years in middle school and three years in high school. Colleges and university courses at the undergraduate level are of four to six years duration. Access is easy and equitable: gross enrolment at the secondary level is at 90 per cent, for both boys and girls. Schools are adequately funded — more than 2.4 per cent of Korea's GDP is spent on secondary education, a third of that privately. Through a massive national literacy campaign and the introduction of compulsory education system in 1948, Korea raised its literacy levels rapidly, vastly reducing education inequality between 1970 and 1995. Korea initially emphasized literacy and numeracy and focused on primary education. Later it emphasized vocational education and still later graduate-level science and technology education. The important point is that these emerged and changed with the economy's changing needs (Ranis 1995).

Six principles are said to have guided the new education system in Korea. The first was the earlier mentioned six years of free and compulsory elementary education. Second, the secondary education system was divided into middle school and high school. The idea was to bring down the number of dropouts and make secondary education more relevant. Third, while secondary education would be on a single track, at the high school level this would split into different streams of study enabling the movement of students between streams. Occupational training courses were included in vocational education. Fourth, in keeping with the various demands in society higher education sector was diverse with differing programme contents and durations. Fifth, adequate provisions were to be made for the supply of teachers at elementary and secondary school levels. Sixth, civic schools were set up with the intent of providing adult education (Lee et al. 2010: 55-56).

In any modernizing society the rules of climbing the social ladder get rewritten. In the pre-modern period, the criteria for one's standing in society or upward social mobility depended on the group or clan one belonged to. Birth determined how far one could go in the social ladder. Opportunities opened up for upward mobility based on one's background. There were instances of someone rising up due to abilities but these would be few and far between. In a society that has stepped into modernization, the social mobility rules get rewritten with achievement taking precedence over ascription. The ability of a person to perform determines how far he would rise in station in life. This ability basically depends on the skill set one has. The social background of the person increasingly becomes irrelevant. The skill set one has is essentially determined by education. If access to education is open to all then education becomes a major determinant of social mobility.

The other aspect is that this is an effective way to reduce existing economic inequalities in society. The existing economic inequalities in a society can be due to wealth inequality and income inequality. Wealth inequality could be because of inequitable distribution of land during the pre-modern times. Land reforms would be the answer to this, though implementation may not be easy because the vested interests would be holding power. The easier thing to tackle is income inequality. Incomes are based on the skill sets that people possess; and if they are given opportunities to acquire skill sets equitably, then incomes too should be equitable. Giving access to education equitably would put people on a level-playing field. The critical point here is that access to education should be given to all sections of society equitably without any discrimination based on geography, gender, clan, economic standing or any other criteria if social mobility is to be facilitated and economic inequities in society are to be reduced. Education would become the greatest leveller.

Korea clearly did exceedingly well in this aspect. The opportunities for education were given to all citizens irrespective of gender, age or regional background. The equality in educational access has strong legal backing in Korea and is considered one of the most fundamental rights of Korean citizens. The centralized system of education enabled the

> . . . equalizing education conditions across the country. Every student in Korea has the same education in terms of curriculum, facility, and quality of teachers whether he or she lives in a city or a rural area. — Lee et al. 2010: 87

This philosophy has gone a long way in reducing social inequality and has led to an increase in upward mobility.

Even after more than forty years of heavy investment in human capital, Koreans are still "over-eager" towards education and are over-investing in education. There was so much expansion of elementary education that the 1950s is called a decade of elementary education and the 1960s one of middle school education.

> . . . Education seems to have been the most effective mechanism to improve equity among citizens. Education has been mostly non-discriminatory as the opportunity to be educated was given equally to all. — Lee 2001

From the earliest days the focus was on access and quality for all, motivated by the desire to bring educated workers into the workforce. It has one of the most impressive Lorenz curves for any country in the world, indicating that Korea's education has been most egalitarian. The Lorenz curve is a graphic representation of the spread of inequalities seen against a situation of absolute equality represented by a 45° diagonal. The larger the inequality, the more the curve is away from the diagonal (Thomas et al. 2000: 15).

During the modernizing phase, when a country tries to create a modern education system, logic dictates that it invests more in the primary sector of education initially. For one, the illiteracy levels would be high; it is the duty of the state to provide large sections of the population with literacy. This would also facilitate the growth of industry in the country. Second, economic logic indicates that the primary education sector should receive more attention as the rate of return to it is the highest, followed by the secondary sector and then the tertiary sector. Thus, the state would try to provide basic education to as large a section of the population as possible rapidly. The share of the population that proceeds to secondary education would be quite low in the initial years of modernization, as even with primary education, a large share of the population would be able to find gainful employment. As the country progresses economically and as industry matures, the secondary education sector would develop in part due to the demand for higher human capital needs and in part because people with basic education and income-earning capacity would try to raise their skill levels further. The tertiary education sector, the universities, colleges and higher institutions would be the last to develop. This would be the natural progression.

Stated differently, an education triangle with a large base comprising of a large section of the population educated at the primary level, with a smaller layer over it possessing secondary education qualifications and an even smaller layer at the top with skills in higher education would be what any country would attempt to have in the beginning. As economic development proceeds, the percentage of people who proceed from the primary to secondary education will increase; likewise those moving from secondary to tertiary education also would increase. With development, the country would be able to afford the setting up of the higher educational institutions which consume much larger amounts of resources. Meanwhile almost the entire population will turn literate and people would keep raising their skill levels in consonance with the rise in development levels. Empirical support for this is available in a study which analysed educational impact on economic development in various countries of Asia and concluded that ". . . early increases in higher education enrolments are not effective as a strategic means of increasing growth" (McMahon, 1999: 50). Korea gave importance to the spread of elementary education in the beginning. This is seen in the fact that during the initial period of 1954-59, 80 per cent of the education budget was set aside for compulsory elementary education (Lee et al. 2010).

Korea focused on one education cycle at a time, starting with basic education. In the 1950s and 1960s, when public funds mainly targeted primary education, secondary schools financed almost half their expenses through parent–teacher associations. However, the rapid expansion of primary education put enormous pressure on secondary schools, and student competition for good secondary schools increased. In preparation for entrance exams students often repeated grades and families paid up to a quarter of their income for private tutoring. Well over two-thirds of the Korean government expenditure on education was spent on primary and secondary schooling. In the forty-year period between 1960 and 2000, illiteracy was wiped out and the mean years of schooling doubled. It is held that the 1950s was the period of elementary education, the 1960s that of middle school, the 1970s that of high school and the 1980s that of higher education (Lee 2001).

The building up the base of the educational triangle broadly and then moving upwards made sense in a number of ways. First, scarce resources were used to give basic education to everyone equitably without the creation of an elite class and introducing inequities in society. Second, this coalesced with the kind of human capital needs that Korea experienced as it moved from the import substitution stage to the export expansion phase. No one was denied access to basic education and in keeping with their capabilities, the population was able to pursue higher levels of education. This sequential pattern of growth of education, it is held was the reason why there was equal distribution of education in the population. This sequential expansion led to a rise in average income levels while reducing income inequalities. This also accounts for Korea's success in attaining rapid economic development without worsening the economic inequalities. The sequential educational expansion was co-ordinated with the trade, industry and labour policies between the 1961-96 period (Adams 2010 and Choi 2009 quoted therein).

This is in stark contrast to what took place in the Indian context, where in the immediate years after Independence the political economy of development ensured that the vested interests of the ruling and powerful classes were well taken care of. The Indian elite bureaucratic and ruling classes made sure that their own offspring did not suffer for want of good quality higher educational institutions and so were very favourably inclined towards their creation. Thus at a time of scarce resources, the higher education sector did not suffer for want of funds. The second reason which prevented the creation of a large base of the education triangle has to do with the economic model that India was following in the initial decades of development. Huge sums of money were invested in state-owned public sector undertakings. The economic models that India tried to follow gave the policy planners indications on how much highly qualified skilled professionals would be required in each sector. This meant substantial investments had to be made in the higher education sector. However a large share of human capital thus created could not be usefully utilized as the original plans went awry. These two reasons meant that the higher education sector got more than what would be considered a fair share in the context of a country at the initial stages of modernization. It has to be remembered that the pie was small; large investments in higher education necessarily meant that the

Table 1: Literacy Rates in India, Selected Years, 1881–2001 (%)

Year	*Literacy Rate*			
	Total	*Males*	*Females*	*Gender Gap*
1881	6.3			
1911	7.3			
1931	9.3			
1951	18.3	27.2	8.9	18.3
1961	28.3	40.4	15.4	25.0
1971	34.5	46.0	22.0	24.0
1981	43.6	56.4	30.0	26.4
1991	52.2	64.1	39.3	24.8
2001	65.4	76.0	54.3	21.7

Source: World Bank 1997: 16, and Government of India 2001.

Note: Literacy rates for 1881–1931 are for persons ten years olds and above, rates for 1951-71 are for persons five years old and above, and rates for 1981 and later are for persons seven years old and above.

primary education sector suffered. For the money spent on educating one student at university in 1950-51, ninety-six students could have been schooled at the primary level (Gounden 1987).

In Korea elementary schools are by and large public and there is no tuition fees. Most middle schools too are public. While a fee had to be paid, it was kept low by the government. By 2002 the government made middle schools too free. The public high schools are supposed to have poor teaching and this is where families start spending heavily on private tuition.

The combined spending on education by the government and private spending by households have been above 10 per cent of GNP in the recent past in Korea with about 7 per cent coming from the private sector. This high figure reflects the importance parents give to education and reflects the perceived returns. Were one to add to this the firms' spending on employees, this rises to 14 per cent of GNP, a truly impressive figure. It is estimated that parents with school age children spend close to 25 per cent of their income on the education of their children. Some of this spending is believed to be wasteful (Lee 2001).

While Pakistan and South Korea were almost equal in GNP per capita in 1960, whereas only 30 per cent of the Pakistani children were enrolled in primary schools in that year, 94 per cent of South Korean children were. Establishing a direct connection between this fact and later growth rates might not be easy, but the implications are hard to miss (The Economist 1996). The heavy investments that South Korea made in education was to favourably impact on the subsequent economic growth. South Korea was able to record 9.4 per cent growth rate in its GDP in the 1980s and around 7.2 per cent between 1990 and 1995.

What are the major conclusions one can arrive at after looking at the role of education in South Korea in the post-Second World War years? First, it is very clearly brought out by the Korean experience that education was exceedingly important for the rapid economic development that it experienced. Without the rapid accumulation of human capital it would have been impossible to have had the fast and sustained economic development. The obvious lesson for India which believes it is an emerging economy today is that not much progress can be made without educating its whole population at least at the basic level.

Second, in Korea, education was the great leveller, the most effective mechanism that improved equity among citizens. Education was non-discriminatory since everyone had equal opportunity to be educated. It is worth recalling that Korea stands out from the other countries in recent times in that it managed the fastest expansion in education coverage while recording the fastest decline in the education Gini coefficient (Thomas et al. 2000). The most important lesson for India is to give equitable access to quality education to everyone. The corollary is that education has to be provided by the state at least at the basic level. There are important implications for gender equity in society when equal access to education is given to everyone (Balatchandirane 2003, 2004 and 2007a).

Third, the sequential nature of educational development in Korea, i.e. spreading primary education to the entire population, followed by secondary education and then tertiary meant that inequalities in the societies were kept to a minimum while economic growth was fostered. The unconscionably large share of budget that was taken up by the higher education sector immediately after Independence in India when resources where scarce and the majority of the population was illiterate only served to worsen existing economic inequalities. Economic growth could have been much faster had large sections of the society were educated at least at the basic level. This is the reason why many of the East Asian economies, including Korea were able to tap the opportunities in the export markets for industrial products in the 1970s and later in a big way. India exports on the other hand were dominated by and large by primary products.

Fourth, initially in the 1950s, it was the tremendous contribution of the parents who sacrificed a great deal to ensure that their children be educated; soon the government was to play a dynamic and central role in fostering an efficient mass education system (Ashton et al. 1999). The detailed planning and execution of various schemes related to education as well as the co-ordination of educational policies with the larger development policies in Korea ensured a smooth spread of education while ensuring steady supply of the human capital needs of the industry without which growth would have suffered. The abdicative role of the Indian state in provisioning education is too well known to be detailed here. Unless that changes, the current privatization drive is not going to be conducive for creating human capital in a meaningful way. Economic growth would slow down and the existing high levels of economic inequalities are going to worsen.

Finally, it is worth remembering that Korea more than made up for its late start by ensuring that everyone had access to education without any discrimination on the basis of gender, geography or clan. The commitment of the State to the diffusion of basic education was impressive. This has relevance in the context of the current globalization process where the privatization *mantra* has pervaded the portals of education and the "market mechanism" is seem as a cure-all for development. Social sectors like education and health have to be nurtured by the state in the initial stages of modernization in India.

References

Adams, Don, 2010, "A Comparative Perspective on the Development of Korean Education", in Chong Jae Lee, Senong-yul Kim and Don Adams (eds.), 2010, pp. 107-48.

Amsden, Alice H., 1989, *Asia's Next Giant: South Korea and Late Industrialization*, New York: Oxford University Press.

Ashton, David, Francis Green, Donna James and Johnny Sung, 1999, *Education and Training for Development in East Asia: The Political Economy of Skill Formation in East Asian Newly Industrialized Economies*, London and New York: Routledge.

Balatchandirane, G., 2003, "Gender Discrimination in Education and Economic Development: A Study of South Korea, China and India", *International Studies* (New Delhi/Thousand Oaks/London), **40**(4): 349-78.

———, 2004, "Gender Discrimination in Education and Economic Development: Lessons from East Asia", in Sushila Narsimhan and G. Balatchandirane (eds.) *India and East Asia: Learning from Each Other*, New Delhi: Manak Publishers, pp. 101-59.

———, 2007a, "Women's Education and Development: East Asian Lessons for South Asia", in Jandhyala B.G. Tilak (ed.), *Women's Education and Development*, New Delhi: Gyan Publishing House, pp. 35-70.

———, 2007b, *Gender Discrimination in Education and Economic Development: A Study of Asia*, China: Institute of Developing Economies, 2007, Visiting Research Fellow Report, pp. 221 + xii.

Choi, A., 2009, "Sequential Educational Expansion, Equity, and Growth in Republic of Korea", *KEDI Journal of Educational Policy*, **6**(2): 21-43.

Economist, 1996. "Those educated Asians: What can the rest of the world learn from the classrooms of Asia?" pp. 29-30., 21st September.

Gounden, A.M. Nalla 1987. "Education and Economic Growth: Lessons from india", in Gosh, Ratna and Mathew Zachariah eds., Education and the Process of change New Delhi: Sage Publications, pp. 103-24.

Lee, Chong Jae, Senong-yul Kim and Don Adams (eds.), 2010, *Sixty Years of Korean Education*, Seoul: Seoul National University Press.

Lee, Chong Jae et al., 2010, "A Korean Model of Educational Development" in Chong Jae Lee, Senong-yul Kim and Don Adams (eds.), 2010, pp. 53-106.

Lee, Jison, 2001, *Education Policy in the Republic of Korea: Building Block or Stumbling Block?*, World Bank Institute Working Paper, Washington: The World Bank.

McMahon, Walter W., 1999, *Education and Development: Measuring the Social Benefits*, New York: Oxford University Press.

Ranis, Gustav, 1995, "Another Look at the East Asian Miracle", *The World Bank Economic Review*, **9**(3), 509-34.

The Economist, 2006, *A Survey of Pakistan*, 8 July.

Thomas, Vinod et al., 2000, *Measuring Education Inequality: Gini Coefficients of Education*, Washington DC: The World Bank.

Tilak, Jandhyala B.G., 1989, *Education and Its Relation to Economic Growth, Poverty and Income Distribution: Past Evidence and Further Analysis*, World Bank Discussion Paper 46, Washington: World Bank.

World Bank, 2006, *World Development Report 2007: Development and the Next Generation*, Washington: The World Bank.

20

Trade, Commerce: Past, Present and the Possibilities
— The Korean Experience —

Lee, Soon-Cheul

Poverty to Prosperity

KOREA was the poorest country in 1948. Japanese occupation and Korea War left few production facilities. After adopting the export and industrial policies for economic development since 1960s, Korea had achieved rapid economic growth. Per capita income grew from US $ 67 in 1953 to US $ 22,000 in 2011 (*fig.* 1). The rapid growth was made possible by the government maintaining macroeconomic stability and heavy investments.

Based on the policy goals of the Korean government, the last sixty years were divided into six eras as:

1. Import Substitutions (1948-61)
2. Export Promotion (1962-72)
3. Government-led Industrialization (1973-79)
4. Economic Liberalization and Globalization (1980-97)
5. Crisis (1997-98)
6. Low growth/establishing a New Growth Momentum (1999-2012.

In the import substitution period, the per capita income grew 2.7 per cent at the time when Korean economy was dominated by the agriculture and other primary industries. During the export-

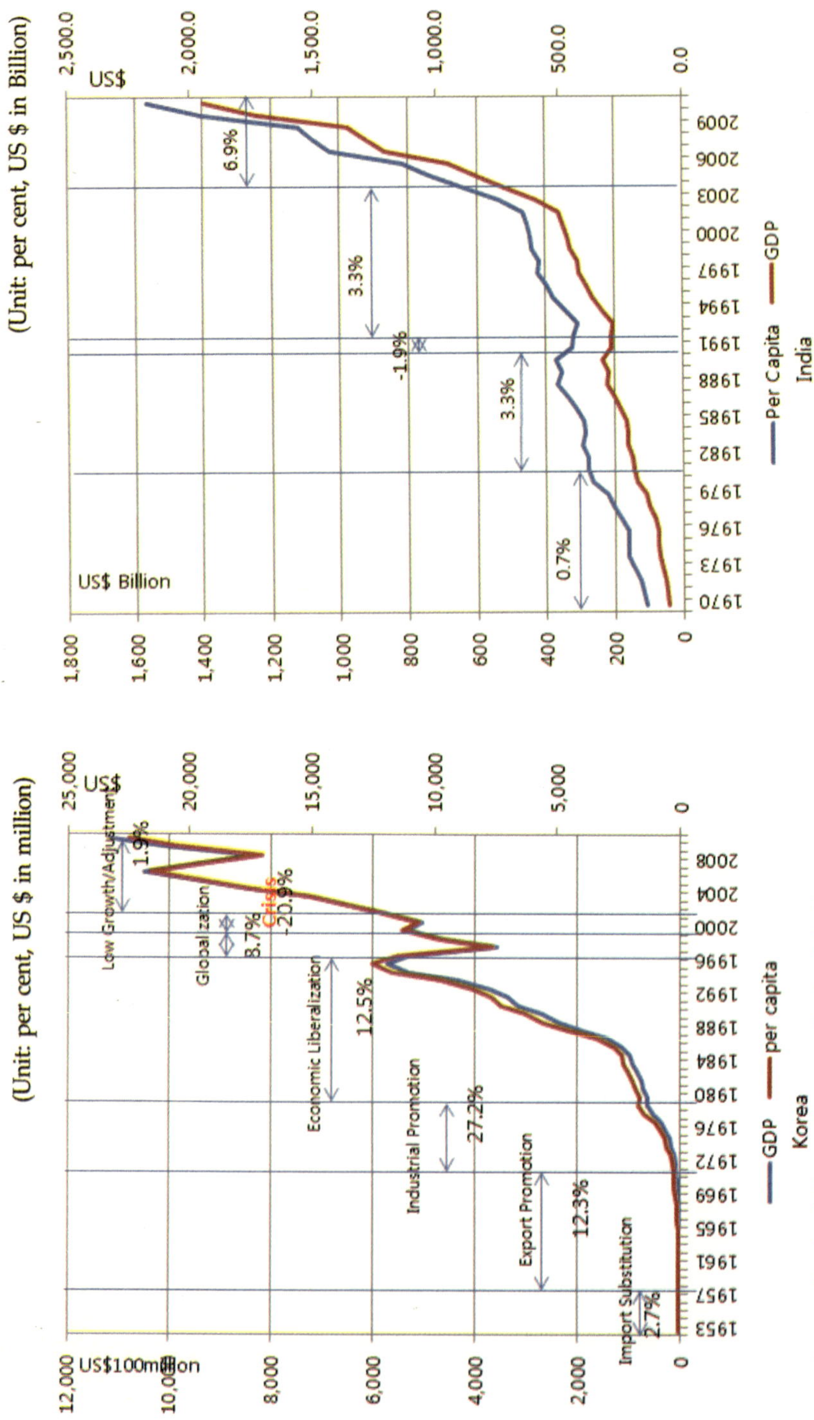

Source: Bank of Korea, Reserve Bank of India

fig. 1: The trend of economic growth of India and Korea

and government-led industrialization eras, the economy grew tremendously on average 12.3 and 27.2 per cent, respectively. The growth rates in the economic liberalization and globalization periods were 12.5 and 8.7 per cent. Facing the crisis in 1997, the Korean economy entered into the low growth era. We can say, the Korean economy has grown the fastest in the 1970s and 1980s.

Meanwhile, the Indian economy grew relatively slow in the 1970s as known as "Hindu growth". Since 2003, India has grown dramatically more than 7 per cent on average, the fastest growth in the world.

Until the 1970s, agriculture was the main industry in Korea. The share of the agriculture was about 50 per cent of the economy. However the agriculture ratio decreased very fast after the Korean government adopted export- and industrial-oriented policies for the economic growth, resulting its contribution to less than 10 per cent during that period. While decreasing the share of the agriculture, the role of manufacturing in contributing to the growth of the economy increased. The share, which was 9 per cent in 1953, increased to 30 per cent in 1988. The industrial sectors including manufacturing began to lead the Korean economy in the 1970s.

In India, the service sector has been leading the Indian economy as the sector has grown faster than other sectors. The share of agriculture in India was 42.2 per cent in 1970 and decreased so fast that it came down to only 9 per cent in 2010, while the share of service sector changed from 42.4 per cent to 62.8 per cent during that period. The share of manufacturing has sustained around 16-18 per cent during the period (*fig.* 2).

All of that, the manufacturing has led the grown of Korean economy while the service sector has led the Indian economy. It also points out that government-led export and industrial policies were important for rapid Korean economic development. Thus, it is worth reviewing the trade and industrial policies how to contribute so prominently the economic development of Korea.

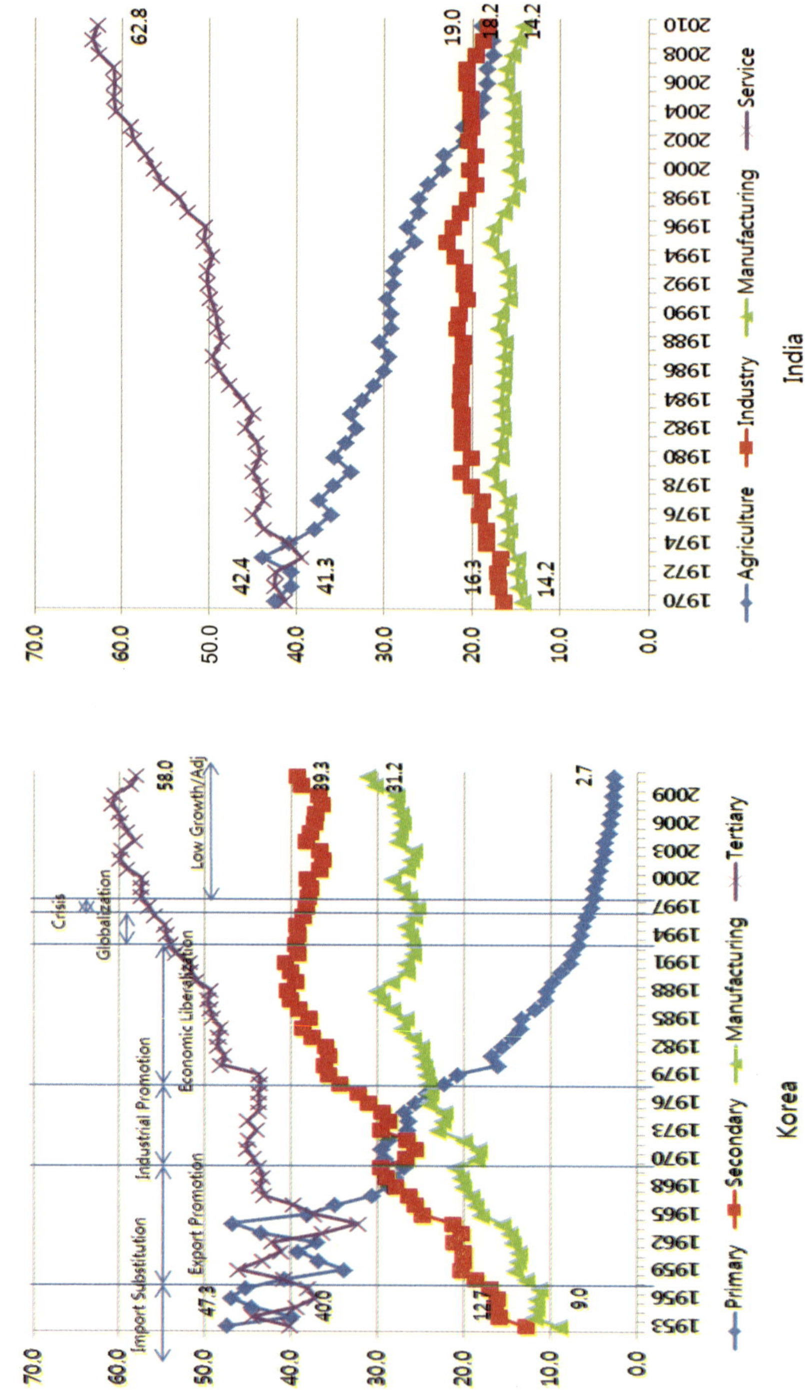

Source: Bank of Korea, Global Insight

fig. 2: The structure of Korean and Indian economy (unit per cent)

Trade and Industrial Policies in Korea

IMPORT SUBSTITUTION: 1948-62

Japan's occupation in 1910 to 1945 had left few domestic power and industrial facilities in the south because the industrial bases were mostly in the north. Korea was split between north and south in 1945-48. Korean War in 1950-53 destroyed 45 per cent of production facilities in South Korea and its people suffered in intense poverty (Kim and Roemer 1979). Korean government did not emphasize on economic growth because of the corrupt government and chaotic politics.

The government tried to reconstruct the national economy with the help of the UN and the US. During 1945-50, a total of US $ 585 million in aid was provided by the UN and the US. Without the sources of foreign exchanges, Korea needed daily necessities, construction materials and fertilizers for agriculture. Korea financed them by aids.

In the 1950s, Korean government adopted an economic policy of "revised capitalism" which allowed private ownership under the government regulations. Exports were mostly agriculture and marine

Table 1: GDP and Trade in Korea

Year	*GDP (bn. Won)*	*Per Capita GDP (US $)*	*Exports (mn. US $)*	*Imports (mn. US $)*
1948			22	208
1949			14	133
1950			29	48
1951			16	155
1952			28	214
1953	48	67	40	345
1954	66	70	24	243
1955	115	65	18	341
1956	152	66	25	386
1957	197	74	22	442
1958	205	80	17	378
1959	218	81	20	304
1960	245	79	33	344
1961	294	82	41	316

Source: National Statistical Office.

products. Trade policies consisted of typical import substitution measures used by many less developed countries of the time. That is, Korean government imposed high tariff rates on imports because most of imports was financed through foreign aid. A high tariff rate between 25 and 30 per cent was imposed on imports with additional quantitative restrictions. Korea government also maintained a positive list import system with about 1,000 type of goods on the list. The government maintained a highly overvalued exchange rate and controlled over it strictly.

Korea's implementation of its import substitution trade policies involved nothing more than building up a huge trade deficit. In 1961, exports were US $ 41 million while imports volume was US $ 316 million, which resulted in about US $ 270 million of trade deficits. These trade deficits required inflows of foreign aid from the US and the UN.

THE ERA OF EXPORT PROMOTION POLICIES: 1962-72

The political chaos ended in military coup by Chung Hee Park, overthrowing the Rhee government. Economic growth was crucial to provide the justification for the political leadership. As the foreign aid decreased sharply, the government needed new initiatives for foreign exchanges. These forced the government to transform the aid-based economy inherited from the 1950s into the export-oriented economy.

1. The government initiated five-year economic development plan in 1962.
2. It stimulated exports for the source of foreign exchange supply.
3. The government focused on light manufacturing rather than trying to build heavy manufacturing and machinery industries as was often done in other countries. Korea took advantages of cheap and abundant labour. The government ensured that focus was placed on developing textiles, plywood, footwear, etc.
4. Korea joined GATT in 1967.

Table 2: Interest Rates (%) in Korea (1964-75)

Year	*Inflation (CPI)*	*1-Year Term Deposit*	*Bank Loan*		*Curb Market*
			Market Average	*Export*	
1964	—	15.0	16.9	8.0	61.8
1965	—	30.0	26.0	6.5	58.9
1966	11.2	30.0	26.0	6.0	58.7
1967	10.9	30.0	26.0	6.0	56.7
1968	10.8	26.0	25.8	6.0	56.0
1969	12.3	24.0	24.5	6.0	51.4
1970	15.9	22.8	24.0	6.0	50.2
1971	13.5	22.0	23.0	6.0	46.4
1972	11.7	15.0	17.5	6.0	39.0
1973	3.1	12.6	15.5	7.0	33.2
1974	24.3	15.0	15.5	9.0	40.6
1975	25.3	15.0	15.5	9.0	47.9

Source: Cho (1989).

Finally, Korean government set up the Monthly Export Promotion Meeting involving the president, ministers and representatives from major exporting businesses. In the meeting, private sector was encouraged to set "target" for export and discussed the needs of the business related to the issues of exports.

Korean government also set up some institutes for supporting business involving exports. For instance, the government established Economic Planning Board (EPB) and Korea Development Institute (KDI) for policy-making and providing the theoretical research and statistics.The Korea Trade Promotion Corporation (KOTRA) was established to promote exports by extending overseas networks.

The government-assisted export businesses with a preferential tax system, automatic credit access and a number of subsidies with administrative supports (Kim and Cheong 1998). The government rationed the limited foreign exchange reserves to the firms and industries involved in exporting. A series of currency reforms were implemented. The government devalued the Korean currency and

Korea's Import and Export (1955-70) (US $ in million)

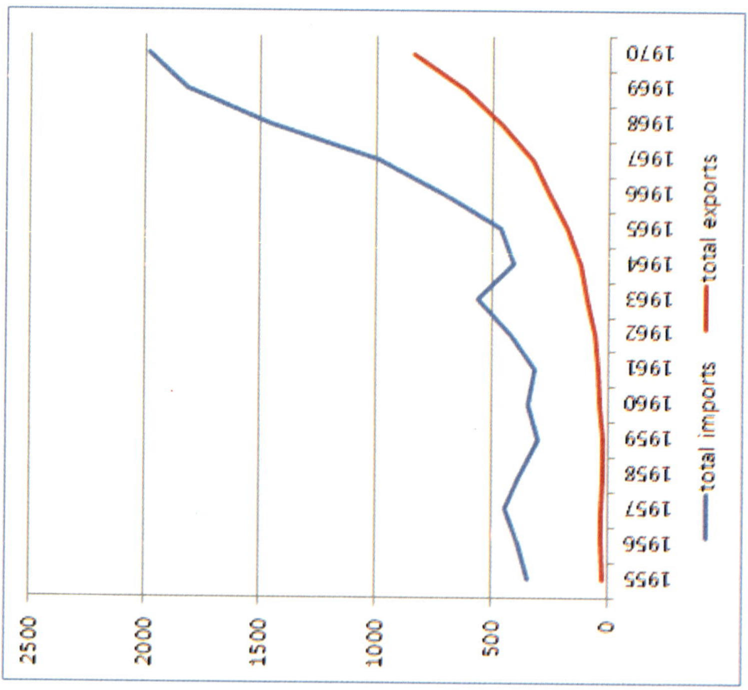

Source: Yoo (2008).

Korea's Export Composition (1955-70)

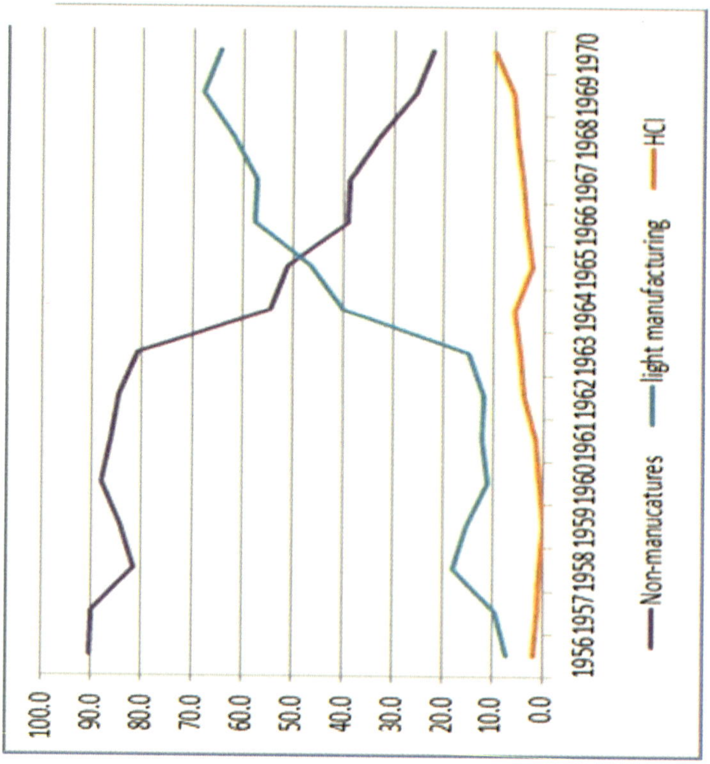

fig. 3: Korean imports and exports during 1955-70

managed foreign exchange reserves. The devaluation of the Korean Won improved the competitiveness of Korean products in the world market. The government also financially backed up exporters with very cheap interest rates. The government also invested heavily in infrastructure: modernizing ports, building power plants and facilities, constructing expressways, etc.

The export-led policies set a solid economic foundation replacing Korea's dependency on foreign aid. Exports began to expand rapidly in the early 1960s, with exports growing by 40 per cent on average in current dollars and reaching US $ 835 million in 1970, more than 40 times as large as in the 1950s (*fig*. 3).

The industrial structure changed dramatically as the portion of manufacturing in the economy grew from 15.5 per cent in 1961 to 23.3 per cent in 1972. The share of exports from light manufacturing increased rapidly while that from non-manufacturing decreased very quickly.

Korean conglomerates — so-called "Chaebols"— was created in this period. Hyundai Group including Hyundai Motors was founded by Joo Young Chung. It started business as an owner of small rice store in 1934 and ran a car repair shop in 1941-43. Chung founded a small construction company in 1947, which became Hyundai Construction later. Hyundai Motors was founded in 1967 as joint venture with Ford, but later with participation from Mitsubishi.

LG/GS Group, which was founded by In-Whe Ku, started business in 1931 as an owner of store which sold cotton and textiles. Lucky Chemicals was engaged in manufacturing cosmetics and toilet articles (e.g. toothpaste) in 1947. Ku launched Goldstar Electronics in 1958, which was manufacturing radios and later TV sets and household electronics. In 1960, LG moved into vinyl and petrochemicals (establishing Honam Petrochemicals with US Caltex-Chevron and Texaco, which became GS Caltex).

SK Group was founded by Joungkun Choi that bought the remains of the Sunkyoung Textiles in 1953 which was a former Japanese–Korean joint venture company in 1939, but managed as the asset belonging to the Korean government in 1948. The factory had been destroyed during the Korean War. In 1962, SK Group established Sunkyoung Industry which was a trading company. In 1960, Sunkyoung moved into artificial fibres that was the first Korean textile exporter to Hong Kong.

GOVERNMENT-LED INDUSTRIALIZATION: 1973-1979

In the 1970s, the government changed industrial policies from the development of light manufacturing to the development of the heavy manufacturing and chemical industries. The Nixon Doctrine had called for the withdrawal of US ground forces from Korea. It motivated Korea government to foster a local defence industry. In the world market, severe competition in labour-intensive sector with less-developing countries also forced Korea to adjust its industrial structure. The balance of payments deficits continued to increase due to increased imports of capital goods. These situations made the government kick off the promotion of heavy manufacturing and chemical industries with the Heavy and Chemical Industry (HCI) Promotion plan in June 1973, embodied in the Third and Fourth Five-Year Development Plan (Choong Yong Ahn and Joo-Hoon Kim 1995; Yeong-koo Park 2005). The government targeted six industries as future core industries: steel,

Table 3: The Trend of KDB[1] Loans by Industry

(unit: Korean Won in Million)

Industry	*1972*	*1973*	*1976*	*1978*	*1979*	*1972-79 AAGR[2] %*	*1980-89 AAGR %*
Manufacturing	25,958	54,975	124,759	263,138	535,751	39.2	12.5
Light industry	12,349	10,883	11,639	21,598	73,751	29.1	12.8
HCIs[3]	13,609	44,092	113,120	241,540	462,000	41.5	12.5

Note: 1. Korea Development Bank. 2. Average annual growth rate. 3. Heavy and Chemical Industries.

Source: Korea Development Bank, 1994, *"40-year History of the Korea Development Bank"*.

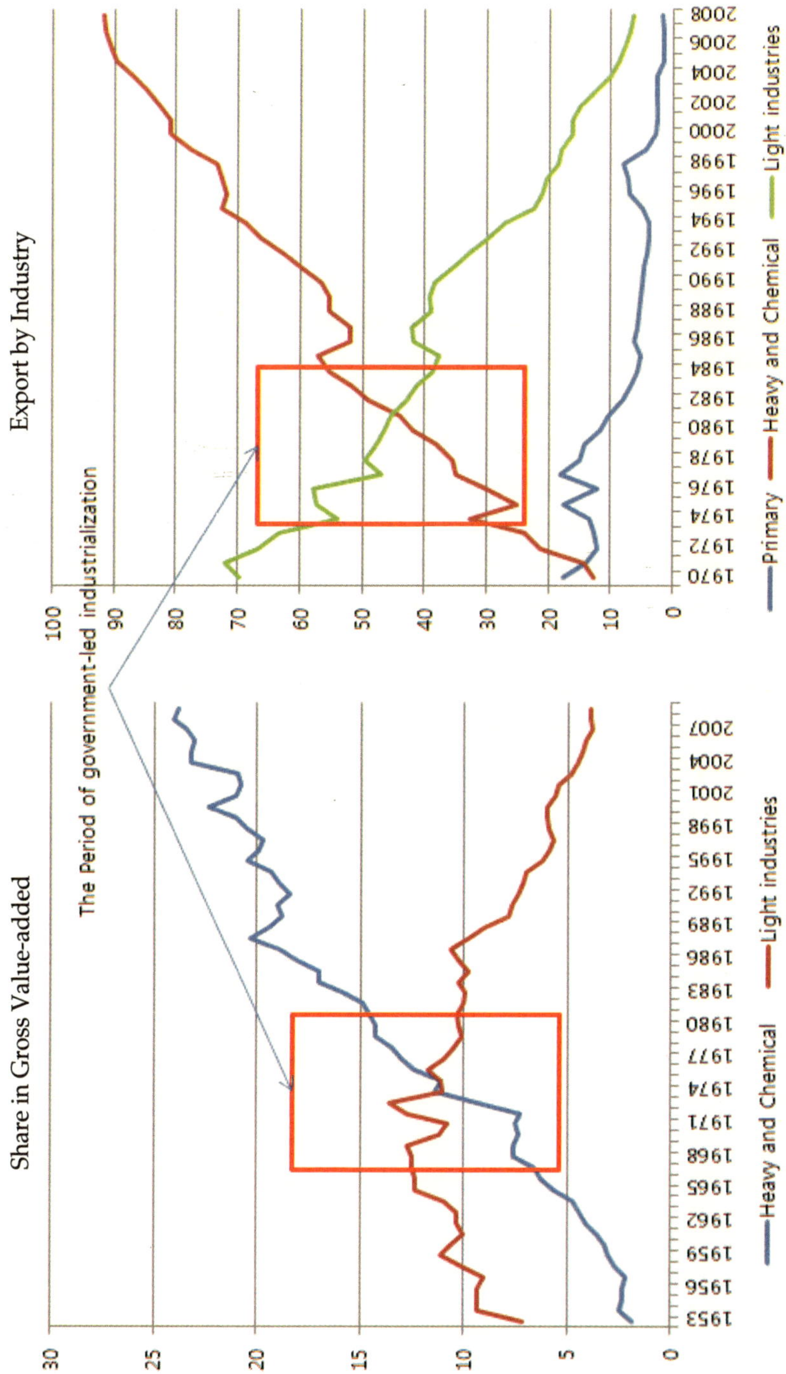

Source: Sankong and Koh (2010).

fig. 4: The share of Heavy and Chemical Industries in GDP and exports in Korea (per cent)

non-ferrous metal, machinery (including automobiles), ship-building, electronics and chemicals. The government invested a total of US $ 9.6 billion between 1973 and 1981 into these sectors.

The government encouraged private enterprises for the implementation of a variety of business projects. Because of the long-term nature and the scale of investment, the construction of heavy manufacturing and chemical industries required massive factor inputs, such as capital, human resources and technology. The government provided the long-term administered credit and tax incentive with educated labour through various specialized vocational and job-training institutions, and technology provided by the government research institutes. The most important incentives for HCI promotion was the financial support. The government promoted HCI by supplying massive capital for construction and development and by allocating virtually unlimited amounts of credit at below market rates by enacting the Tax Reduction and Exemption Law in 1975. Import policies were tightened to protect domestic HCI-related industries.

These industrial policies during the 1970s nurtured companies to become Korean conglomerates of today, Chaebols. The firms that went through the government made huge profits and expanded. These firms turned into the now-famous Chaebols. The government narrowed down the relationship with large and major firms in the economic development process.

For example, Hyundai Group established Hyundai Shipping Co. in 1972 and moved into ship-building under encouragement of President Park. Hyundai Group also engaged in maritime transportation services in 1978. LG/GS group also entered into business calculators and office machinery in 1974 and established LG Semiconductors in 1979. SK Group expanded to various industries such as construction, machinery, metal, and tourism through 1970s.

ECONOMIC LIBERALIZATION AND GLOBALIZATION: 1980-97

In 1979, President Park was assassinated, bringing political chaos. Presidency of Doo Hwan Chun and Taewoo Roh took powers in 1980-

83. The second oil shock caught Korea as fuel prices skyrocketed. Furthermore, the worldwide recession revealed some of the problems stemming from HCI promotion policy. As a result, Korea experienced negative GDP growth in 1980 and current account deficit of 8.7 per cent of GDP.

Realizing the problems brought about by excessive HCI promotion, Korea began fundamentally reorienting its external and internal policies in the early 1980s. Korean economic policies shifted to technology-intensive industries from heavy manufacturing and machinery industries in the 1980s. The government implemented the policy based on the market mechanism rather than industry-specific, selective intervention by the government.

The government reduced its role in the market for economic development and promoted competition. Preferential credit and foreign exchange allocation were reduced and/or eliminated. All subsidized loans were eliminated and the government no longer formally targeted areas of the economy with preferential treatments. The government pursued more import liberalization designed to embody the market mechanism to improve the quality of Korean products. Tariff levels for manufactured goods fell substantially during the period. By 1996, a number of restrictions as well as average tariff

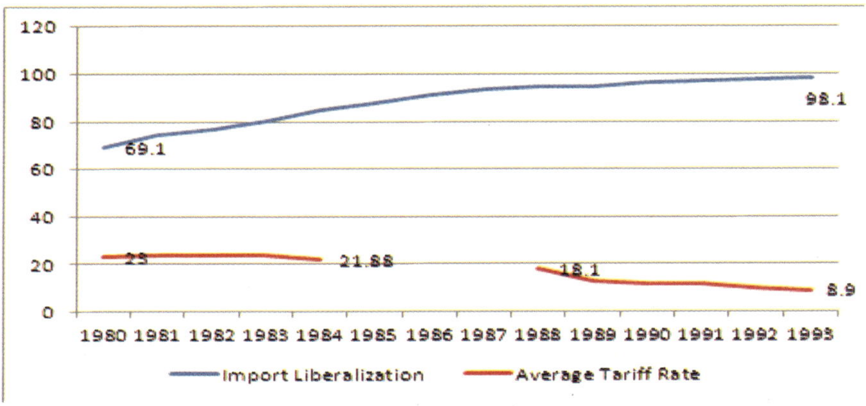

Source: Sohn, Yang and Yim 1998.

fig. 5: Import liberalization and average tariff rates in Korea (per cent)

rates for manufacturing goods were comparable to those of most industrialized countries. The exchange rate system was revamped as the government gave up the pegged system and introduced the Multi Currency Basket Peg System, which was replaced by the official rate for the day based on the transaction volume-weighted average of the rate for the previous business day.

Korea joined the OECD in 1996. After the launching WTO and joining OECD, Korea's industrial and trade policies were modified to be consistent with WTO and directed toward implementing and enforcing the multilateral free trade order. Korea abolished the directed subsidy system for export activities as well as some traditionally managed and controlled trade systems including reduction of concession tariff rates and amending domestic laws (copyright, patents, food hygiene, industrial subsidy policy, tax exemption policy, etc.) to conform with WTO requirements. Korea was committed to liberalizing goods and capital markets following the principles of the WTO.

By joining the WTO and OECD, Korea done much to accelerate globalization of the economy and encouraged both imports and market liberalization. But, with liberalized capital flow, commercial banks and corporations made excessive short-term foreign borrowing, leading to overexpansion and overinvestment.

FINANCIAL CRISIS 1997-98

The negative terms-of-trade for the Korean export products had deteriorated as semi-conductor prices plungedin the international market in April 1996. Terms of trade was lower by 20 per cent campared to a year ago. Furthermore, Korean banks, especially the newly-licensed merchant banks, had engaged in massive borrowing from foreign banks. These banks were able to take advantage of low international interest rates, made possible partially by Japan's recession, which had lowered interest rates by Japanese banks close to zero per cent; and partially by Korea's increased credit rating after joining the OECD. These merchant banks then lent money to Chaebols without properly considering the risks or the financial status of the recipient firms. These banks assumed that the Chaebols had an implicit guarantee from the government derived from close ties. The Chaebols used those funds in unproductive projects, or overinvested in what they mistakenly thought would be productive areas. These made the structure of the debts very inappropriate, leading short terms held too big share, which was 58.8 per cent of total external debts. Short-term external dents relative to foreign reserves went to up to 280 per cent in 1996 from 200 per cent in 1992.

In Korea, large conglomerates went bankruptcy as Hanbo Group in January 1997, Sammi in March 1997, Jinro in April 1997, and Kia in July 1997. In October 1997, rating agencies (S&P, Moody's) downgraded Korea's ratings and sudden withdrawal of foreign funds and run of foreign creditors.

Economic shock from other Asian countries swept through Korea and aggravated its debt problems in 1997. The capital flight out of Korea accelerated and Korea's foreign exchange reserves fell to dangerously low level. The sharp depreciation and the drain on foreign exchange reserves became so critical and the Ministry of Finance and Economy asked the IMF for assistance and Korea and IMF agreed on $ 57 billion support package: elimination of trade-related subsidies, phasing out of the import source diversification programme, adjusting tariffs and review the existing import certification procedures as well as existing subsidy programmes, financial services liberalization, allowing M&A, especially full liberalization of money market instrument issued by non-financial institutions.

The government had conducted drastic structural reforms, reducing the thirty-three banks in 1997 to twenty-three in 1999. Banks became healthy enough to meet the BIS requirement, 7 per cent in 1997 increasing 10.8 per cent in 1999 and 12.4 per cent in 2005. The government restructured the corporate sector. Financially unstable firms were sold, closed down or merged from other firms, resulted in improving firms' financial soundness. Twenty-nine out of thirty merchant banking corporations, which were directly responsible for the outbreak of the crisis, disappeared.

Other reform measures dealing with almost every aspect of the Korean economy were initiated or announced immediately. FDI was liberalized in most sectors and more prudential financial regulations were taken and labour market reformed.

ESTABLISHING AN ADVANCE MARKET ECONOMY: 1999-2012

Through the restructuring process, corporations and financial institutions improved their financial health significantly. In the corporate sector, latent non-performing assets were estimated at Won 18.6 trillion, or 3.4 per cent of GDP, at the end of 2001. This ratio was much lower than the level observed before the crisis (over 20 per cent), and government intervention was deemed no longer necessary. Debt-to-equity ratios and other financial indicators also improved dramatically. Of particular importance was the disappearance of implicit state guarantees to business.

The Korean economy emerged from the crisis in an entirely different shape. First, it became much more open to international capital flows. Most of the restrictions on inward FDI were lifted at the end of 1997. Foreign exchange trading was liberalized in two stages between April 1999 and January 2001, which helped the daily trading volume to jump from 4 billion dollars (1 per cent of GDP) in 1998 to 30 billion dollars (3 per cent of GDP) in 2006. The government also abolished the ceiling on foreign shareholdings in listed companies in May 1998. The foreigners' share of total market capitalization rose sharply and exceeded 40 per cent in 2004, up from less than 15 per cent in 1996.

Second, the transparency of corporate management was substantially enhanced. Accordingly standards were revised, the Chaebol were required to prepare consolidated financial statement, and external auditors and corporate accounting officers were subject to stiffer penalties. In corporate governance, outside directors became a permanent part of the governance structure and the rights of shareholders were significantly strengthened.

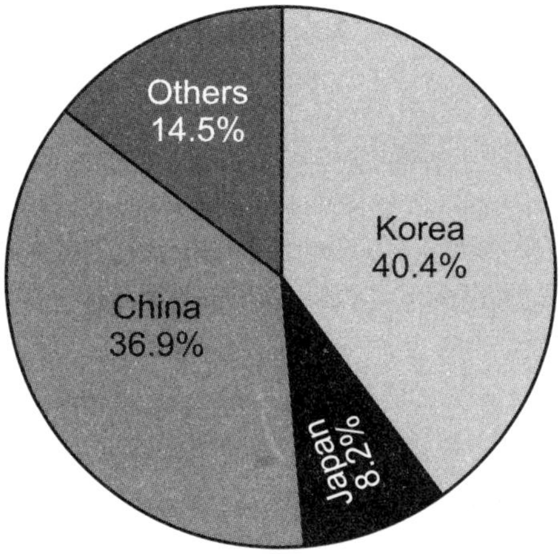

fig. 6: Share of New Orders Received (2007, per cent)

Third, the working of the financial market improved substantially. Most importantly, interest rates were fully liberalized and could play their proper role as a price mechanism. In wake of the crisis, Bank of Korea shifted to a policy of inflation targeting, discontinued its control of the money supply, and began to influence the interest rate directly through open market operations.

However, the annual growth rate declined from 7.9 per cent in 1990-95 to 4.5 per cent in 2000-05. The decline was accompanied by a noticeable fall in investment rates. Most of decline in the aggregate growth came from the slowdown in the growth of capital and labour (Hahn and Shin 2007). In contrast, the TFP growth rose from 0.8 per cent in 1990-95 to 2 per cent in 2000-05, slightly above the 1.5 per cent recorded in 1960-90. It shows that the structural reforms contributed to improved efficiency of the Korean economy.

From the late 1990s, Korea began pursuing a Free Trade Agreement (FTA) policy, turning away from a trade policy that focused only on the WTO's multilateral trade liberalization. In an environment where FTAs were rapidly spreading all over the world, it was vital that Korea improved its economic efficiency. In addition, Korea needed to pursue FTA policy in response to the regionalization trend in other regions, such as the EU and NAFTA, which posed the threat of trade discrimination in European and the US. The FTA policy also was seen as necessary to secure export markets and promote the efficiency of Korea's economic system. With the launch of the FTA policy, Korea concluded FTAs with Chile, Singapore, EFTA, ASEAN, the US, India and the EU.

Korea now ranks very high in terms of trade openness, although its FDI openness still ranks very low. The openness of the Korean economy measured as the sum of exports and imports as a percentage of GDP increased from 79 per cent (exports 45 per cent and imports 34 per cent) in 1998 to 92 per cent (exports 45 per cent and imports 47 per cent) in 2008. Over the past several decades, Korea has taken actions to lower tariffs and to remove non-tariff barriers.

The investment in R&D has increased since the crisis. The ratio of R&D expenditure to GDP has increased to 2.63 per cent in 2003, 3.47 per cent in 2007, from 2.48 per cent in 1997. These results augmented the global brand values. Total brand values of Samsung, Hyundai and LG rose from UD $ 6.4 billion in 2001 to US $ 24.4 billion in 2007.

With investment in knowledge-based industry, IT industry grew fast and worldwide market share of Korea in IT industry was remarkable. The share of LCD panel was 52.2 per cent, Dram 56.2 per cent, mobile phone 28 per cent in 2009. Korea was sixth in e-Government Readiness Rank of the UN. Korea stands tall as a global IT powerhouse. Korea developed WiBro (Wireless Broadband internet) and launched the world's first commercial service in 2006. Korea ranks first in the world in the average download speed (Japan 2nd, Sweden 3rd).

Korea is a world leader since 2003 in terms of new orders received in shipbuilding. Korea has seven of the world's top ten shipyards. Korea also ranks sixth in the world steel market. POSCO is the fourth steel producer in the world.

Summary and Implications

In the last sixty years, Korea was able to achieve a phenomenal economic growth through its export promotion and rapid industrialization policies. Primary industries that dominated the Korean economy up to the 1950s gave way first to labour-intensive industries in the 1960s and then to capital-intensive industries in the 1970s and now knowledge-based industries, leading the economy.

The progress was made possible not only by the massive mobilization of labour and capital but also by the heavy investment in technology at the level of development and the flexible reallocation of resources from less to more productive sectors.

Foreign trade played a pivotal role in this aspect by encouraging innovation and accelerating resource allocation. It also enabled Korea to learn from advanced countries and take advantage of the vastly expanded global market. Entrepreneurs responded to the changing circumstances by committing themselves to pioneer new markets and new products. The government provided institutional and physical infrastructure essential for their activities.

One distinguishing feature of Korea's industrialization process is that it has depended critically on the dynamism of the private sector. The government intervened in the market heavily but relied mostly on private enterprises for the actual implementation of the projects, taking full advantage of their creativity and minimizing deadweight cost that was associated with bureaucratic control. All government interventions had clear criteria for success and failure, and target activities but not sectors. It eliminated rent-seeking opportunities and encouraged positive-sum activities by entrepreneurs with the exchange rate reform (Jones and Sakong 1980). It provided export subsidies, which can be considered as a compensation for the knowledge spillover exporters generated for other domestic producers by finding new markets or products. The subsidies were given in proportion to the export performance, which acted as a clear and objective criterion for success. They were given to all export activities regardless of the sectors or industries. The government held a monthly cabinet-level meeting with representatives from the private sectors to discuss and solve export-related problems. The government also focused on education and training to support export industries.

Policies of Korean development are generally considered very successful, but we can find that there are also so many mistakes in the policy. Industrial policy can be useful, but it must be used very carefully. A pragmatic approach is required to correct policy mistakes. The goal is to encourage successes, but not to protect failures. The exit strategy is also prepared because the government can't assist firms forever.

Many tasks lie ahead for Korea to sustain its growth and adapt its industrial structure to the changing environments. Efforts are required to develop new growth engines in such areas as the advanced technology sectors, parts and materials, and knowledge-based service industries. It is also important to enhance the competitiveness of Small and Medium Enterprises (SMEs) and domestic-oriented industries and reconcile industrial development with environmental protection.

Korea's development experience may give some lessons to India. India has high-quality labour, based on a large population. India needs more industrial reforms to foster a market-oriented, market-friendly economy. The future efforts must be directed to establish regulatory framework to encourage market competition. It will reduce entrance barriers for start-up businesses and privileges held by state-owned enterprises. Encouraging competition also raises the levels which are playing for new and established firms, and eliminating disincentives on light manufacturing. The industrial policy must be expanded to foster and encourage exports, especially manufacturing, taking comparative advantages of cheap and abundant labour.

The establishing infrastructure is important for economic development. More roads and transportation facilities need to come up. To reduce corruption and rent-seeking are to improve governance, especially in economic development institutions.

References

Ahn, Choong Yong and Joo-Hoon Kim, 1995, "The Outward-looking Trade Policy and the Industrial Development", in Dong-Se Cha and Kwang Suk Kim (eds.) *The Korean Economy 1945-1995: Performance and Vision for the 21st Century*, Korea Development Institute, pp. 312-69 (in Korean). Seoul.

Hanh, Chin Hee and Sukha Shin, 2007, "An Empirical Evaluation of Korea's Slower Economic Growth After the Crisis", in Chin Hee

Hahn (ed.) *Understanding the Economic Growth After the Crisis Evaluation and Implications, Research Monograph 2007-05*, Korea Development Institute, pp. 23-76 (in Korean). Seoul.

Jones, Leroy P. and Il Sakong, 1980, *Government, Business and Entrepreneurship in Economic Development: The Korean Case*, Harvard Univesrity Press.

Kim, Kwang Suk and Michael Roemer, 1979, *Growth and Structural Transformation, Studies in the Modernization of the Republic of Korea: 1945-1975*, Harvard University Press.

Kim, Sang Kyum and Inkyo Cheong, 1998, "Asian Exports: Past Trends and Future Prospects: Country Case Study — Korea", unpublished paper to be published by the Asian Development Bank, Korea Institute for International Policy. Seoul.

Korea Development Bank, 1994, *40-year History of the Korea Development Bank.*

Park, Yeong-koo, 2005, "Structural Changes and the Drive to Heavy and Chemical Industry", in Dae-geun Lee (ed.) *New Korean Economic History: From the Late Joseon Period to the High-growth Period of the 20th Century*, Na-nam, pp. 403-28 (in Korean). Seoul.

Sakong, Il and Youngsum Koh, 2010, *The Korean Economy: Six Decades of Growth and Development*, Korean Development Institute. Seoul.

Sohn, Chan-Hyun, Junsok Yang and Hyo-Sung Yim, 1998, "Korea's Trade and Industrial Policies: 1948-1998: Why the Era of Active Policy Is Over?", KIEP Working Paper 98-05, Korea Institute for International Economic Policy. Seoul.

Yoo, Junbgho, 2008, "How Korea's Rapid Export Expansion Began in the 1960s: The Role of Foreign Exchange Rate", Working Paper 08-18, KDI School of Public Policy and Management. Seoul.

Valedictory Speech

21

What India Has Given

Geshe Samten

India–Korea relations are not new. In fact they are as old as the relations of India with Tibet. Korea responded positively to both Buddhism and Hinduism. It was Māhayāna Buddhism and not Hinayana Buddhism that reached Korea to influence the people and their life there. We in the Central University of Higher Tibetan Studies have established collaboration with many Korean universities. For the last six years we have collaboration with Tongokon Digital University under which every year in February a group of students is given training in Tibetan agriculture, medicine and meditation.

Tibetan Buddhism is nothing but a vibrant maintainence and continuation of the intellectual traditions of Nalanda and Takshila. It is a holistic tradition of culture which had been there in India for millennia but came under stress and virtually disappeared. With a galaxy of scholars Tibet sustained intellectual, cultural relations for centuries with India and the world's centres of learning.

India has been a source of wisdom and light which spread across the world in different forms. Tibetan culture is a renewed Indian culture, popular among common people and in the universities. Indian culture today is flourishing in different parts of the world and Tibet's monastic scholarship has made it possible and India owes to that extent a debt of gratitude to Tibet.

The world needs an alternative to the economic system of Communism. Communism could not succeed because the very idea behind Communism (equality for all) is not practised, is beyond practicability. The system has developed economic culture but not mental culture. The change has to happen in our psyche. Equality has to be in the mind and not in the external world. The attitude of equality of everybody has to be achieved through mental training. Communism does not provide that training. Materialistic approach has not been successful to provide peace to individuals or to society. We need to devise alternate mechanisms.

Twentieth century has been the century of bloodshed and a lot of new inventions. Now we need to work for making this world violence-free. There should be a change in the educational system. The culture of mind has to be developed. The culture of violence has to be replaced. Modern education system trains in violence and selfish motives, and not in peace and equality. In the Chicago University a questionnaire was circulated to UG students. At the end of Fourth Semester, same questions were circulated. The result was shocking — Economics students became more selfish, miser and much else.

So we have to educate in values and turn our students into holistic persons. We have to make them skilled and professional. Professionalism is very important in universities. Our curriculum has to include these traits of a holistic person. The students should be able to contemplate another mental culture. Our curriculum and training methods should replace negative elements with positive traits in a person. As educationists and scholars, it is important for us to contemplate on these issues.

Buddhism is of interest to scientists. For the past twenty-five years His Holiness Dalai Lama made numerous dialogues with scientists and Buddhist scholars. This has led to a paradigm shift in interaction between science and Buddhism. There are neurosciences laboratories where experiments are conducted on Buddhist psychology and neuroscience. Highly trained Buddhist meditators have discovered neuroplasticity. Earlier, neuroscience believed that neurons once dead cannot be revived, but recent phenomena like mindfulness based stress reduction (MBSR) and alternate deficiency crises (ADC) have proved this belief wrong. Especially, these have been very successful with children. Now meditation is not a religious practice. It is a natural process of transformation towards happiness. Many Western universities are researching on neuroscience labs and other related projects. While accepting the Templeton Award, His Holiness Dalai Lama emphasized on the establishment of interaction between science and spirituality. We should encourage these factors to promote science-tradition, spiritual-tradition and to human closeness.

I thank Prof. Kapil Kapoor, Director CIAS and Dr Pankaj Mittal, Vice-Chancellor, Bhagat Phool Singh Mahila Vishwavidyalaya for inviting me here. I am happy to know the development of the Centre for Indic–Asian Studies, a very important and innovative programme.

Thank you very much.

Appendix I

Cultural Interflow Between India and Korea
Morning Calm and the Pensive Beyond

Lokesh Chandra

THE confluence of India and Korea for the last two millennia is fine and firm, "a stone niche woven like silk", a song, a sky, a spring, the caress of a keen coming together. It prompts a journey to an interior that we can never leave, the light of *dharma*'s eyes. Our journey begins in the rocky remains of 2,000 years ago, when Korea, the Land of Morning Calm, found its identity, its Self-being in a new syndrome. A princess of Ayodhyā, India, arrived in Korea in CE 48 at Kimhae aboard a ship, with the Three Treasures of statues, *sūtra*s and *śramaṇa*s (monks). She became the queen of the founder of the first Korean state of Karak. She established the first national capital and named it Gaya. From a tribal order, Korea emerged as a state. Its spirit and beauty are visible in the sportive play of nature and the simple subtlety of the heart. In gratitude to the sea that allowed safe passage to the queen to his shores, the king built the Haeunsa "Temple of Sea Grace" that stands to this day near the top of Punsongsan Mountain.

Buddhism was officially introduced into Korea during the period of the three kingdoms: Koguryo received it in CE 372, Paekche in 384, and Silla in 527. It was the Indian master Mallānanda who brought Buddhism to Paekche in 384. It gave the three kingdoms a new meaning: they became a civilization. In its first energy and freshness it filled the country with benefits, nourished art, diffused education, made roads, established resting places, promoted beneficence and multiplied comforts in many forms. It was a humane system of morals and of aspirations to nobility. It made vivid and tangible the presence of a profound social and cultural order.

In 535 the first great cathedral of Buddhism was founded and called Pulguksa. It is the oldest surviving Buddhist monastery of Korea. It means: *Pul* "Buddha", *guk* "land", *sa* "monastery", a monastery that springs from the deeps of Buddhism, to celebrate the new dynamic and vital order that was to determine the tonality of Korean life for centuries. The most skilled workmen were summoned to make it a monument of restrained dignity and quiet peace.

In the middle of the eighth century, Pulguksa was rebuilt and enlarged by King Kyongdok. The same master architect built the rock chapel of Sokkuram a mile away, on the crest of mount Tohamsan. From the rock chapel the pilgrim greets the Eastern Sea facing Japan. It signifies crossing over the sea of life to bliss. It is a pearl of East Asian cave temples in its overall planning. It enshrines the best Korean sculptures of all times. Superb examples of warm naturalism in spite of the hard medium of stone, they remain unsurpassed in East Asian lands. They sprout from the passion of everything that the eyes embraced, celebrating its essence in the eternity of stones. The piety of the patron and the tender love of the sculptor sink into the silent rapture of live sculptures in their kissed limbs, smiling in flowing drapery and deep solitude.

The pensive images of Maitreya are coaeval with the period of the consolidation of the Korean state. Maitreya cult was practised at the Silla court by young aristocratic warriors who formed a fraternity known as the Hwarang — perfumed followers of the dragaon flower. This name is an allusion to the *nāgapuṣpa* tree under which Maitreya Bodhisattva would become a Buddha. They had an enormous importance in the government both during the three kingdoms and the unified Silla dynasty. They were responsible for national unity. The Buddhist kingdom of Silla accomplished the unification of the three kingdoms and formed the nation state of Korea for the first time in history. Ever since, Korean Buddhism was the destiny and the defence of the land. Monk Wolkwang formulated the "Five Worldly Commandments" to form the basis of national ethos.

The Korean Hyecho became a disciple of the Indian teacher Vajrabodhi at the age of sixteen. Later, he travelled to India by the sea route and returned in December 727 via Central Asia. In Samarkand he records one Buddhist monastery with one monk. Hyecho is the last pilgrim on the historic Sūtra Route, before the monasteries and monks perished in the onslaught. He records this wounded time in his *Travel Records* which are on par with those of his celebrated predecessor Hsuan Tsang.

To ward off the Mongol invasion, the king of Korea had 81,258 wooden blocks of the *Tripiṭaka Koreana* engraved. Completed in CE 1251, they have been preserved in perfect condition to this day at the Haeinsa monastery on Mount Gaya. They reflect the glory of national unity. Befitting its reputation as a Sūtra-Vihāra, Haeinsa is the foremost meditation centre of the Chogye sect. Stillness reigns where monks meditate to encounter their inner self. As the evening mist pervades the valleys, and mountains dull into darkness, the windows of the monastery are lit by monks preparing to cross over the 108 passions to the sea of Buddha's wisdom. The Korean Tripiṭaka, done for the defence of the country, is a marvel of Korean technology eight centuries ago. It is important for the excellence of its editing and for its beautiful block-printing.

Zen (Son) Buddhism with its distrust of words was in tune with the ideographic system of Chinese writing. Its aim was direct experience without the mediation of words. The quest for wordless truth has been the spirit of Zen Buddhism. It has sunk deep into the national consciousness, and Korea thus has silent workers and noiseless machines.

The last Indian *ācārya* to visit Korea was Chikong (Dhyānabhadra). He arrived in Korea in the 1340s and established the Juniper Rock Monastery on the pattern of the Nālandā University. Its foundations can be seen near Seoul. He wrote Sanskrit *Dharaṇī-mantra*s on the gigantic Yonboksa Bell for the liberation and peace of the Korean people from Mongol domination. An inscription at the Juniper Rock Monastery dated 1378 records the life and work of Dhyānabhadra and informs us that the king of Kāñcī was his nephew. The mill for making *sattu* installed by Dhyānabhadra still lies at the site of this monastery.

In 1446 the sage-like emperor Seijong invented a new Korean alphabet and moveable printing types. This alphabet continues to this day as the Hanguel or "Proper Writing". Kei Won Chung in his dissertation to Princeton University says that the Korean alphabet was composed on the principles of the Sanskrit alphabet. With the new alphabet learning became accessible to a large number of people.

Seoul has the only Buddhist Broadcasting Station in the world: it exalts the glory of Korea's identity. A restaurant called "Perfume of Grasses" recalls the cuisine of Ācārya Dhyānabhadra. It serves "tea of honey-stick". Honey-stick is liquorice (*madhuyaṣṭi* in Sanskrit and *mulehṭhī* in Hindi).

In 1991, Korea dedicated the world's largest bronze image of Maitreya at Popchusa monastery. This 100-ft high statue embodies the aspirations of the Korean people for national re-unification. The Popchusa was built in 553, two centuries later, in 776, monk Yulsa erected a 40 ft gilt bronze Maitreya for national prosperity and unity of the people. During the eye-opening ceremony in April 1991, three rainbows appeared in the clear sky:

> Isn't this a sign that we can even move heaven when we are truly devoted? When we build an image of Maitreya in our hearts too, all lives on earth will turn into lotus flowers, and the very world around us will become a pond of joy.
>
> — Chief Abbot Yu

Appendix II

Buddhism as the Creative Vision of Korea

Lokesh Chandra

KOREA, the land of morning calm, found its sense of being and eternity 1,600 years ago when Buddhism gave her a new meaning. Buddhism became the civilization for Korea. In its first energy and freshness it filled the country with benefits, nourished art, diffused education, made roads, established resting places, promoted beneficence and multiplied comforts in thousand forms. A humane system of morals and of aspirations to nobility, it made vivid and tangible the presence of a profound social and cultural order. The high water-mark of Korean civilization was reached under Buddhism. Come to mind the words of the great poet Basho:

Ah! The grass and the wind!
And here among these stones
The shadow of a dream.

The eternal plane became the earthly plane. The quest for enlightenment supreme became the flying banner of perfection that has conditioned Korea's miracle during the last four decades. Buddhism became the interior world whose individual roots went back to one's infancy and social roots were embedded firmly into the centuries. It coloured all thoughts and feelings, decisions and actions. A Korea torn from the spiritual soil of its being by dominating Western influence is now moving beyond them. The European world itself has glimpsed the limits of modernization. The post-modern era means cultural development beyond the contradictions of traditionalism and modernism. Access to tradition, understanding the assimilable positive in the European model and to move beyond into the creativity of the new will become a major cultural instrument that interacts with a living future. Buddhism lives like a flower in Korea, which is its earth and sky, its home, its humanized immensity.

Buddhism was absorbed by East Asia from missionaries of diverse ethnic and linguistic origins, especially in the early period. In the second and third centuries CE, eighteen foreign missionaries were active in China: four were Indians, four Indo–Scythians, three Parthians, four Sogdians and three Khotanese. Thousands of scriptures, five codes of monastic discipline of five different schools, bewildering rituals stimulated diversity in Chinese thought. Focus on devotionalism in Pure Land Buddhism stood in sharp contrast to the radical rejection of the validity of the scriptural teaching in Zen Buddhism in its wordless intuitive way to enlightenment. Patronization of Buddhism by some non-Chinese dynasties tended to political polycentrism *vis-à-vis* imperial unification of Confucianism. Confucianism catered to elite, while Buddhist ideas with their devotionalism were part of popular religion. Monasteries provided basic education at the grass-root level. In the *yin–yang* system women represented darkness, but they became nuns in Buddhist monasteries and permeated society. Buddhism merged into the East Asian systems and enriched the East Asian lands spiritually and materially. Buddhism was officially introduced to Korea during the period of the three kingdoms: Koguryo received it in 372, Paekche in 384 and Silla in 527. It brought with it an advanced culture and provided a unifying political force to each kingdom.

Buddhism became naturalized in the East Asian context to such an extent that the platform Sūtra attained the status of "sūtra", a term for classics spoken by the master himself. In this Sūtra, Hui-neng proclaimed the universality of Buddha-nature: "Although people are distinguished as northerners and southerners there is neither north nor south in Buddha-nature". He wrote:

The mind is the tree of Perfect Wisdom.
The body is the clear mirror.
The clear mirror is originally clear and pure.
Where has it been affected by and dust?

Our age with its overwhelming stresses and rocketing consumerism needs calm and discipline which can come only from Buddhism:

> Meditation is achieved when one is externally free from phenomena and calmness is achieved when one is internally unperturbed. Meditation and calmness mean that externally meditation is attained and internally calmness is achieved.

Zen Buddhism has its distrust of words. Its aim was direct experience without the mediation of words, and Korea has silent workers and noiseless machines.

The intellect has to be sobered and softened by cultivation through non-cultivation in the tradition of Zen masters. Behind all solemnity is the sportive play of nature which becomes the heart of Zen in its simple subtlety.

Devotional Buddhism of the Pure Land and other related forms add "other help" to "self-help" and develop salvation by grace besides by effort. Doctrine, discipline and devotion become the flourishing fields of the Buddhist world-view. Appeal to and dependence on Amitābha Buddha to deliver beings replaces the emphasis on inner contemplation. The paradise of a gracious and loving Amitābha Buddha becomes the expectation of the faithful. The importance of right attitudes and the danger of false values is stressed. *Dhammapada*, a collection of sayings, reflects Buddhism in simple profundity.

> For hatred does not cease by hatred at any time;
> hatred ceases by love: this is an old rule.
>
> They who imagine truth in untruth, and see untruth in truth,
> never arrive at truth but follow vain desires.
>
> The virtuous man delights in this world, and he delights in the next; he delights in both. He delights and rejoices; when he sees the purity of his own work.

The ideal of the *bodhisattva* embodies compassion, a readiness to assist others and help those in distress, to render all kinds of service. They strive to win the affection of all creatures, and in their modesty they are aware:

> As it is not possible for any bird to reach the confines of the sky, so it is not possible for any man to comprehend the good qualities of the self-becoming Buddhas.

Suffering (*duḥkha*) arises out of the realization that man can never fully find himself. Eternity is vaster than moments of time: the rustling breeze of Buddhist fragrance has awakened the sensitivities of our peoples to the ideal of the *bodhisattva*. Collective life can transcend individual death. Such is the ideal of the *bodhisattva*. The *bodhisattva* says:

> The whole world of living beings I must rescue, from the terrors of birth, of old age, of sickness, of death and rebirth, of all kinds of moral offence, of all states of woe, of the whole cycle of birth-and-death, of the jungle of false views, of the loss of wholesome *dharmas*, of the concomitants of ignorance.

The selfless love, the infinite compassion, the universal redemption of the *bodhisattva* alone can free men and nations from hate, fear and insecurity of existence. Through the last twenty-five centuries Buddhism has spread the message of understanding and resolution, communion and compassion, in fact a universal human loyalty, a new horizon and a paradigm of a new universe.

The lay ideal is enshrined in the *Vimalakīrti-Nirdeśa*. It was translated from Sanskrit into Chinese by Kumārajīva in the fifth century CE. Ever since it has influenced all the countries of East Asia. It identifies *saṁsāra* and *nirvāṇa*. As the two are one, a person can be free from ills by a re-evaluation of the world, and not by withdrawing from it. It depicts the ideal lay person, Vimalakīrti, who renders benefit to all beings.

Buddhism arose as a spiritual force against social injustice and advocated the equality of all men irrespective of their birth. It gave spiritual freedom to women. The welfare state created by the Buddhist emperor Aśoka is an outstanding example of the spirit of its perennial teachings. In the *Aṅguttara-Nikāya* the Buddha says:

> He who has understanding and great wisdom does not think of harming himself or another, nor of harming both alike. He

> rather thinks of his own welfare, of that of others, of that of both, and of the welfare of the whole world. In that way one shows understanding and great wisdom.

The individual self merges into the continuity of life. The dying words of the master to Ānanda were:

> We are leaves fading while the tree lives. Be then, O Ānanda, your own lamp. Be your own Refuge. Cling to the Lamp of Truth, that is Sincerity.

The translation of thousands of Buddhist *sūtra*s from Sanskrit to Chinese produced a profound effect on the intellectual creativity of East Asia. The inner space of man, reflected in the myriad mirrors of the written ideogram, evoked a deep response from the people. The need to multiply the written word was imperative. In moments of unknowing at long last man was on the threshold of proto-technology of printing. The texts had to be multiplied for recitation and hundreds of thousands of *mantra* scrolls had to be deposited in the temples of the realm. Buddhism gave birth to printing. It flourished as an integral part of Buddhist requirements of vast quanta of printed *mantra*s for ensuring their grace of liberation, and also for mass scale distribution of *sūtra*s by the bereaved descendants so that their deceased parents may acquire full merit. The 81,258 printing blocks of the Korean Tripiṭaka done for the defence of the country, preserved in the Haeinsa Temple, are a marvel of Korean technology and national will. It is important for the excellence of its editing and for its beautiful block-printing.

In the latter part of the seventh century Shul-ch'ong invented the Yi-do script to denote case-endings in the margin of Chinese texts. It was to aid the reader in Koreanizing the system of the Chinese sentence. At first he composed eight case-endings, i.e. nominative, accusative, instrumental, dative, ablative, genitive, locative and vocative. He probably based them on the Sanskrit case-endings. His father was a great Buddhist scholar and he must have taken his help. The book *Kyun yu Chun*, written in CE 1075 says: "The Yi-do resembles the Sanskrit in its inflections".

The great Korean pilgrim to India, Hyecho translated a hymn to the Thousand bowl Mañjuśrī in CE 741. It is still available and is one of the rare works of Korean scholarship accorded the honour of being canonized in the Buddhist Tripiṭaka. Buddhism contributed to the evolution of Korean literature, specially in prose. The Buddhist works were based on stories from the Buddhist canon. They were not merely translations but often new writings. Their tone is devotional, and in a strange way elusive. Their language is both rich and direct. Their poems are inspiring, and their narratives are interesting and detailed.

Along with Buddhism, Korea got her social and political insititutions, arts and sciences from China. It led to remarkable development in painting, frescos, sculpture and architecture. Music and musical instruments evolved in Korea under Buddhist influence. Indian Buddhists served on the imperial Bureau of Astronomy in China. In the seventh century three schools of Indian astronomy were prevalent at Ch'ang-an. They were headed by Gautama, Kāśyapa and Kumāra. Since 721, the Buddhist monk I-hsing adopted a new calendar based on Indian sources. He has the credit of inventing the first mechanical clock. The astrological influences of the nine planets resulted in special temples to them. All the learning was transmitted to Korea. The Korean Tripiṭaka preserves the *Ts'i Yao Jang Tsai Kiue* to avert evil influences of the seven planets. The Korean Tripiṭaka has medical texts on curing the diseases of children, pregnant women, and those that arise in meditation.

The Sokkuram is an outstanding monument of Korean architecture. From this rock chapel the pilgrim greets the Sea. It signifies the crossing over the sea of life to bliss. Built as an act of filial piety to parents, it celebrates their absence, distance, dream and destiny. It is a pearl of East Asian cave temples in its overall planning. It enshrines the best Korean sculptures of all times.

In the Confucian world-view of *yin* and *yang*, *yang* signifies heaven, light, male, while *yin* stands for earth, darkness, female. *Yang* is the superior or male principle and it produces *yin*, the inferior or female principle of nature. Hence goodnesses of Buddhism were replaced by masculine names and symbolic forms in the Chinese version of the

Vajradhātu-maṇḍala. On the other hand, women could not worship male deities. Hence the male Avalokiteśvara was replaced by the feminine White-Robed Kuan-yin or Pāṇḍaravāsinī, the consort of Amitābha, who dominated East Asia. In the long course of twenty-five centuries, in the processes of its universalization, Buddhism accorded rights to women, which was long denied to them. Women have enjoyed freedom in Tibet, Thailand, Laos, Sri Lanka and other Buddhist countries as marriage was not a religious ceremony, and consequently not a sacrament but a social event. Feminine freedom goes back to Lord Buddha himself. On the very day of his enlightenment, Sujātā offered food in a golden bowl to the Buddha still seated under the tree of illumination. The positive attitude of the Buddha towards women "ranks as one of his greatest claims to fame as a benefactor of the human race". A prince by birth and at heart, he was for open attitudes, not a closed fist but an open hand, and a mind open to the logic of life.

The air of Korea is full of obscure menace. With the increasing integration of global markets, the world is on the threshold of a long-run economic boom. Besotted by Japanese economic conquest, the Americans have started joint ventures. They have larger stakes or higher scales than their major Japanese partner. The power balance within the company is shifting to the American subsidiary. Europe triumphantly enters its "Fortress 1992" to become the most powerful group in terms of finance and technological innovation. The Eurocentric "comeuppance", and "our European home" advocated by the Soviet leadership, pose a challenge to non-European systems, be they cultural, or economic, or political. The manipulation of symbols in the financial and technological segments will be the invisible but superpotent onslaught, a cause for grave concern. The question arises: will technology and economy conspire with Hegel, Heidegger and Wilhelm Halbfass in the Europeanization of the world, as they seek the self-representation and self-assertion of Asia in contexts created by Europe? Shall Asia understand the "otherness" of the "other" in shaping the real world? To Hegel, European thought was the measure of all things. As a rigorous critic of the Romantics, he disapproved of their contempt of the European present. Martin Heidegger refers to the "complete Europeanization of the earth and of mankind". To Wilhelm Halbfass "the Europeanization of the earth continues to be inescapable and irreversible". The "global restructuring" of industry and the universalization of consumerism are fast becoming the gale of creative destruction.

The Korean environment of centuries seeks its essence in the spontaneity of the flowering of Buddhism. To Buddhists the land where they are living is a pure land, the Buddhakṣetra, the Paradise. "Participation in realities" was a more widespread phenomenon than "ascetic life in mountains". The founder of the ancient state of Karak married a princess of Ayodhyā who arrived from India in CE 48 at Kimhae aboard a ship, along with her brother monk Bo-ok. She came with Buddhist statues and *sūtras*. She established the national capital and named it Gaya. The Buddhist kingdom of Silla accomplished the unification of the three kingdoms and formed the nation state of Korea for the first time in history. Ever since, Korean Buddhism was the destiny and defence of the land. The 81,258 blocks of the Korean Tripiṭaka were the Buddhist omnipotence to repel the Mongolian invader. The three scriptures for defending the nation were the *Lotus Sūtra*, the *Heart Sūtra* and the *Golden Light Sūtra*. In them *dharma* was the infrastructure of a strong national defence system.

Buddhism with its many gods and goddesses represents pluralism, which is going to be the new sensibility. It is the openness to multiple forms of reality. They are the many structures of meaning and being in which we constantly live. No universal proposal for human meaning can come up: the depths can be lived out of the many. Pluralism gives depth, a resonance of the transcendent function. Buddhism teaches an acceptance of the variousness of ourselves and of others. Buddhism announces and owns expanding consciousness, a new humility in the diversity of our modern existence. Contemporary life can have no fixed horizons, fences, boundaries. The emerging pluralistic universe seeks relevance in theodiversity to purify, perfect and ennoble our existence. In theodiversity man's free-thinking and many-sided thinking have the power to create for himself new and individual eyes, always newer and ever more individualized.

Buddhism has kissed this world with compassion, enwoven light and love in the hearts of men, kindled lamps in the forlorn recesses of somber shades of life, enlivened dead dogmas with logic, offered flowers and lit lamps in place of rituals of slaughter, tendered mercy to a dancing-girl when she lay under the shadow of a wall, struck with black pestilence, her body spotted with sores, a body once drunk with the wine of her youth. Buddha, the prince of peace, brought silence to the arid heart of men who ceaselessly run in furious chase of victory. From the surging centuries of noise rises the prayer of lover immeasurable: "Let Buddha be my refuge".

石 窟 庵

Appendix III

Gaṇḍavyūha and the Korean Cave of Sokkuram

Lokesh Chandra

BUILT as an act of filial piety to parents, Sukkuram celebrates their absence, distance, dream and destiny. It is a pearl of East Asian cave temples in its overall planning. It enshrines the best Korean sculptures of all times. They are reminiscent of the sculptural glories of Tang China, and yet are unique in their ethereal quality. They sprout from the passion of everything that the eyes embraced, celebrating its essence in the eternity of stones:

> There is a tradition that the sculptor who carved these bas-reliefs was in love with the King's daughter and used her as the model for the image of Kwanum/Avalokiteśvara in order to immortalize her beauty. — Ha 1972: 386 n. 4

The piety of the patron and the tender love of the sculptor sink into the silent rapture of these live sculptures in their kissed limbs, smiling in flowing drapery and deep solitude.

Construction of Sokkuram

The history of the three kingdoms of ancient Korea, entitled *Samguka-Yusa*, written by the Buddhist monk Ilyeon (1206-89), gives an account of the foundation of Buddhist temples and pagodas. In a chapter on filial piety, he narrates how Kim Tae-song, the Prime Minister of King Kyongdok commenced the construction of Sokkuram in CE 742, and repairs of and additions to the Pulguksa monastery which was founded about CE 535.

> His heart moved by heavenly grace, Kim Tae-song built the beautiful Pulguk Temple in memory of his two sets of parents and also founded the wonderful grotto of Sokkuram. He invited the two distinguished monks Sillim and Pyohun to supervise these temples. He had his fathers and mothers represented among the images in these temples in gratitude for bringing him up as a useful man.
>
> After the great stone Buddha for Sokkuram was finished, Kim Tae-song was working on the lotus pedestal when suddenly it broke into three pieces. He wept bitterly over this, and at length fell into a trance. During the night gods and goddesses descended from heaven and restored the stone to its original condition. Tae-song awoke in joy and climbed the southern peak of Mt. T'oham where he burned incense and worshipped the celestial deities. People thereafter called the place Hyang-nyong (Incense Peak). . . .
>
> The two stone bridges of the blue and white clouds, the seven-treasure lotus flowers and the two pagodas, Tabo-t'ap (Pagoda of Many Treasures) and Sokka-t'ap (Pagoda of Śākyamuni) at Pulguksa, in addition to the seated image of Buddha and the bas-reliefs of Kwanum on the walls and ceiling of Sokkuram, are unsurpassed in exquisite workmanship among the art works in the temples of Korea. — Ha 1972: 381-82

It is clear that the grotto was constructed in memory of his parents by Kim Taesong. This was to ensure their being born in the Pure Land or Sukhāvatī of Amitābha, his Western Paradise. It raises the question of the identity of the central statue of Sokkuram.

Plan of Sokkuram

The ground-plan of the Sokkuram cave consists of a small open-sky rectangular antechamber which is joined by a narrow vestibule to the circular main chamber. It is a unique cave-temple with a domed ceiling. The plan is given in *fig*.1 (HS 2.35).

In the antechamber there are eight stone slabs on which the *hachibushu* (eight kinds of beings who protect Buddhism) (JEBD 1965: 95) are carved in low relief:

nāga *gandharva*
yakṣa *deva*
kinnara *mahoraga*
asura *garuḍa*

On the walls of the antechamber, facing the entrance, are the Two Guardian Kings (Jap.ni-o) whose images appear on both sides of the temple gate: Kongō-misshaku on the left and Narean-kongō on the right. This custom of placing guardian deities at the temple gate began in India (JEBD 1965: 221).

The vestibule has the four *lokapāla*s on its walls, two on each side:

Virūpākṣa Vaiśravaṇa
Virūḍhaka Dhṛtarāṣṭra

The walls of the main hall bear fifteen images in relief on rectangular

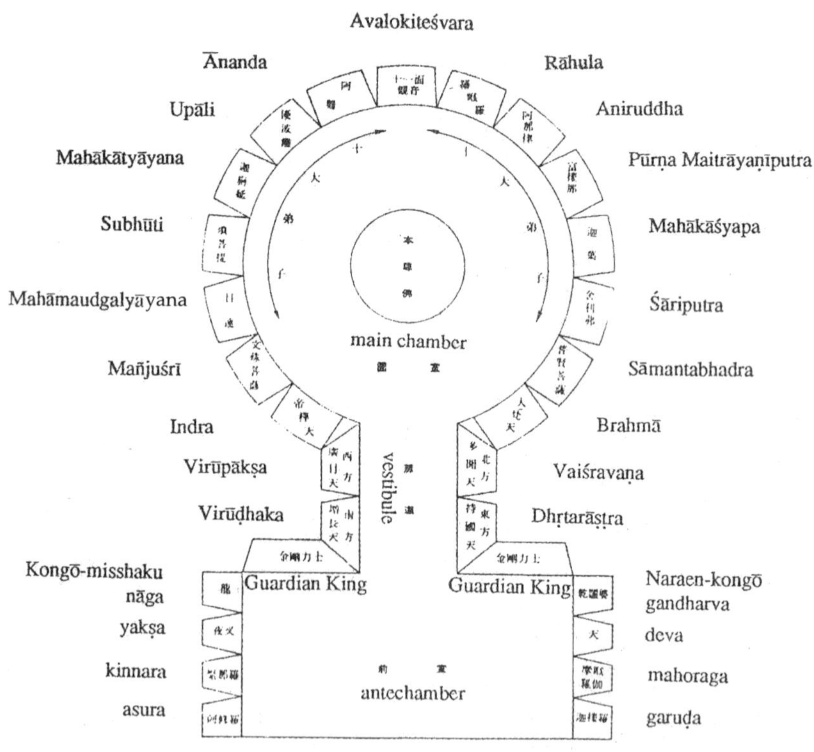

*fig.*1: The plan of Sokkuram cave temple.

stone panels:

Indra			Brahmā
Mañjuśrī			Samantabhadra
	Mahāmaudgalyāyana		Śāriputra
	Subhūti	Main Image	Mahākāśyapa
Ten arhats	Mahākātyāyana		Pūrṇa Maitrāyaṇīputra
	Upāli		Aniruddha
	Ānanda		Rāhula
		Avalokiteśvara	

Atop the panels of the *arhat*s are ten deep niches with images of seated *bodhisattva*s. Two of the images have disappeared. Four of them have been tentatively identified as the layman Vimalakīrti holding a fan, Avalokiteśvara with a Buddha in his crown, Kṣitigarbha in monk's attire and Mañjuśrī facing Vimalakīrti.

Correspondence of Sokkuram and the Gaṇḍavyūha

> In the middle of the eighth century, during the reign of King Kyongdok, Pulguksa (Temple of the Buddha Land) and the shrine of Sokkuram were built by the Hwaom sect of Buddhism. The rise of this sect marked an important stage in the centralization that was taking place in the Korean political system. The *Hwaom Sūtra* was an important group of religious writings first brought to Korea from China in the mid-seventh century. These scriptures honoured a new Buddha, the Vairocana or Creating Buddha, from whom all others were thought to emanate. . . .
>
> The ruling caste, first in Korea and then in Japan, saw an analogy between such a religious concept and a governmental system, the king being equated with the Vairocana and his officials with the minor Buddhist deities. In Japan, at the time that Pulguksa was going up, the emperor built the great temple of Todaiji and housed within it the Vairocana Daibutsu, which is still there in spite of several fires and numerous earthquakes.

> In 748 he decreed that the *Avataṁsaka Sūtra* was to be the state scripture. In Korea, King Kyongdok made a similar effort to glorify his own position through patronage of the Hwaom sect. Both countries and their rulers were drawn into close connection through this sect by means of the tie of international Buddhism. Hwaom (*Kegon* in Japanese) Buddhism became so important in these countries that the royal courts took from it many of their ceremonials, their new art forms, their literature, and their music. — McCune 1962: 92

The scheme of the Sokkuram pantheon corresponds remarkably to the *Gaṇḍavyūha* of the *Avataṁsaka-sūtras*. The Lord (*bhagavān*, *Gaṇḍavyūha* 2.11) was staying in the *mahāvyūha kūṭāgāra* (pavilion) in the Jetavana Ārāma (monastery) at the city of Śrāvastī with 5,000 *bodhisattvas* led by Samantabhadra and Mañjuśrī. The Lord attained *siṁha-vijṛmbhita samādhi* (6.13). The *bodhisattvas* of the ten directions assembled to witness the miracle:

Page	Direction	Name of the Bodhisattva
8	East	Vairocana-praṇidhāna-nābhi-raśmi-prabha
9	South	Duryodhana-vīrya-vega-rāja
10	West	Samanta-śrī-samudgata-rāja
11	North	Asaṅga-śrī-rāja
11	NE	Dharmadhātu-sunirmita-praṇidhi-candra
12	SE	Dharm-ārciṣmat-tejorāja
13	SW	Sarva-māra-maṇḍala-vikīraṇa-jñāna-dhvaja
13	NW	Vairocana-praṇidhi-jñāna-ketu
14	Nadir	Sarv-āvaraṇa-vikiraṇa-jñāna-vikramī
15	Zenith	Dharmadhātu-praṇidhi-tala-nirbheda

The ten seated *bodhisattvas* in the niches atop should be the above ten *bodhisattvas*. As in the niches, so also in the *Gvy* they are seated (*nyasīdat paryaṅkam ābhujya* 15.14-15).

The identification of the niche *bodhisattvas* as given by earlier scholars has to be reconsidered.

The great apostles (mahāśrāvaka, Gvy 17.22) Śāriputra, Maudgalyāyana, Mahākāśyapa, Revata, Subhūti, Aniruddha, Nandika, Kapphiṇa, Kātyāyana, Pūrṇa Maitrāyaṇīputra could not visualize the miracle of the Tathāgata at Jetavana, nor did they see the congregation of the bodhisattvas: "assembled there in Jetavana, itself, seated in the very presence of the Lord, in front, at his back, left and right, why did they not see the miracles at Jetavana" (19.17-19). And these great apostles neither visualize nor know as they are devoid of the *bodhisattva* vision (*bodhisattva-cakṣur-virahitatvāt* 21.2). The *śrāvaka*s had to know the path of the *bodhisattva*s to partake of the emerging world: from the way of *śrāvaka*s they had to progress to the course of *bodhisattva*s, i.e. from Theravāda to Mahāyāna. The ten *arhat*s on the walls of Sokkuram are these ten *mahāśrāvaka*s: Revata, Nandika and Kapphiṇa have been replaced (?) by Upāli, Ānanda and Rāhula if the present identifications are correct. The *bodhisattva*s of the ten directions recite laudatory verses to enlighten the beings.

Samantabhadra thereafter proceeds to illuminate the meaning of the *siṁha-vijṛmbhita samādhi* of the Lord (33.25). Mañjuśrī speaks *gāthā*s highlighting all the miraculous deeds (43.2). He also refers to Brahmā and Indra (43.11). After his enlightening exposé, Mañjuśrī is praised and eulogized by Brahmā, Indra, and the kings of *nāga*s, *yakṣa*s, *gandharva*s, *kumbhāṇḍa*s, *garuḍa*s, *asura*s, *mahoraga*s and *deva*s. Samantabhadra and Mañjuśrī, Indra and Brahmā, and the eight beings are carved at Sokkuram. The identification of *kinnara* will have to be changed to *kumbhāṇḍa*.

Thus far we have the introductory basis of the *Gaṇḍavyūha* for Sudhana's quest for knowledge and his pilgrimage to fifty-two (*dvāpañcāśat* 548.21) or fifty-three teachers (so numbered in the edition on p. 549), or fifty-four in the Chinese tradition (which added the name of Fo-kuo as the fifty-fourth to make it half of the auspicious number 108: 54 x 2 = 108, Lokesh Chandra 1975: 63). At the end *Gaṇḍavyūha* (548.3...) categorizes the basic pantheon (*sarvāvatī parṣat* 548.8) as follows:

From this analysis it is apparent that the Sokkuram was planned to be the stereomorphic paradigm of the *Gaṇḍavyūha*. The pilgrimage of Sudhana has been so central and intrinsic to the *Gaṇḍavyūha* that absence of its stone carvings is particularly striking. In ancient times it must have been painted on scrolls and hung in the cave temple (see further below).

	Headed by
Bodhisattvas	Mañjuśrī
Bodhisattvas of Bhadrakalpa	Maitreya
Mahābodhisattva	Samantabhadra
Mahāśrāvaka	Śāriputra and Maudgalyāyana
Loka	*Deva, mānuṣa, asura, gandharva.*

Samantabhadra and Mañjuśrī "go in pairs and are the chief *bodhisattvas* in the Avataṁsaka conception of the world" (Suzuki 1974: 161). Mañjuśrī went out from Pratiṣṭhāna to the human world and preached Mahāyāna. In the city of Dhānyakara, he perceived a handsome youth of noble family, Sudhana. He advised him to visit Sāgaramegha. Sudhana visited Sāgaramegha, who taught him and sent him on to another friend.

> In this way he was sent from one friend to another until he had visited fifty-three. At last he came to Samantabhadra, under whose teaching he perfected his vow and entered into the Dharmadhātu (Supreme Reality). In this story of Sudhana, Samantabhadra plays the chief part as master.
>
> — Suzuki 1974: 94-95

The last part of the *Gaṇḍavyūha* is devoted to Samantabhadra's ten vows and his desire to be born into Sukhāvatī. This part is known as Bhadracarī. It is integral to the *Gaṇḍavyūha*. In a number of passages, the *Gaṇḍavyūha* emphasizes that the vows and practice of the Bodhisattva Samantabhadra are its *summum bonum*:

16.24	*Samantabhadra-bodhisattva-caryā-praṇidhāna-niryātāḥ*
44.02	*Samantabhadraiś carita-prakārair viśodhitāḥ*
527.25	*kathaṁ Samantabhadra-caryā-maṇḍalam avataritavyam*
528.12	*Mañjuśrīḥ kumāra-bhūtaḥ sarva-vimokṣa-nayeṣu avatīrṇaḥ Samantabhadra-bodhisattva-caryāyām*
529.16	*Samantabhadra-caryā-maṇḍala 'vatarayitvā*

What is the ultimate wish of Samantabhadra? It is to visualize Amitābha face to face and to attain to his Pure Land of Sukhāvatī (*sammukha paśyiya tam Amitābham taṁ ca sukhāvatī-kṣetra vrajeyam* 547.18:st.57 of the *Bhadracarī*). Thus the path is: Mañjuśrī–Samantabhadra–Amitābha. The culmination of the *Gaṇḍavyūha* is the way of Samantabhadra and its consummation is Amitābha and His paradise of Sukhāvatī. The main image at Sokkuram reflects a syncretic representation of Bhagavān [= Śākyamuni] as well as of Amitābha. His aspect as Śākyamuni is featured by the ten *arhat*s and the two *deva*s Brahmā and Indra. His manifestation as Amitābha is highlighted by Avalokiteśvara standing right at his back. As Amitābha, the *ūrṇa* on the forehead of the main image receives the first rays of the rising sun. Korean poems celebrate the splendour of this moment shimmering in divine light. The recitation of the *Bhadracarī* is immediately followed by and consummated in the recitation of Amitābha hymns, to this day in daily recitation at Korean monasteries of the Chogye order. The transition of *Bhadracarī* to the Amitābha hymn is natural, as it ends with *tena jagad . . . yatv amitābhapurīm varam eva* (548.2 st. 62).

The Unique Iconography of Samantabhadra and Mañjuśrī at Sokkuram

At Sokkuram Samantabhadra holds a boxed manuscript, most probably of the *Bhadracarī*, symbolizing his vow to attain the paradise of Amitābha. I have checked the Indian, Indonesian, Nepalese, Tibetan, Mongolian, Chinese and Japanese traditions of the iconography of Samantabhadra and have not found him holding a manuscript. Mallmann (1975: 331-35) too does not specify the manuscript as an attribute. This form must have been created to emphasize his association with the *Bhadracarī* which embodies his vow to go to the world of Amitābha.

The form of Mañjuśrī at the Sokkuram cave is again unique. He holds a bowl in his hand. A form of Mañjuśrī with a thousand hands holding thousand bowls is known from the Chinese text *Ta-shang* (Mahāyāna), *yu-ch'ieh* (*Yoga*), *Chin-kang* (*Vajra*), *Hsing*

(*Prakṛti*), *Hai* (*sāgara*), *man-shu-shih-li* (Mañjuśrī), *ch'ien-pei* (*sahasrabhuja*), *ch'ien-po* (*sahasrapātra*), *ta-chiao-wang* (*mahā-tantra-rāja*), *ching* (*sūtra*), 大乘瑜伽金剛性 海曼殊室利千臂千鉢大教王經 translated from the Sanskrit original by Amoghavajra into Chinese in CE 740 (Nj 1044, STP 16.6378, K 1272, T 1177[a]). T 1177[b] is a hymn of 108 names of thousand-bowl Mañjuśrī (Jap. Kem-pastu Monju). This *sūtra* was studied by the well-known Korean monk-pilgrims to India, Hyech'o. On the morning of 1 January 733 he was initiated into it by Vajrabodhi. Since 5 May 740 Hyech'o copied the text. After studying it for eight years, on 6 January 741 he took up its translation as an assistant to his teacher Vajrabodhi. The plan was suspended in 741 on the death of Vajrabodhi. According to the will of Vajrabodhi the original Sanskrit *sūtra* was returned to India on 30 March 741. Therefore Hyech'o went to Ta-hsing-shan monastery and studied the remaining part of the *sūtra* with Amoghavajra (Yang 1969: 38).

The manuscript of Samantabhadra reminds us of the Vedas held by Brahmā in his hand (Danielou 1964: 237). Brahmā is the *pitāmaha* "grand-sire": The Lhasa xylograph of the Tibetan *Bhadrakalpika-sūtra* illustrates *Rgyal kun mes-po Kun-tu-bzan-po* = Skt. *Sarva-jina-pitāmaha Samantabhadra* "Samantabhadra the grand-sire of all Jinas" (NTMP 16.3). The bowl of Mañjuśrī has a parallel in the drinking bouts of Indra. It should be noted that Indra with a *pātra* occurs in the Raghu Vira manuscript of 108 Lokeśvaras: Indrapātra Lokeśvara is the forty first Lokeśvara. It is equivalent to Piṇḍapātra Lokeśvara in the other two series. The *lectio dificilior* Indrapātra was simplified to Piṇḍapatra. It is interesting to note that Indra and Mañjuśrī are placed on the right of the main chamber of Sokkuram, while Brahmā and Samantabhadra stand on the left. The development of Brahmā and Indra of the early Pāli Theravāda tradition into different iconographic forms under new names reflects the devlopments of Buddhist sects which provided both the impetus and context. The situation can be tabulated as under:

A detailed study of the transformations of Brahmā and Indra in the Buddhist sects is called for.

Theravāda	Brahmā	Śākyamuni	Indra
Amitābha-sūtra	Avalokiteśvara	Amitābha	Mahāsthāmaprāpta
Bhadracarī of the Avataṁsaka	Samantabhadra	Amitābha	Mañjuśrī

Popularity of the Avataṁsaka in Korea

It is important to bear in mind that the *Avataṁsaka-sūtras* (plural, not *sūtra*) are a collectaneum. They are not a single *sūtra* but a whole genre of texts spread over time. The loose translation of the Chinese character as chapters of the *Avataṁsaka* has given rise to the erroneous feeling that it is one large text. It comprises various texts of the Avataṁsaka class, which are designated in the Chinese Tripiṭaka. Moreover, in Chinese *ching* can be singular as well as plural: *sūtra* or *sūtras*. The *Daśabhūmika*, *Gaṇḍavyūha* and *Bhadracarī* of the Avataṁsaka circulated as independent works in China, as they did in India. The *Gaṇḍavyūha* occurs at the end of the Avataṁsaka, but that does not mean that it is final in the development of Avataṁsaka. The *Gaṇḍavyūha* is its oldest component (Fontein 1967: 18) and as such it ends with the eulogy of Amitābha. In the *Avataṁsaka*, Rocana is the Supreme Buddha.

It is relevant to emphasize the popularity of the *Avataṁsaka* texts both in China and Korea, whence it was introduced into Japan. The partial and complete translations of the *Avataṁsaka* are detailed below:

- CE 147-86 Tou-sha-ching "epithets of the buddha", tr. Lokakṣema (Nj 102, T280, K90).

  Equal to text 3 in Buddhabhadra's old translation (Nj 87).

  Equal to text 7 in Śikṣānanda's new translation (Nj 88).

- 373-395 Lo-mo-chia-ching = *Gaṇḍavyūha*, incomplete translation attributed to Sheng-chien (Nj 106, T294, K102).

- 418-422 First translation of the entire *Avataṁsaka-sūtras*, by Buddhabhadra (Nj 87, T278, K79).

  Known as the Old Translation, or Translation in 60 Chuan.

- 685 Divākara retranslated part of the *Gaṇḍavyūha* to fill a gap in Buddhabhadra's translation. (Nj 101, T295, K104) (gives the correct date CE 685). See Fontein 1967: 176 n.14 for details of the gap.

- 699 Second translation of the complete *Avataṁsaka*, by the Khotanese monk Śikṣānanda (Nj 88, T279, K80).
- 798 *Gaṇḍavyūha* translated by Prājña (Nj 89, T293, K1262) (repeated twice: KS 16, 52: this shows the popularity of the *Gaṇḍavyūha* in Korea).

The *Gaṇḍavyūha* was translated twice as a separate text and another time to complete the lacuna in Buddhabhadra's rendering. This is a clear proof of its high vogue in East Asia as the core of the Avataṁsaka School.

A century after the translation of the complete corpus of Avataṁsaka texts by Buddhabhadra, it became a full-fledged school of Buddhism. The first patriarch of the Avataṁsaka School was Fa-shun (557–640), followed by Chih-yen (602-68). The Korean Monk Uisang (625–702) studied with the second patriarch. The third patriarch Fa-tsang (643–712) systematized the doctrines (Fontein 1967: 17). Uisang founded the Avataṁsaka sect in the Korean kingdom of Silla along with Monk Wonhyo (617-86). The story of these two monks is illustrated in the famous Japanese Kegon Engi scrolls (Fontein 1967: 84). In 739 the Korean monk Simsang (d. 742) was invited to lecture on Avataṁsaka at the Todaiji. He was a disciple of Korean Masters Uisang and Wonhyo. The Japanese Avataṁsaka tradition considers the Koreans as its spiritual masters (Fontein 1967: 78, 84). In 742 Monk Doji presented an embroidered *Avataṁsaka* scroll of seven places and nine assemblies to the Daianji Monastery (ibid.: 78). The Todaiji owns a hanging scroll which depicts Sudhana and his *kalyāṇamitra*s (ibid.: 87, 108...). Three points emerge from the foregoing discussion:

1. Korea was prominent in the Avataṁsaka tradition in the seventh and eighth centuries, the period of the construction of Sokkuram.
2. It was but natural that when Prime Minister Kim chose to create the Sokkuram as an act of filial piety to his parents he should have chosen the latest popular school of the Avataṁsaka whose finale was a prayer to attain the paradise of Amitābha. The blending of Amitābha devotion with

Avataṁsaka learning had developed in the *Bhadracarī* (Fontein 1967: 57, 63).

3. Sudhana and the *kalyāṇamitras* were depicted on scrolls in Japan, a tradition which must have been derived from Korea. The Sokkuram should have had Sudhana and his *kalyāṇamitras* on scrolls.

The Avataṁsaka continued to flourish in Korea. Choe Ch'iwon (857 -?) wrote the authentic biography of the third and the greatest of all Chinese patriarchs Fa-tsang (T2054, Fontein 1968: 177 n. 4). The Korean patriarch Uich on (1055–1101), the fourth son of the Koryo King Munjong, studied Avataṁsaka. He travelled to China to study Buddhism and from there he collected Buddhist works. Among them is Yang Chieh's eulogies on the *Gaṇḍavyūha*. The biography of Yang Chieh stresses his devotion to Amitābha (Fontein 1967: 52-53).

Evolution from Śākyamuni to Rocana in Avataṁsaka

Gaṇḍavyūha was the nucleus whence the *Avataṁsaka* developed. The later parts of the *Avataṁsaka* describe the mystic doctrines of (Vai)Rocana. Thus we can trace the following stages in the transition from the historic Śākyamuni to Rocana to Vairocana:

1. Bhagavān.
2. *Gaṇḍavyūha* subordinates the cults of Avalokiteśvara (28) and Maitreya (52) to the emerging world of the Avataṁsaka. They are reduced to mere cogs in the machine like other *kalyāṇamitras* (Fontein 1967: 21-22).
3. Amitābha is the logical finale of Sudhana's pilgrimage. Samantabhadra leads Sudhana to Amitābha.
4. The emerging presence of Vairocana can be detected in several compounds with Vairocana in the *Gaṇḍavyūha:* Vairocanottara-jñānin (2.17), Vairocana-dhvaja (2.19), Digvairocana-mukuṭa (3.5), as names of two *bodhisattvas*, Jagad-virocana-vyūha (6.13-14), the night-goddess Pramudita- nayana-jagad-virocanā of the Vairocana-bodhi-maṇḍa (thirty-fourth *kalyāṇamitra, Gaṇḍavyūha* 254), five more goddesses (*kalyāṇamitras* 35-39) of the Vairocana

Bodhimaṇḍa, the Bodhisattva Maitreya of the Vairocana-vyūh-ālaṁkāra-garbha mahākūṭāgāra (*kalyāṇamitra* 52).

5. Māyā recites the names of Buddhas to whom she gave birth in previous incarnations beginning with Vairocana (Fontein 1967: 13). In a carved teakwood Chinese pilgrimage column "we find Sudhana's final meeting with Samantabhadra and an assembly with the Buddha Vairocana and attendants" (Fontein 1967: 66).

6. Vairocana emerges supreme:

> In the Mahāyānistic world of ideas the Buddha Gautama was of course no longer regarded as a unique historic figure and his attainment of enlightenment was not thought of as a unique event. He came to be incorporated in an infinite series of *Tathāgatas*, the appearance of whom was thought to extend over an eternity of innumerable *kalpas* backwards into the remote past as well as forwards into the distant future. In the *Avataṁsaka-sūtras* these *Tathāgatas* are all manifestations of one supreme Buddha, the Buddha Vairocana. . . . — Fontein 1967: 22

7. The traditional classification of Tantras into four divisions reflects the same development that the cult of Amitābha evolved into that of Vairocana:

Division of	**Main Deity**
Kriyā Tantras	Amitābha
Caryā Tantras	Vairocana in Amitābha's *mudrā*
Yoga Tantras	Vairocana in bodhyagrī-mudrā
Anuttara-yoga Tantras	Heruka

In the *Sarva-Tathāgata-Tattva-Saṁgraha* the presiding Buddha is occasionally referred to as Śākyamuni as well as the more usual name of Vairocana (*STTS*, ed. Lokesh Chandra and D.L. Snellgrove: introd., p. 52).

Transition from Rocana of Avataṁsaka to Vairocana of Vajrayāna Reflected in the Sokkuram and Pulguksa Complex

Just as the Avataṁsaka was an earlier stage in the evolution of Vajrayāna, so also the Sokkuram culminated in the Vairocanas of

Pulguksa monastery. Vajrayāna had become known in Korea as soon as it was introduced into China. The famous Silla monk Hyonch'o had been the personal disciple of both Vajrabodhi and Amoghavajra who laid the foundations of Vajrayāna in China. Hyonch'o had already studied under Śubhākarasiṁha. Hyonch'o became the teacher of Hui-k'o who had transmitted the doctrine to Kobo Daishi. The Korean monk Uirim was the teacher of Shun-hsiao (Kim/Lee 1974: 76).

The Pulguksa monastery contains two seated gilt-bronze life-size statues. They "share the same technique of casting and workmanship. They even share the reversed order in the positioning of the hand gesture".

> Such features as these point to the possibility, at least, that the two images may originally have been members of a group of the five Buddhas of the Esoteric Buddhist Maṇḍala, in which the Mahāvairocana occupies the centre of the diagram. On the other hand, no other Buddha images are known that might complete the group, and no record exists either to lend positive support for their interpretation or to provide a clue for their dating. The style, however, in its relaxed treatment of the garment folds and the apparent lack of interest in modeling of the full face and the expansive body suggests a data posterior to that of the Sokkuram Buddha of *c*. 751. Yet the facial expression lacks the serenity found on the Paengnyul-sa Bhaiṣajyaguru mentioned earlier (Pl. 108), which dates from the last decades of the eighth century. So these two Pulguksa bronze statues are generally assigned by Korean scholars to the second half of the eighth century, between the dates of the Sokkuram Buddha and the Paengnyul-sa Bhaiṣajyaguru, both on stylistic grounds and in the light of the historical development of the cult of esoteric Buddhism in Silla as well.
>
> — Kim/Lee 1974: 77

The perception of Kim/Lee can be specified only in the light of Japanese Shingon which has preserved the tradition intact up to our times in all its details. That the date of these two figures is posterior to the Sokkuram Amitābha of *c*. 751 is natural and in tune with the logic of spiritual evolution: the Avataṁsaka converging into Vajrayāna.

The seated gilt-bronze statue of Vairocana in the *bodhyagrī-mudrā* is a clear-cut and certain indication that it pertains to the Vajradhātu. The *bodhyagrī-mudrā* is unique and exclusive to Vajradhātu Vairocana. The two Vairocanas of the Garbhadhātu and Vajradhātu occur together as a pair of the two *caryā* and *yoga* divisions of Tantras which are known in Japan as the *ryobu* (twin divisions). The complementarity of the duo is integral in East Asian Vajrayāna. The other image, identified so far as Amitābha, should be the Garbhadhātu Vairocana. The Vajradhātu, in fact, presupposes the Garbhadhātu Vairocana. The hands of the Garbhadhātu Vairocana are in *dhyāna-mudrā* of meditation. The *mudrā* of Amitābha was also *dhyāna*, for instance, in the gigantic staute of Amitābha at Kamakura. In fact, the *mudrā* of Amitābha had been carried over to the Garbhadhātu Vairocana in the evolution of Tantras. Amitābha of the first division of Kriyā Tantras developed into Garbhadhātu Vairocana of the second division of Caryā Tantras. So another *mudrā* of Amitābha in the Pulguksa Garbhadhātu Vairocana is in order. Garbhadhātu Vairocana acquired in addition a crown of five *Tathāgatas*. So also the Vajradhātu Vairocana wears the same crown of five *Tathāgatas*. Both the Vairocanas at Pulguksa are bereft of crowns. In former times, they must have worn separate crowns which have disappeared over the centuries.

The pagoda to the right of the Pulguksa is Tabo-t'ap, which means the pagoda of many treasures or of Prabhūtaratna of the *Lotus Sūtra*. McCune (1962: 93) says:

> The first story is a platform provided with four stone staircases leading up to an enclosed area which is thought to have accommodated a Buddhist image at one time.

It should and must have, enshrined the image of Prabhūtaratna Tathāgata, while Śākyamuni was in the other Sokka-t'ap or pagoda of Śākyamuni. In China and Japan these two pagodas occur together. These pagodas were modelled after the Stūpa-Sandarśana chapter of the *Lotus Sūtra* and they became popular in China since CE 732 (JEBD 1965: 310b).

Conclusion

In this chapter we have tried to bring more precision in the interpretations of previous scholars, by comparing them with the Buddhist traditions elsewhere, especially in Japan. At Pulguksa: (i) the two pagodas did have the images of Śākyamuni and Prabhūtaratna, and (ii) the twin gilt-bronze statues are the Vairocanas of the two *maṇḍalas* known in Japan as the Ryobu Maṇḍala.

The Sokkuram represents the *Gaṇḍavyūha*. Its central image is Amitābha. The images in the niches are the *bodhisattvas* of ten directions who flock to listen to the teachings of the Bhagavān (Lord) of the *Gaṇḍavyūha*. The pilgrimage of Sudhana to fifty-four *kalyāṇamitras* must have been depicted on scrolls, lost in the passagfe of centuries.

Literature Cited

Daniélou	Daniélou, Alain, 1964, *Hindu Polytheism*, London: Routledge & Kegan Paul.
Fontein	Fontein, Jan, 1967, *The Pilgrimage of Sudhana*, The Hague: Monton & Co.
Gvy.	*The Gaṇḍavyūha Sūtra*, ed. Daisetz Teitaro Suzuki and Hokei Idzumi, Tokyo.
Ha	*Samguk Yusa*, 1972, tr. Ha Tae-hung and Grafton K. Mintz, Seoul: Yonsei University Press.
HS	*Han-guk ui sa-chal*. "Monasteries of Korea", vol. 2 (Sokkuram), Seoul, 1974.
JEBD	*Japanese–English Buddhist Dictionary*, Tokyo: Daitō Shuppansha, 1965.
K	(Korean Tripitak), Lancaster, Lewis R., 1979, *The Korean Buddhist Canon: A Descriptive Catalogue*, Berkeley: University of California Press.
Kim/Lee	Chewon, Kim, and Lena Kim Lee, 1974, *Arts of Korea*, Tokyo: Kodansha International.
Lokesh Chandra	Chandra, Lokesh, 1975, *Sudhana's Way to Enlightenment*, New Delhi: International Academy of Indian Culture.
Mallmann	Marie-Thérèsse de Mallmann, 1975, *Introduction à l' iconographie du tantrisme bouddhique*, Paris: Adrien-Maisonneuve.
McCune	McCune, Evelyn, 1962, *The Arts of Korea: An Illustrated History*, Tokyo: Charles E. Tuttle Co.

Nj	Bunyiu Nanjio, 1883, *A Catalogue of the Chinese Translation of the Buddhist Tripiṭaka*, Oxford: Clarendon Press.
NTMP	*New Tibeto-Mongol Pantheon*, part 12, by Raghuvira and Lokesh Chandra, New Delhi: International Academy of Indian Culture, 1967.
STTS	*Sarva-tathāgata-tattva-saṁgraha*, ed. Lokesh Chandra and David L. Snellgrove, New Delhi: International Academy of Indian Culture, 1981.
Suzuki	Suzuki, D.T., 1974, *Manual of Zen Buddhism*, London: Rider & Co.
T	*Taishō Daizōkyō*, ed. Takakusu Junjirō and Watanabe Kaigyoku, Tokyo, 1924-29.

Contributors

Balatchandirane, G.: Teaches economic history at the Department of East Asian Studies, University of Delhi. He has lectured at various universities in India, South Korea, USA and Japan as well as made presentations in a number of international seminars. He has been a Visiting Professor at the University of Kanazawa and at the Yokohama National University, Japan. Balatchandirane is a member of the Job Migration Task Force of the Association of Computing Machinery (ACM), USA, and wrote part of the report on the *Globalization and Offshoring of Software*. He has publishsed about eighty papers in journals and books. He has also edited two books.

Chandra Lokesh: is a contemporary scholar of Buddhism and the Indian arts. He is the son of the famous Sanskrit scholar Raghu Vira. He has also served as a member of the Indian Rajya Sabha, Vice-President of the 'Indian Council for Cultural Relations', and Chairman of the 'Indian Council of Historical Researdh'. In 2006 he was recognized with India's Padma Bhushan award. He has to his credit over 360 works and text editions. Among them are classics *Iconography of Tibet*, and his *Dictionary of Buddhist Art* in about 20 volumes. Presently he is Director, International Academy of Indian Culture.

Chel, Ko-Myeong: A literary critic and scholar, he is an Associate Professor in the Department of Korean Language and Literature in Kwangwoon University, Republic of Korea. He was awarded the "Young Critic" award of 2011. His main publications include *Realist Can't Sleep* (2010); *The Politics of Radical Resistance* (2010), *Bone Flowers Bloom* (2009); and *Controversy, Respond to the Criticism* (2006).

Cheul, Lee Soon: Is Associate Professor of Economics in the Department of Russia–India Business, Busan University of Foreign Studies, S. Korea. She was awarded her PhD from Oklahoma University in 2002. She was a member of delegation, India–Korea Comprehensive Economic Partnership Agreement during 2006-09. She also headed the South-East and South Asia Team, Korea Institute for International Economic Policy which is a government-funded research institute from 2005 to 2009.

Dutta, Alokka: Is Assistant Professor in Bhagini Nivedita College, University of Delhi. She has presented and published many research papers. Apart from publishing book reviews in various journals, she has contributed chapters in books relating to India's Foreign Policy. She has visited South Korea two times — (i) presenting a research paper on Globalization of Indian Folk Culture, and (ii) as a delegate from University of Delhi in International Next Generation Leaders Programme in 2008.

Gargesh, Ravinder: Is Professor and Head, Department of Linguistics, University of Delhi. In the teaching career spanning thirty-nine years, he has taught linguistics to postgraduate students of Linguistics, English, Hindi and Punjabi. He has been involved in the teaching of Hindi as a foreign language to students from Korea since 1993. He has also been a Visiting Professor to the Departnment of Indian Studies at the Hankuk University of Foreign Studies in Seoul, Korea in the years 2006-07 and 2009-11. He has published three books and has edited another two. He has published over fifty research papers and has supervised ten PhD thesis. He was on the editorial board of the seven volume series on the *Studies in Language and Linguistics: Selected Writings of Prof. R.N. Srivastava* (1992-99). He has been actively involved in the field of lexicography by being one of the compilers and editors of *Persian–Hindi Dictionary* (2 vols. 2002), *Koriyaayi–Hindi Shabdakosh* (Korean-Hindi–Dictionary, 2008) and *Persian–Hindi–English–Urdu Dictionary* (since 2008; and 3 vols. published, work still in progress). He is on the editorial boards of the following international journals — *World Englishes* (USA), *Journal of English Language Studies* (Tehran) and *Iranian Journal of Applied Language Studies* (Baluchistan, Iran).

Kwang-su, Lee: Is Professor in the Busan University of Foreign Studies, Busan, Korea. He is also the Co-Director of "Solidarity of Peace and Human Rights of Asia", Busan, Korea. He is the author of *Buddhist Ideas and Rituals of Early India and Korea*. He got his PhD in Indian History from University of Delhi.

Lee Kyung, Hee: Is a PhD researcher at Centre for Linguistics, School of Language, Literature and Culture Studies at Jawaharlal Nehru University (JNU), New Delhi.

Mishra, Ravikesh: Is Assistant Professor of Korean Language and Literature at the Centre for Japanese, Korean and North-East Asian Studies, School of Language, Literature and Culture Studies, Jawaharlal Nehru University, New Delhi. His area of interest and study include Korean language and literature, comparative poetics and aesthetics. He has been awarded the "Korean Government Scholarship" (2000) and "Korea Foundation Fellowship" (2004). He has published *Korea: Ek Jhalak* (tr. and ed.) supported by the Ministry of Culture and Tourism, Republic of Korea in 2006, a book titled *India and Korea: Perspectives on Language, Literature and Culture* (ed.) supported by the Korea Foundation (2008) and *A Textbook on Korean Culture (Raju in Korea)* (co-authored) published in 2008 by Manak Publications, New Delhi.

Paranjape, Makarand R.: Is Professor of English in the Centre for English Studies, Jawaharlal Nehru University, New Delhi. He was educated at St. Stephen's College, University of Delhi (BA Hons.) and at the University of Illinois at Urbana-Champaign, USA (Masters and PhD). He is the author/editor of over thirty-five books which include works of criticism, poetry and fiction, and has also published over 100 academic papers in books and journals published from India and abroad. His latest work includes *Another Canon: Indian Texts and Traditions in English* (2009), *Altered Destinations: Self, Society, and Nation in India* (2010) and *Acts of Faith: Journeys to Sacred India* (2012).

Sharma, R.C.: A passionate photographer and an author of two books and several papers and articles to his credit, Sharma has been teaching Linguistics since 1976. Professor of Linguistics at University of Delhi since 1995, he has been a member of the faculty there since July 1985. Prior to this, he was teaching at Kurukshetra University. With an MA in Linguistics and another in Philosophy from Kurukshetra University, he did his PhD in Linguistics from University of Poona. He has also taught as a Professor at Hankuk University of Foreign Studies for a year at its Seoul and Yongin campuses (September 2007 to August 2008) and is currently a Professor of Indian Studies at the Seoul Campus since March 2012. Prof. Sharma has held positions of Head of the Department of Linguistics, Dean of the Faculty of Arts, Chairman of the large inter-faculty Board of Research Studies in Humanities and Social Sciences, Chairman of the Publications Advisory Committee, Dean of Examination and many other responsibilities at University of Delhi. A widely travelled person, he has delivered lectures at several universities in India and abroad. A Life Member of the Linguistic Society of India, Dravidian Linguistic Association and Indian Academy of Social Sciences, he has also served as Editor of *Indian Linguistics*.

Shrivaastav, Sanjeev Kumar: Is a Researcher at the Institute for Defence Studies and Analyses (IDSA), New Delhi. He specializes in American studies. His areas of research are mainly: India–United States Strategic Partnership; United States Foreign and Security Policies Towards Asia; Indian Foreign Policy; and International Relations: Theory and Practice. He was invited to an International Programme — Next Generation Leaders from India 2010 — held in Seoul and other cities in South Korea in April 2010. His current project is on "India-United States Strategic Partnership Focusing on Its Nature and Various Dimensions". He is also pursuing his doctoral research from American Studies division at School of International Studies, Jawaharlal Nehru University, New Delhi.

Singh, Avadhesh Kumar: Is Professor and Director, School of Translation Studies and Training, Indira Gandhi National Open University (IGNOU), New Delhi. He was Vice- Chancellor, Dr. Babasaheb Ambedkar Open University, Ahmedabad (2006-09). He was Convener, Knowledge Consortium of Gujarat, Government of Gujarat, Gandhi Nagar (Gujarat). He has published more than 120 papers in various anthologies, national and international journals of repute. He has authored fifteen books till now. His recent publications include *Indian Knowledge Systems* (2 vols) with Kapil Kapoor) (2005); *Ramayana Through the Ages* (2007); *Voices of Woman: Gārgī to Gaṅgāsatī* (2008); *Interventions: Critical and Literary Discourses* (2009); and *Towards Interdisciplinarity: (the) University, Social Sciences and Humanities* (2010); and the latest *Revisiting Literature, Criticism and Aesthetics in India* (2012). He has been in various UPSC, UGC and NAAC Committees and is associated with many literary, critical and cultural projects. He has been a British Council Visiting Fellow to Corpus Christi College, Oxford (UK) and has delivered lectures in various universities in India and abroad, he has been the editor of *Critical Practice,* a biannual journal of literary and critical studies since 1994.

Soon, Young Kim: Is working at the Cultural Centre, Embassy of the Republic of Korea to India. She has been a Guest Lecturer in Korean Programme in the University of Delhi from 2004 to 2011. Earlier she worked at Jawaharlal Nehru University as Guest Lecturer from 2000 to 2002 and Assistant Professor from 1996 to 2000. She completed her MA in Linguistics and PhD in English from Jawaharlal Nehru University, New Delhi.

Yaruingam, A.S.: Is presently working in the Department of African Studies, University of Delhi.

Young, Kim Do: Is Professor of East Asian Studies at the University of Delhi. He has been Korea Foundation Professor there since 2002. Earlier he has been a Korea Foundation Professor at Jawaharlal Nehru University, New Delhi, from 1996 to 2002. He had his postgraduation and Doctorate from Jawaharlal Nehru University itself. He has been instrumental in opening programmes such as BA, MA in Korean language, in India.

Index